LEADERSHIP IN WAR AND PEACE

This book offers a gendered perspective on leadership in war and peace, considering leadership in its complexity and presenting a practical examination of both leadership successes and failures.

The work challenges readers to think through and discuss specific aspects of leadership, including how and why leadership diversity matters and the ethical challenges presented by the revolving door of the military–industrial complex. Further, leaders responsible for decisions involving war and peace must be able to understand, appreciate, and communicate effectively with everyone they work with and have a repertoire of leadership styles to use depending on context. The book represents an excellent tool for developing such skills, as it uniquely considers leadership through both male and female lenses, along with the experiences and perspectives of multiple military, government, and industry leaders interviewed by the author, making it both relatable and informative.

This book will be of much interest to students of gender studies, leadership studies, defense studies, and military studies in general, as well as military and security practitioners.

Joan Johnson-Freese is a University Professor Emeritus at the US Naval War College. She is the author of several books, including *Women, Peace and Security*, Second Edition (2023), and *Educating America's Military* (2012).

"Leadership in our national security agencies takes place in a highly structured, process-driven environment. Thus, to achieve positions of leadership, especially in the State Department, where I served for 40 years, management skills are prized; effective leaders are identified by results, not by how results are achieved. Even the Department's leadership and management skill set, which was not codified until a decade ago, lists prudential skills as the last four of ten. As Professor Johnson-Freese opened eyes and horizons with her study of women, peace, and security, she has taken a step forward with this assessment of leadership – and the different ways women and men manifest it. I highly recommend this study for students (and practitioners) of leadership and for those who aspire to provide better national security leadership going forward."

—Ambassador (ret.) Gene Christy

"The reality is today's military is integrated and has been for some time. Most every ship, squadron, or unit today has both men and women and benefits from this diversity of perspectives and experiences. A leader guiding a modern military organization must be able to understand, appreciate, and communicate effectively with everyone in their command. This book represents an excellent tool for developing such skills, looking at leadership through both male and female lenses. But even more importantly, it's simply a superb book on leadership in general, eschewing the pithy aphorisms and recycled generalities of most leadership books, instead treating important themes and presenting practical examples that examine both the successes and failures of complicated figures relevant and familiar to the reader."

—Captain David Reynolds, USNR (ret.), *former Naval Aviator and Commanding Officer of four Navy Reserve commands*

"*Leadership in War and Peace* is a must-read book for leaders seeking to foster great people, leaders, and teams. Dr Johnson-Freese diligently examines how a diverse force – particularly women and men – should be valued for their differences and how that contributes to a high performing team. This book delves into practical "how-to" specifics that many leaders frequently request, and is sure to be highlighted and dog-eared by leaders across the force."

—Andrea N. Goldstein, *former Director for Force Resiliency, Department of the Navy*

"Leadership is in crisis. To effectively confront the complex and evolving security threats of the 21st century, leaders will have to adapt – using both masculine and feminine leadership styles, in the right measure, with the right people, and at the right time. This groundbreaking book will empower them to do so."

—Nicholas Tomb, *Institute for Security Governance, Defense Security Cooperation University*

"A brilliant fusion of ideas, examples, and practical recommendations, this book should serve as a primer for anyone who is leading now or in the future! In an increasingly complex and polarized world, Professor Johnson-Freese has identified the key issues – and solutions – for all men and women who live in the crucible of leadership."

—Jeffrey Harley, Rear Admiral, US Navy (ret.)

"This is a must read for all! Dr Johnson-Freese's refreshing take on leadership highlights the importance of utilizing a variety of leadership characteristics to meet the moment, providing historical examples of success and failures interwoven with common sense leadership principles and ethical considerations. She shows why looking at leadership through a gendered lens strengthens not only the leader's ability to lead but also more effective mission outcomes. Her methodology equips leaders to leverage all the talent in their workforce and implement key Women, Peace and Security principles. This book should be a staple in any leader's toolkit."

—Major Samantha Arrington Sliney, US Air Force

"Dr Johnson-Freese's latest work provides a much-needed modern reframing of leadership. Drawing on examples and data from across government, business, sports, and political arenas, *Leadership in War and Peace: Masculine and Feminine* offers vivid insights on the criticality of understanding gender dynamics in leadership and why it matters to our national security. The author demonstrates the nuanced interconnectedness between the two, filling a blind spot in the crowded and often redundant philosophies on leadership and national security studies. *Leadership in War and Peace* provides readers with a new tool – a superpower – they can use in building and leading the strongest teams possible. Unique, fresh, and compelling – a must read."

—Cathleen Pearl, *Chief Impact Officer, Military Women's Memorial*

LEADERSHIP IN WAR AND PEACE

Masculine and Feminine

Joan Johnson-Freese

Routledge
Taylor & Francis Group
LONDON AND NEW YORK

Designed cover image: Cover imagery by Lizzy Phenix.

First published 2025
by Routledge
4 Park Square, Milton Park, Abingdon, Oxon OX14 4RN

and by Routledge
605 Third Avenue, New York, NY 10158

Routledge is an imprint of the Taylor & Francis Group, an informa business

British Library Cataloguing-in-Publication Data
A catalogue record for this book is available from the British Library

ISBN: 9781032915883 (hbk)
ISBN: 9781032915852 (pbk)
ISBN: 9781003564065 (ebk)

DOI: 10.4324/9781003564065

Typeset in Times New Roman
by Deanta Global Publishing Services, Chennai, India

CONTENTS

ACKNOWLEDGMENTS

First and foremost, I want to thank my students and colleagues at the Naval War College and Harvard Extension and Summer Schools for the conversations we have enjoyed, and for the observations and insights about leadership they have shared over many years. I have learned from every one. I've also been fortunate to have remarkable teaching assistants who helped me push forward with research and teaching. Most recently, Chuck Houston, Melissa Deehring, and Maryruth Belsey Priebe, you've made teaching a pleasure.

I also want to thank all of those in the many organizations I've worked with for their invitations, the insights of members, and the opportunities that have been provided to share and learn about leadership and the role of gender in both leadership and security. Jess and Mary at AllTru, the work you have done and the work you continue to do is awesome and inspiring. Meg and Christina at The Valkyrie Project, thank you for introducing me to the amazing work being done by your organization and for the connection to the Joint Women's Leadership Symposium. Attending JWLS and having the opportunity to speak at JWLS is always awesome. The leadership lessons offered there abound. Ariana, Karin, and Roksana at Women in International Security (WIIS), you've been great as a venue to help spread awareness of the Women, Peace, and Security framework and the contributions women make to national security. Katherine at Solar Sister, you are a personal hero. Your story and the organization you created demonstrate what can be done to change the world, one person at a time. Phyllis and Cathleen at the Women's Military Memorial, thank you for showcasing the additive value of diversity and the sacrifices being made by real-life heroes who just wanted to serve their country and do their jobs. Yasmine, you strode from the world of fashion to that of women's empowerment with ease and phenomenal success. Thank you for giving me the opportunity to join in your journey. Hanifa, you too are a personal hero. You inspire every person you meet, and if I've been helpful with your incredible work with CERESAV, it's been my honor and pleasure. Nick, Cary, and Blair at the Institute for Security Governance, the work you do is so important. I can't thank you enough for having included me. Saira Yamin, you have taken the WPS program at the Naval War College to a new level.

I first became interested in the relationship between gender and security after hearing Valerie Hudson speak. I'm likely not the only person to have had that experience. Other authors and speakers, some of whom I have had the pleasure to work and write with, who I would like to acknowledge include Heather Huhtanen, Kitty Pilgrim, Jim Minnich, David Smith, Stephenie Foster, Susan Markham, Jacqui True, Dui Turner, Andrea Goldstein, and Tahina Montoya.

These "thank yous" don't begin to reach all of those who have been so accommodating and generous at various institutions I've been invited to, but please know I'm grateful.

PREFACE

Teaching the "leadership" course at the Naval War College during the Iraq War was a challenge, in a good way. There are three things I found the military especially skeptical of: civilians, academics, and women. I was the trifecta. Walking into a seminar of, at that time, mostly men, as their "leadership instructor" brought stares and glares, understandably. The students' cross-armed, tilted-head body language spoke volumes. Who was I to teach them, just back from avoiding improvised explosive devices and firefights, anything about leadership? And they had a point. But leadership isn't just about convincing individuals to face a barrage of bullets. (Many of the military students, by the way, would much rather do that than write an academic paper.) So, I would begin by saying that I wasn't sure leadership could be taught, but I was sure leadership could be learned, and that with their on-the-ground experience and my book-learned knowledge, I was certain we could have interesting and useful discussions if they would allow me to be their "sherpa" – instead of the word "teacher" – on their learning journey. Almost invariably, we had great discussions, and I remain in contact with some of those once-skeptical officers to this day. Education is always most successful if everyone, teachers and students, enters with an open mind to learning something new.

I had not intended to write another book. But in classes, lectures, and keynote addresses over the years, and especially of late, I have found myself talking more and more about leadership, regardless of whether the actual subject matter focuses on security studies generally; grand strategy; Women, Peace, and Security; space security; or professional military education, all subjects I've taught and/or I'm regularly called upon to address. Besides teaching leadership at the Naval War College, I've also taught a class called Leadership in War and Peace through Harvard Extension and Summer Schools. The similarity in the name of that course and this book, with only "Masculine and Feminine" added, is not an accident. This book brings together various aspects of my academic career through leadership, including strategy for achieving national security-related goals, the importance of gender equality to national security, education, space security, and policy. Consequently, parts of the book are drawn from previous works when pertinent.

My intent in writing the book is simple: to generate useful discussions on leadership among a broad swath of students, practitioners, and individuals in the general public, as I firmly believe that such discussion is desperately needed when the news seems to indicate daily that the world is falling apart and leadership is too often in crisis. The book is deliberately constructed to be relevant to not just members of the military or security communities interested in leadership, but also those interested in such subjects as international relations, business, gender studies, social justice, civics, and more. Examples of issues and leaders are primarily but not exclusively American, with international examples deliberately included in each chapter as well, and analogies drawn from various fields, including business and sports.

I was very fortunate to be able to interview a wide variety of male and female leaders from both the public and private sectors as part of my research for the book. Indeed, once I began conducting interviews, some individuals heard about my project from friends or colleagues and reached out to me to offer their views, for which I am very grateful. Some chose to speak on background, without attribution, while others allowed attribution. I also drew from discussions and debates I've had with students and colleagues over the years regarding leadership. All provided incredible insights that are integrated throughout the book to provide perspectives, raise questions, and make issues interesting and relatable. I truly would have been unable to write this book earlier in my career, without their input.

I wish I could thank every one of those individuals, but alas there are simply too many to recount and acknowledge, and many prefer not to be named. So, I thank all of you collectively.

While I gained immeasurably from the remarks and insights of others, including those who took the time to read and make comments on parts of earlier drafts, responsibility for all the material presented is, however, mine alone.

INTRODUCTION

I often begin my leadership classes by asking whether the US Civil War Confederate General Robert E. Lee was a good leader, and a lively debate regularly ensues. Lee was a West Point graduate and married to the great-granddaughter of American Founding Father George Washington's wife, Martha. Though he said he was philosophically against slavery, he owned slaves inherited upon the death of his mother and believed in the legal right to ownership, including the use of violence to enforce ownership. While he favored keeping the Union intact, when the South seceded, Lee chose to follow his home state, Virginia, and so fought for the Confederacy. Lee was undoubtedly a brilliant tactician, decisive, and an inspiration and hero to his troops through his personal courage, battlefield integrity, and intelligence.

But the military most often measures "good" in terms of whether or not a mission was successfully completed, and "winning." Lee was in charge of the Confederate Army, and the Confederacy lost. Some students defend his leadership, arguing that the Confederacy lost, and so Lee was on the losing side, by virtue of his circumstances; specifically, a lack of supplies, and consequently, losing was not his fault. Others argue that he was a traitor by virtue of leaving the Union, and so inherently a bad leader. Controversy about Lee's position as a leader has reached down to the halls of West Point regarding what to do about displays of his name and image.[1] As part of my class discussions about Lee, consideration of the difference between a good leader and an effective leader is also raised. The overall idea is to establish early on in class discussions that leadership is complex. So too will be the case in this book.

Discussions in this book also challenge traditional considerations of leadership, down to and including physicality. When you think of a leader, what kind of person do you picture in your mind? Traditionally, leaders were assumed to be tall,

DOI: 10.4324/9781003564065-1

either muscular Rambo-types or dignified John F. Kennedy-types – men of some intrepid and virile variety. But that has never been the case. From Napoleon to Gandhi, even male leaders came in many physical and intellectual varieties. And now, women are added to the mix of leaders in numbers that make them more than historical oddities, à la Joan of Arc and Catherine the Great. But just as women veterans struggle for acknowledgement and recognition as veterans – veterans being not just men in hats telling where they served – women still struggle for acknowledgement and recognition as leaders, especially those who don't "fit the picture" of a leader in terms of voice, stature, race, even hair style, or a multitude of other attributes. Recognizing the differences between men and women, and the value of combining talents, often begins with expanding their images in our minds.

Perhaps the most difficult aspect of developing the book content was avoiding the pitfalls of polarized partisan politics that have gripped the United States of late. I would be remiss, and there would be an obvious hole in my examination of leadership without consideration and inclusion of events and personalities since the 2016 presidential election because they are significant. But the focus of the book is on leadership, not politics, and I have tried hard to keep the focus there.

The thesis of the book is that future great (and even good) leaders will need to utilize both masculine and feminine styles, traits, and skills, and understand when to use each, to maximize their personal effectiveness, and subsequently that of their organization, institution, or nation. Diversity matters in the leadership of both war and peace. In support of that thesis, the book is divided into eight chapters, though I deliberately weave people and points of analysis among chapters, rather than only silo them.

Chapter 1, "Why a Gendered Lens on Leadership in War and Peace," begins with consideration of L. Paul "Jerry" Bremer's role as head of the Coalition Provisional Authority in Iraq. Was he a leader or a manager/implementor of decisions that had been made in Washington? The intent is to point out the differences between leadership and management, the importance of the differences, and the "grey areas" between them. Then the first of several instances throughout the book of how men and women are different is made through a sports example, as part of building a case in support of my thesis. Recognizing the value of inclusive diversity for the sake of national security, different from the diversity, equity, and inclusion (DEI) efforts that have soured many individuals on the human resources push for diversity, is also introduced by way of the Women, Peace, and Security framework, consideration of the relationship between conflict and gender, and gendered approaches to conflict resolution. The chapter concludes with consideration of how balancing the gender traits prevalent in both men and women, individually or as part of a leadership team, increases the potential for effective decision-making and leadership.

Chapter 2, "Theories and the Context of Leadership," begins with consideration of the different roles that Generals Dwight D. Eisenhower and George S. Patton played during World War II, illustrating the importance of context to leadership. That is followed by a brief review of past academic trends in trying to categorize, indeed theorize about leadership, toward an understanding of different macro trends in leadership studies. That review is followed by further consideration of the "context" of leadership, including a comparison of Aung San Suu Kyi and Nelson Mandela to demonstrate the difficulties some leaders have had, and what it takes to be successful in transitioning between different leadership roles. A general overview of feminist theory in relation to leadership is then provided, including an explanation of intersectionality. The difference in defining gender equality as seeing men and women as the same, and the perils that definition holds, or as different but with each sex bringing traits of value to leadership, is explained. Finally, leadership and the lesbian, gay, bisexual, transgender, queer, plus (LGBTQ+) community is introduced, with attention given to both Pete Buttigieg and Kyrsten Sinema as LGBTQ+ leaders.

Chapter 3, "Leadership Styles," examines the various styles leaders use as leaders, in terms of their conduct, decision-making, and relationship with those who work for or with them. The chapter begins with a mini-case examination of Donald Rumsfeld as a one-dimensional leader and the pitfalls of that approach. That is followed by consideration of emotional intelligence as a key aspect of leadership. The chapter then moves to a review of Daniel Goleman's six "leadership styles" and the competencies required to effectively use them, particularly in combinations according to context, with many of those competencies often being "gendered." Mini-cases of Admiral Hyman Rickover, father of the US nuclear Navy, and former British Prime Minister Margaret Thatcher are offered to illustrate the many (often controversial and ambiguous) considerations that come into play when evaluating or pigeonholing a leader's style. The chapter ends with a short description of the avenues available to build emotional intelligence and the prerequisites for successfully doing so.

Chapter 4, "Ethics and Leadership," examines the ethical challenges of leadership, beginning with the relevance of the "revolving door" between government officials and military officers and lucrative private sector positions. Then, Jeffrey Matthews' seven categories of unethical (and sometimes criminal) activity are individually considered: war crimes (with special attention paid to the examples of My Lai and Abu Ghraib), insubordination, moral cowardness, toxic leadership, obstruction of justice, public corruption, and sex crimes, with institutional betrayal also added. Included in the consideration of sex crimes is the continuing prevalence of sexual assault as an issue in the security community generally and in the military specifically, and how that affects women attempting to rise into and be accepted in leadership roles.

Chapter 5, "Men and Leadership," addresses issues related explicitly to masculine considerations of leadership. The chapter begins with a mini-case regarding General David Petraeus, once considered a "rock star" general, to exemplify the demands and contradictions of masculinity. That is followed by consideration of the challenges facing men in society generally as their gender stereotypical roles as protector and provider fade. An explanation is given regarding the difference between "good men" and "real men," and how that affects leadership. Comparisons of good men and real men are then drawn through several national leaders: US President Jimmy Carter, Canadian Prime Minister Justin Trudeau, Senator John McCain, Brazilian President Jair Bolsonaro, and Philippine President Rodrigo Duterte. The chapter concludes with consideration of men in patriarchies, drawing on an example of the Democratic Republic of the Congo, and an important but too often ignored discussion of developing positive, healthy forms of masculinity.

Chapter 6, "Women and Leadership" focuses on women's leadership experiences, beginning with a look back at Admiral Grace Hopper's career. That is followed by a mini-case called "Two Paths to Three Stars," considering the careers and experiences of two American women who each achieved the rarefied rank of a three-star general military officer, pointing out that there are many different paths to leadership roles for women. The chapter then reaches back to examine how women have historically achieved leadership roles and women's leadership in patriarchies, with a focus on former Liberian President Ellen Johnson Sirleaf. The structural and cultural challenges to women in leadership are then considered, including what has changed from the past and what hasn't. Women's leadership styles, including when women try to adapt masculine traits, are examined through style analyses of British Prime Minister Theresa May and German Chancellor Angela Merkel. A snapshot of former New Zealand Prime Minister Jacinda Ardern's leadership style is also included as someone considered a new brand of women leaders, and to point out the several types of violence faced by women politicians.

Chapter 7, "Gender Diverse Leadership in Practice," addresses gendered leadership through the lens of three mini-cases: US nonproliferation efforts with Iran, the intelligence community, and the creation of Space Force. All contribute to demonstrating the positive impact of gendered leadership and the obstacles that still need to be addressed in diversifying leadership. The rationale for including these specific areas of examination is that skeptics, and individuals who are merely "blind fish"– oblivious to their environment, including bias – to the importance of inclusive diversity and gendered policy, are most often convinced by example.

Chapter 8, "The Future of Leadership," begins by reiterating the assertion that leadership is in crisis and delves into that assertion further. That is followed by a discussion on the importance of authenticity in leadership. In that context, the chapter considers Senator Josh Hawley and Congresswoman Elise Stefanik as two politicians who have significantly "rebranded" themselves, and what that rebranding perhaps says or doesn't say about them as leaders. Then the discussion moves to an examination of two leaders who have faced extraordinary challenges: General Mark Milley and Congresswoman Liz Cheney. One male, one female, one military leader, one political leader, both were swirled in situations that challenged their ethics, their styles, and their futures. The intent is to task readers to look forward regarding what they want and expect from future leaders.

The discussion then moves to the cost of leadership in physical, and emotional terms, as increasingly, leaders are paying high personal prices for their service. Finally, the chapter concludes by returning to the issue of "learning leadership" that prompted the writing of the book.

Whether reading the book alone or as part of the group, it is my hope that the issues and examples raised will be the basis for discussion and sharing of views. Leadership is in crisis, and only by recognizing, discussing, and addressing the challenges, faults, and foibles that have jeopardized leadership, and potentially national security, of late will that crisis be abated. Additionally, while acknowledging the non-binary nature of gender, given that data has been and remains most often gathered and differentiated by sex in a binary nature, that binary characterization will be utilized throughout.

Note

1 Byrn, Jimmy and Gabe Royal. "What Should West Point Do About Its Robert E. Lee Problem?," Modern War Institute, June 22, 2020. https://mwi.westpoint.edu/west-point-robert-e-lee-problem/

1

WHY A GENDERED LENS ON LEADERSHIP IN WAR AND PEACE

American diplomat L. Paul Bremer, nicknamed Jerry, arrived in an already chaotic Iraq in May 2003 as head of the Coalition Provisional Authority (CPA), less than two months after the US military mission to topple Saddam Hussein had begun with a "shock and awe" show of overwhelming US military force. That military mission was completed in less than six weeks. Bremer arrived with what he felt was clear guidance from President George W. Bush, conveyed by Bremer in a 2006 interview: "Let's see if we can get the Iraqis on a path to democracy, to representative government, and help them rebuild their economy, help them reconstitute their economy."[1] Bremer has been described as "a modern potentate. As administrator of the CPA, which governed Iraq at the time, he wielded full legislative, executive and judicial authority."[2] Bremer was "the most powerful American citizen outside the United States comparable only to General Douglas MacArthur who commanded US occupational forces in Japan after its defeat in 1945."[3] He held the power to rule by decree.

After receiving a Master of Business Administration degree from Harvard in 1966, Bremer joined the State Department and held several overseas posts, including as an assistant to Henry Kissinger, but never in the Middle East. He did not speak Arabic. When he left the foreign service in 1989, he became managing director of Henry Kissinger and Associates. His lack of practical experience in the Middle East was considered a plus by the Bush Administration that appointed him because he would not have "the Middle East mindset of the State Department and wasn't contaminated by the Clinton-era thinking."[4] He would, administration thinking went, approach the Middle East like a business problem.

Bremer issued two critical orders almost immediately after his arrival in Iraq, decisions that would soon thereafter get Bremer blamed for the quagmire in which the United States quickly found itself. He signed Order Number 1, banning the

DOI: 10.4324/9781003564065-2

Baath Party and dismissing its members, and initiated the de-Baathification of Iraqi society. At the time of the banning, the party had 1.5 million members from all walks of life, from high government officials to teachers and doctors, thereby gutting a fair number of Iraqi institutions necessary to keep the country moving. The decision had been discussed prior in Washington and supported by Bush Administration officials like Secretary of Defense Donald Rumsfeld's Deputy, Paul Wolfowitz, who equated the Baath Party in Iraq to the Nazi party in post-World War II Germany. In a letter to his wife, Bremer wrote, "There was a sea of bitching and moaning...[but] the president's guidance is clear: de-Baathification will be carried out even if at a cost to administrative efficiency."[5]

CPA Order Number 2 disbanded the Iraqi Army and the entire accompanying Iraqi institutional security apparatus. That sent disgruntled soldiers home, with their weapons, and left a security vacuum that domestic militias and terrorist groups like Al-Qaeda (AQ) were happy to quickly fill. Firing the military was, again, however, not a Bremer initiative. According to one account, "an order to that effect had been drafted and cleared through the Pentagon, approved by Secretary of Defense Donald Rumsfeld, presented to President Bush and his National Security Council, and even discussed with British officials before Bremer issued it."[6] While the maze of decisions and decision-makers behind the origination and the intended breadth and finalization of both orders is complex, it is clear that neither order was original to Bremer.[7]

Bremer, the US "Viceroy,"[8] lasted 13 months in Iraq, leaving on June 28, 2004, the same day he handed sovereignty back to the Iraqi Interim Government. At an early point during Bremer's time in Baghdad, then Secretary of State Colin Powell was meeting with Henry Kissinger and asked him about Bremer's management style. "He's a control freak," Kissinger said.[9] But from Bremer's perspective, he would say to people, "I don't want to deal with the Washington squirrel cage. I don't want somebody in Washington with an 8,000-mile screwdriver interfering with what we do here."[10] Chaos needs a leader to address it, not a committee. Was Bremer a leader – certainly the descriptions of his power would imply he was – or was he a manager?

This is a book about leadership, not management, but it's sometimes difficult to draw a clear line between the two, though there are important differences between them. American computer scientist and mathematician Rear Admiral Grace Hopper, instrumental during World War II for her software programming work, famously stated: "Manage things. Lead people."[11] Leadership is an interpersonal process toward "getting people to act without coercion."[12] Not all leaders are good managers, and few managers are good leaders. The qualities, capabilities, and tasks characteristic of each diverge considerably. In simplest terms, managers focus on planning, processes, and resource use related to successfully completing incremental tasks related to a larger goal, while leaders inspire, motivate, and empower people to work together toward a larger goal, as well as setting goals. Some people are better at one than the other, and gender matters to both.

Why Gender Matters

Women are not men. Let me repeat that: *Women are not men.* Among other ways, women are physiologically different, communicate differently, hear differently, are motivated differently, and self-reflect differently, and all of those differences will affect how they manage and lead. Not necessarily better or worse, but often differently. And when speaking in generalities about differences among and between the sexes, I am referring to propensities, a bell curve distribution based on studies and statistics, while recognizing that there are outliers and differences among women's and men's leadership styles, traits, and skills, as well as between them. That does not mean, though, that assumptions can or should be randomly made because all individuals are different.

A senior woman leader I spoke with said that when she arrived at a new command, an individual welcomed her and said how happy he was that the command would have a compassionate leader. To that, she said she thought to herself, "You don't know that about me." Likewise, Amber Mitchell, who retired as a Chief Master Sergeant from Space Force, said that as often the only female in her squadron, certain assumptions were frequently made about her that she had to counter. "The assumption was that I was going to be soft or 'emotional'…I found myself working really hard to make sure I was great at my job and didn't need any extra comforting measures or their help in general."[13]

Assumptions about individuals, both men and women, can be very wrong. Assumptions are based on societal and cultural expectations regarding learned gender roles. Some are learned through the home, families and friends, some through enculturation, or what we see around us. Institutional hallways full of pictures of men as leaders, for example, sets the expectation that men will be leaders. Advertisements and cinematic portrayals of women as domestic goddesses, damsels in distress or fashion-fixated shopaholics creates assumptions about women. Specifically, those portrayals create the assumption that "women will be more caring and relationship oriented than men…the basic idea that accounts for approaches to women's leadership that differ from those traditionally established for men – normally more competitive and controlling."[14] But that may or may not be true because while women and men have different proclivities in terms of traits and approaches to leadership, all individuals are different, and different traits are more or less appropriate for different situations and contexts. Recognizing and knowing when to use each is key.

Rear Admiral Kristin Acquavella was on the University of North Carolina (UNC) women's soccer team in college, a championship team that included teammates like World Cup champion and Olympic gold medalist Mia Hamm. In an interview with her, Acquavella[15] frequently referenced her time on the team and how much she learned about being part of a team and leadership as an athlete, lessons which she has carried over to her highly successful naval career. When I asked her about the differences between leading men and women, she referred me to a short 2012 YouTube video featuring her UNC coach Anson Dorrance.[16] It's a video every leader would benefit from watching to understand the differences between men and women.

Dorrance coached both the UNC men's and the UNC women's soccer teams, and in the video, he (self-effacingly) discusses his learning process toward understanding how to deal with each. He began coaching the men in 1976 and the women three years later in 1979. He says that being a man, he was confident about how to coach men but knew nothing about coaching women. The literature available to him in 1979 told him, he said, that men and women are equal, so he decided to treat both teams the same. He describes the results as an unmitigated disaster.

Dorrance describes a soccer game where his men's team was going into overtime. To motivate them, he said he drew from a movie he had watched the night before, *The Great Santini*, about a tough, unrelenting Marine warrior frustrated during peacetime, who wanted his children to have "the gift of fury" and to "eat life before life ate them." So Dorrance told his male players to charge back onto the field like a bunch of Neanderthals and unleash their fury against their opponents. He said the men thought that was the best coaching they had ever received. They didn't have to think, just go out and act like a bunch of crazies. They won. He thought he had hit upon the greatest motivational speech ever. But when he was tasked to coach the women's team as well three years later, he confidently tried using that speech with them and said he got only vacuous stares in return. They lost.

He describes another halftime motivational speech used with the men when they were tied with a (new) team Dorrance felt was inferior to the seasoned UNC team. He said it began with him pacing back and forth like a caged tiger in the noisy locker room until somebody finally noticed – "this is my men's team, they're not the most sensitive creatures on the planet"[17] – that he was livid. Then, when the room quieted to where you could hear a pin drop, he let go with his fury. His vocal outburst, he said, was followed by him kicking a wastebasket through a locker room window and walking out. It worked. He had effectively communicated with the men. But, he continued, had he used the same approach with the women, they would have correctly surmised that he was psychotic and that they should flee the room. The women, he said, would have sensed his anger immediately, and what would have mattered to them was the tone of his voice. Further, he felt that simply, quietly asking the women what they thought was going wrong on the field would have been followed by a chorus of self-flagellation as every woman in the room took full responsibility for whatever nightmare was happening.

And showing game videos, Dorrance suggested, was used and only necessary with the men, as when criticism was being meted out, each man regularly assumed that it was for somebody else. "I've never met a male athlete who's ever felt he's made a mistake in athletic competition in his life…It's incredible how little responsibility they would like to take in athletics."[18] Videos, he said, were used as proof of screwups with the men. With the women's team, though, he emphatically felt that, "If you make a general criticism about your women's team, every woman in the room thinks you're talking about her."[19] Highlight reels were used with the women only to show them how well they were playing, to build their self-confidence. Men and women are different.

It is the thesis of this book that future great (and even good) leaders will need to recognize and understand both masculine and feminine styles, traits, and skills, and how and when to use each, as Dorrance did, to maximize each individual's personal potential effectiveness and hence the team or organization's effectiveness. Diversity matters in the leadership of both war and peace.

Substantively as well, diversity among leadership and decision-making groups decreases the potential for groupthink – considered highly prevalent in much of the thinking behind the United States' decision to invade Iraq – and thereby increases the potential for strategic goal achievement. Nobel Prize-winning economist and psychology professor Daniel Kahneman has referenced groupthink as both a phenomenon and a danger.

> One of the major biases in risky decision making is optimism. Optimism is a source of high-risk thinking. Furthermore, doubts are suppressed by groups. You can imagine the White House deciding on Iraq. That's a situation where it's easy for somebody in the administration to think, "This is terrible." It's equally easy to understand how someone like that would suppress himself. There is a tendency and the incentive to support the group. That underlies the whole class of phenomena that go by the label of *groupthink.*[20]

Research has shown that diverse groups assess information more carefully, resulting in superior performance on complex tasks, and smarter, more balanced decisions.[21]

Whether in the military or in public or private national security-related roles, only relatively recently have women been the focus of leadership research, as only relatively recently have leadership positions been open to many women. Traditional gender stereotypical "spindle and spear" roles for men and women have prevailed: men have been responsible for providing for and protecting their families and communities through relationships outside the home, while women were expected to be caregivers and child bearers inside the home. While sex and gender are often thought of as interchangeable, sex is a physiological attribute while gender is a social construct regarding expected roles, behaviors, expressions, and identities, and therefore gender can change.

Gender specialist Heather Huhtanen[22] describes gender as affecting a person's thinking, being, and doing; where "thinking" refers to how an individual understands the world around them and the importance of conforming to sociocultural expectations in the private and public spheres, "being" refers to how a person subsequently manifests themselves, their role, and identity, and "doing" refers to how the individual behaves, reacts, and responds. Bangladesh, a country often struck by cyclones and flooding, can be used to illustrate how gender informs thinking, being, and doing in the context of a natural disaster. Women in Bangladesh traditionally "think" they must stay close to home, "be" responsible for the home and children, and avoid risks associated with the public sphere. In contrast, men are traditionally taught and expected to be brave and protective. This translates into women not evacuating on their own but waiting for men to rescue them. Indeed, the data show that it was mostly women who died during cyclone Sidr in 2007 (70% of the deaths were women)[23] and Gorky in 1991 (90% of the deaths were women).[24]

Huhtanen also explains how gender is one of many aspects of culture that can be used to tease out what is really going on in a conflict (or problematic phenomenon). She looks for how gender is operating as a driver or amplifier of conflict, and how gender is being used as a strategy of conflict. For example, in South Sudan, young men are encouraged to demonstrate their bravery and masculinity through cattle raiding – the results of which they can also use to secure a young woman to wed. Yet this practice routinely results in significant death and injury and feeds ongoing cycles of retaliatory violence and cattle raids.[25] This represents an example of how gender roles – for men and women – are mutually reinforcing and together drive cycles of needless violence that contribute to the current conflict in South Sudan.

In parts of Yemen, owning a gun is considered an integral part of being a man. This close association between masculinity and gun ownership has arguably been an amplifier of the current conflict – the mere fact that weapons are widely available and that young men are often gifted a rifle at 11 or 12 years of age.[26] Finally, the civil war in Bosnia and Herzegovina provides two examples of how gender is used as a strategy in conflict. In 1995, more than 8,000 Bosnian Muslim men and boys were rounded up and executed by the Bosnian Serb Army – this was a strategy of conflict used explicitly to eliminate future or potential war fighters. In contrast, somewhere between 20,000 and 30,000 Bosnian Muslim women experienced militarized or systematized rape during the same conflict. In some cases, women were held until they were pregnant – the strategy, in part, was to disrupt ethnic and religious composition through childbirth.[27] Gender stereotypes can be broken, but women's voices remain in the minority across the board in national security communities, still hindered by both structural and cultural barriers.

Structural barriers are those that can be addressed through laws or policies. Cultural barriers are those that are ingrained due to bias and custom, and often persist after structural changes are made. Culture is ultimately about control. When Captain Kristin Griest and Lieutenant Shaye Haver became the first two women to pass the Army Ranger course in 2015, for example, they were allowed to take the course subsequent to structural policy changes. The backlash they faced when they passed, however, including online death threats, sprung from cultural resistance to their mere presence in a traditionally all-male domain. Similarly, a retired male US Ambassador pointed out that State Department policy in the

1970s required that when two Foreign Service Officers married, one of them had to resign their commission. Most often, he said, it was the woman who did so, for cultural stereotype reasons of men being the family "breadwinner," though he felt, the woman was sometimes the more competent of the two.

Cultural barriers are most often associated with negative stereotypes and simple negative biases. A retired female US Ambassador I interviewed stated: "As an ambassador my biggest challenge was from US Government males who did not like working for a female."[28] Cultural bias and associated cultural barriers can both inhibit females as leaders and their effectiveness in positions of authority.

Cultural barriers to women's inclusion in security-focused leadership exist both within the organizations where they work and in the public. Barriers within organizations are evidenced first and foremost by low numbers of women, especially in leadership positions. In many organizations, women and men enter in approximately the same numbers, but women's numbers decline with organizational advancement. In terms of the public, researchers have found, for example, that the public is willing to accept women as leaders, especially those with military bona fides. But even with those bona fides, women still struggle to be seen as having the "authority" to identify and address national security threats that will be acted upon in terms of policy support.[29] Yet women, and the role of women in society, are known to play key roles in the security and stability of a country.

As part of a career teaching various security and leadership-related courses, I have taught a course titled Women, Peace, and Security (WPS) for several years. It is a national security-focused course, not a gender studies or social justice course, and not focused only on women. From its civil-society-based origins culminating in the passage of United Nations Security Council Resolution 1325 (2000), known as the Women, Peace, and Security resolution, in many countries, WPS has evolved into both an analytic tool and a framework acknowledging that gender equality for men, women, boys, and girls is a matter of national security and it advances ways to abate gender inequality toward positive, sustainable peace that supports human development. WPS connects the dots between human security and state security.

In the course, I initially offer students statistics in support of the gender-related premises of WPS, statistics based on decades of research. That research includes evidence that if a nation scores high on gender inequality, it is more than twice as likely to be a fragile state; more than three times as likely to have a more autocratic, less effective, and more corrupt government; and more than one and a half times as likely to be violent and unstable,[30] and that violence within the "first political order" (the home) correlates to violence becoming the *de facto* method of problem-solving nationally.[31] Those numbers make it difficult to refute that gender matters to national security. Once that relationship is seen, it cannot be unseen. It's everywhere.

Recognition of this linkage between gender equality and security has encouraged countries to adopt approaches such as the WPS framework to alleviate gender inequality and promote gender equality, internally and externally. As of

May 2024, 109 countries have adopted National Action Plans to implement WPS (though some with more teeth, and budget, than others). The United States is the only country in the world to have legislatively mandated implementation of WPS principles through the 2017 Women, Peace, and Security Act. Built upon four pillars: participation, prevention, protection, and relief and recovery efforts, WPS emphasizes the need for inclusive diversity (women having not just a seat, but a voice at decision-making tables) and consideration of how policies and programs affect men, women, boys, and girls differently.

The four US executive departments charged with the implementation of the 2017 Act are the Departments of Defense, State, and Homeland Security, and the US Agency for International Development (USAID). Their designation clearly indicates the security-focused nature of the Act. It is imperative to recognize as well that the implementation of the WPS principles is intended as both domestic and foreign. That first requires awareness. The bumper sticker for my WPS class is "you can't implement what you don't know about." National Security Advisor Michael Waltz, appointed by Donald Trump soon after his 2024 re-election, served as co-chair of the bipartisan WPS Caucus during his time in Congress, so certainly he is aware.

A male student in one of my WPS classes, an Army Major and career intelligence analyst, well stated the importance of "seeing" gender. He said he had taken every course offered by the military to intelligence officers over the course of his career and nobody had ever talked about gender before. Now, he said he felt like he had done a disservice to those who relied on his reports and analyses because so much potentially useful information had been left out of his assessments by not considering gender-related information, perspectives, and issues. Others have confirmed that gender considerations can be left out or minimized in intelligence courses and assessments, and gender considerations are rarely included in international and security-related academic curricula. Hence the importance of talking about the importance of gender within the context of security-related leadership studies.

My emphasis focuses on learning leadership through consideration of examples and discussion. Many, if not most, of the great leaders in war and peace have been avid lifelong students of leadership. While intuition plays a part in leadership, it is often primarily through experience and study, formal and/or informal, supplemented by data, that leadership is learned. Further, while leadership is often a very individual exercise, effective leaders recognize the importance of teamwork, and of receiving honest information and feedback from their team members and mates.

Psychologist Irving Janis posited in his seminal 1972 book *Victims of Groupthink: A Psychological Study of Foreign-Policy Decisions and Fiascoes*, that groupthink occurs when members of an often-prestigious decision-making group prize their group membership more than the quality of the decision they are making – effective goal achievement – or its consequences. The group often follows a directive leader's preconceived agenda without expressing doubts, disagreements, or considering alternative courses of action, and rejecting outside opinions. Their commitment to the group is such that regardless of the outcome of their decision, even if disastrous or counterproductive, group members will defend and stand by their actions. Janis believed that structural faults in organizations, including (but not limited to) lack of diversity, fostered groupthink.[32] Janis considered foreign policy decisions relatively contemporary to his time, such as the Pearl Harbor bombing, the Bay of Pigs invasion, and the Vietnam War. More recent assertions of groupthink negatively influencing decision-making continue, groupthink that might have been avoided with more group diversity – acknowledging that diversity can come from many considerations, including age, religion, ethnicity, socioeconomic background, etc. Here the focus is on including more women.

But political scientist Francis Fukuyama questioned the wisdom of women's involvement in international affairs as related to national security. In fact, his 1998 *Foreign Affairs* article "Women and the Evolution of World Politics"[33] created a firestorm of debate in that regard. Fukuyama argued that while women would tamp down violent and aggressive tendencies in international relations, women would likely be in positions to do so only in democratic states, while autocratic states would more likely be led by aggressive men. In other words, because it's a tough global neighborhood, it takes a tough, aggressive male to deal with another tough, aggressive male. That debate has not abated, with added considerations today focused on the pros and cons of diversity, equity, and inclusion (DEI) – and more recently added, "belonging" (DEIB) – initiatives and mandates. DEI has also been mistakenly confused with WPS. While there are DEI components associated with WPS, DEI is a personnel issue, while WPS is an operational consideration.

DEI programs evolved from social justice movements in the 1960s, focused on equal employment laws. In the United States, DEI began being structurally implemented with the passage of the 1964 Civil Rights Act, making it illegal for employers to discriminate on the basis of race, sex, religion, or national origin, and established the Equal Employment Opportunity Commission (EEOC). Employers subsequently began providing affirmative action training, often to prevent litigation rather than due to a belief in its benefits. Workers' rights were expanded and loopholes closed through later legislation, including the Americans with Disabilities Act (1990), the Family and Medical Leave Act (1993), and the Lilly Ledbetter Fair Pay Act (2009). Culturally, DEI has often met with resistance, some of it self-inflicted.

Organizational attempts to implement DEI goals have often been clumsy at best, with two approaches most common. The first was to outline workplace dos and don'ts, conveyed through mandatory training of one sort or another, training frequently viewed by employees as overly controlling and a waste of time. A 2019 *Harvard Business Review* article concluded that bias-focused training was especially ineffective regarding the behavior of male or white employees,[34] unfortunate given that white males typically hold predominant power within organizations. Not surprisingly, the programs proved largely ineffective and sometimes even counterproductive. Any event intending, directly or indirectly, to change the attitudes of attendees where attendance is forced is unlikely to have a positive result. Those events are often efforts to show compliance to policies, box-checking, rather than actually accepting and committing to implementing them. Bureaucracies are historically very good at compliance.

The second popular approach to DEI was to employ hiring tests, toward eliminating bias and focusing on merit-based hiring. That approach was largely a failure too, as managers resisted being told that they couldn't hire whoever they wanted. Test results were sometimes ignored or cherry-picked. Specifically, employers often ignored test results for white men, but weighed them heavily when minorities fared poorly. Intentionally or not, testing amplified bias rather than suppressing it.[35] Similarly, rules and requirements for hiring and promotion, and toleration for circumventing those rules or subjectively interpreting them, may vary according to who is doing the circumventing and interpreting,[36] again with minorities more likely targeted for rule infractions widely tolerated otherwise.

Initially, DEI initiatives were most often the responsibility of human resources offices within organizations. Beginning around 2010, however, they took on a life of their own, with many organizations hiring DEI officers and expanding both DEI responsibilities and authorities. Between bureaucratic overreach, what critics called too much attention to "woke" activities (alertness to social inequities) often claimed to be attained at the expense of merit, bumbled DEI initiatives, and the comfort of the status quo for some individuals, a rollback of DEI offices and initiatives began around 2022 in educational institutions,[37] and then spread to others. Legislatures in some states have even approved bans on DEI efforts in higher education and in public offices, though some are also now "re-branding" DEI offices with new names. DEI generally is looking to reinvent/rebrand itself toward more of an evolutionary process rather than a revolution,[38] in some cases, for the sake of optics.

Lesson learned: you can't simply outlaw bias. DEI programs have been most successful when found to be in the organizations' best interest. Repeated studies have shown that there is a correlation between businesses ranking high in gender, racial and ethnic diversity, and financial returns.[39] DEI provides organizations serious about their DEI efforts an advantage in talent acquisition simply because the talent pool expands. Research has also found that in organizations serious about DEI, there is increased employee satisfaction among women and minority groups, and so less turnover. Not surprisingly, employee satisfaction is unchanged where DEI programs are superficial, compliance-aimed efforts. And workplace diversity has been shown to improve decision-making and organizational innovation because diversity yields more diverse perspectives, ideas, and solutions.[40] Counterproductive groupthink is avoided.

But financial returns are not the goal of national security affairs. Skeptics argue that national security is "different," and regarding the military, for example, that DEI detracts from a needed focus on lethality[41] and inhibits recruitment.[42] The pithy mantra, "A woke military is a weak military" is often put forth by critics.

Actually, however, there is considerable overlap between private and public organizations, including the military, regarding the benefits of DEI. The benefits to private, profit-driven organizations address challenges very similar to challenges faced by the military. Those challenges are sometimes referred to in the military as the "5 Rs": recruitment, retention, readiness, resources, and risk to force/risk to mission.

The origins of that 5 Rs model are insightful. In 2019, Air Force Lieutenant General (ret) Mary O'Brien was working on the Women's Initiative Team (WIT), toward bringing down barriers to career development for women in the Air Force. She explained:

> It became obvious we needed to make the business case for policy change with some of our mid-level and senior leaders. This led to our "5R" model – a rubric for evaluating each WIT proposal using Readiness, Resources, Risk, Retention, and Recruiting. Once senior leaders understood how these proposals were directly tied to our warfighting capability through quantifiable metrics for the five criteria, the criticisms of "diversity for diversity's sake" were negated, and the floodgates opened for a wide variety of changes. Three examples, from among dozens to choose from, include (1) awarding a contract to produce body armor specifically designed for women; (2) removing administrative policies preventing pregnant and postpartum women from attending professional military education, eliminating a barrier to leadership development, career progression, and promotion opportunities; and (3) revising acquisition policy for all future weapon systems to accommodate the 5th-to-95th percentile of the height and body proportions of our recruiting population (men and women).[43]

The third issue addressed by Lt. Gen. O'Brien is illustrative.

Air Force Lt. Col. (ret) Jessica Ruttenber has spent much of her career as an advocate for removing unnecessary barriers to women and minorities in aviation. Her research cites that large numbers of women have sometimes been excluded from fields due to arbitrary standards and cultural biases resulting in the use of outdated engineering designs based on limited human factor metrics. For example, even with a chronic shortage of pilots, the US military excluded many women from pilot training due to height requirements that were part of the Air Force medical flying physical. The required standing height was 64–77 inches (basically 5'4"), and a sitting height of 34–40 inches. The restriction was based on cockpits being designed around the average size requirements of an American man: according to Department of Health and Human Services data, an average 20-year-old American man stands about 5 feet, 9 inches tall, while the average 20-year-old American female stands about 5 feet, 4 inches tall. Working from the average, that policy meant that 44% of American females were automatically eliminated from the talent pool[44] and the sitting height, due to differences in body types, eliminated 74% of black women, 72% of Hispanic women, and 61% of Asian women.[45]

Equally as counterproductive, the same height requirements were applied to individuals who worked in the body of aircraft, including linguists on reconnaissance planes intercepting and listening to foreign communications. With China as a key focus of US security efforts since turning from Middle East insurgencies to Great Power Competition in the 2018 National Defense Strategy, finding and training able-bodied individuals fluent in Asian languages is both critical and has proven consistently difficult, with shortfalls common. At one point, there was a 70% washout rate among those who trained for those positions at a very expensive training cost of approximately $125,000 per person. From a common-sense perspective, filling those shortfalls was made especially difficult because the military had categorically eliminated a wide pool of individuals fluent in Asian languages – typically short women of Asian heritage (the average height of Asian women is 5'2"). Including women have nothing to do with being "woke" or detracting from lethality; quite the contrary including them strengthens national security.[46] Though waivers could be granted previously, the height requirement policy was not fixed until 2022, and there are many other arbitrary barriers still needing to be addressed. Certainly, recruitment is, or should also be, part of the military's overall business considerations because things are not going well.

Army Maj. Gen. Johnny Davis, commanding general of the Army Recruiting Command, described the 2023 recruiting landscape as "one of the toughest I've seen in over 33 years of service."[47] The Navy failed to reach its 2023 recruiting goal by 7,464 sailors and is projected to miss its 2024 recruiting goal by 6,700.[48] The 2022 National Defense Strategy states that "people execute strategy" and mandates diversity.

> To recruit and retain the most talented Americans, we must change our institutional culture and reform how we do business. The Department will attract, train, and promote a workforce with the skills and abilities we need to creatively solve national security challenges in a complex global environment.[49]

Lethality depends on a skilled workforce, and there is no evidence that women are less skilled than men; in fact, sometimes just the opposite is the case. Whether, however, any of the military services are getting any useful "lessons learned" from those recruiting challenges, or that they recognize who will actually be needed in the future and how to appeal to them, is questionable.

Future wars will likely be "information technology" heavy, thereby requiring not primarily brawn, but brains. Individuals with interests and capabilities in science, technology, engineering, and math (STEM), intelligence, and linguistics, among others will be needed to plan and execute strategy.[50] Accordingly, with its 2021 recruiting campaign "What's Your Warrior," the Army seems to be placing less emphasis on combat jobs and more on high-tech. Similarly, Navy recruiting ads visually depict daring, sexy – but mainly high-tech – jobs,[51] all to a high-tempo, bass-heavy background beat. Whether, however, the military services have actually changed their recruiting strategies to appeal to a broader spectrum of individuals remains limited. In January 2024, the Navy lowered its standards (including individuals without high school diplomas) to be able to accept individuals who were previously rejected, though it did offer more and higher signing bonuses[52] for linguists, cyber specialists, and cryptologists. In still too many instances, the military does not seem to be paying enough attention to its actual needs and what is blocking it from meeting those needs.

Recruitment and retention issues sometimes go hand in hand. There are also workforce shortages in critical areas like cyber; cyber being referenced 30 times in the 2024 Threat Assessment issued by the US Director of National Intelligence[53] and consistently similarly referenced in global assessments. As of 2023, it is estimated that 25% of US government military, civilian, and contractor cyber positions are unfilled.[54] Yet little has been done to alleviate workforce shortages in the cyber career field by recruiting and retaining qualified women who want to work as cyber warriors, conducting offensive and defensive cyber operations. Due to advanced training and promotion opportunities, those positions are seen as more desirable than network administrative and network operations jobs where women in the cyber field are most often placed, resulting in women subsequently leaving. Additionally, many (mostly male) leaders foster a nerd-boy culture within the cyber-warrior community,[55] a culture unattractive to many women.

And if brawn is needed, women have shown themselves capable there as well. Traditionally, less than half of those who attempt the physically and mentally grueling Army Ranger course succeed. In the 2015 class, 380 men began and 94 graduated. Nine women began and two graduated, the first women to graduate.[56] That means that those two women did better than 286 men. While not all women are as physically strong as men, some clearly are. Tradition tells us that men are stronger than women, but that is a cultural stereotype. As of March 2022, 100 women had passed the Army Ranger course. While men and women are different, all individuals are different, including within sexes.

Integration vs. Inclusion

Women have cracked the glass ceiling in high-level government positions. Trailblazing women abound, but too often remain trailblazers rather than the first of many, with women still statistically less common in national security roles than in roles considered more gender-appropriate. Globally, women share an average of 26% of parliamentary (congressional) seats worldwide in 2024, up from 11% in 1995. The number of women as executive heads of state increased from 4 to 17 during the same period. As of January 2023, 22.8% of policy-leading Cabinet Ministry (Executive Departments) positions were held by women, with women represented in 50% or more of those positions in only 13 countries. Notably as well, the five most commonly held Ministerial positions by women are in "soft" or "human security" areas, dealing with individuals, not geopolitics, including women and gender equality, family and children's affairs, social inclusion and development, social protection and social security, and indigenous and minority affairs[57] rather than Ministries involved with "hard," geopolitical security issues.

In the United States, a woman, Kamala Harris, became the first woman elected to the office of Vice President in 2020. Democrat Nancy Pelosi served as Speaker of the House, the third highest position in the country, from 2007 to 2011 and again from 2019 to 2023. Pelosi was the first woman to lead a major political party in either chamber of Congress. A woman has never served as Secretary of Defense, though several have served as Secretary of State, or as president (though Hillary Clinton won the popular vote in 2016). As of 2023, American women make up 28% of the voting Members of Congress. While a record number, it is still relatively small given that women make up 50.4% of the general public.

In militaries, the percentage of active-duty women in NATO member states ranges from 0.3% to 20%.[58] In leadership positions, women are severely underrepresented. For example, not all NATO countries yet have female generals, air marshals, or flag officers.[59] (The terms general and flag officers, or GFOs, refer to the highest-ranking officers in the military, including one, two, three, and four-star officers.) Vice Admiral Louise Dedichen has served as the Norwegian Military Representative to NATO since January 2020, when she became the first woman to serve on the NATO Military Committee. Women hold only one in five NATO civilian staff leadership positions, and in UN peacekeeping operations, only 11% of commanders are women.[60]

Barriers or inhibitors to women in the military have a direct bearing on women rising to leadership levels, as well as recruiting and retention. A 2020 study in the United States by the General Accounting Office, for example, found that women are 28% more likely to leave the US military after one or two tours than their male counterparts,[61] for reasons ranging from family concerns to harassment and feeling isolated and stalled in their careers. Shortages and high turnover rates affect readiness, deplete resources to train new people, and affect risk to force/risk to mission, meaning that the military may lack the capability to achieve its objectives, now or in the future.

Fixing organizations that adhere to rigid gender stereotyping means moving beyond organizational integration to organizational inclusion. A 1994 study focused on male and female leaders in the male-dominated Catholic Church argued that "traditional male-dominated organizational contexts require women to conform to masculine norms and expectations and, therefore, suppress women's values and strengths and mask gender differences."[62] Retired Army Colonel James Minnich has explained and extended the important differentiation between integration and inclusion and how inclusion is key to building strong national defense forces and, hence, national security.

> Inclusion and integration are used interchangeably. They are not the same. Yes, both bring women into the security sector, but integration expects women to

> adapt to an existing system, while inclusion ensures that the system adapts to women. A gender-integrated approach permits women to serve alongside men in masculinized units with some accommodations but little acceptance. Such organizations are male-dominated, exhibit deep-seated masculine cultures, forge obstacles to women's full participation, and experience high levels of sexual violence. A gender-inclusive approach is different as it merges men and women with full system access. In these organizations, the default culture is not male, all are valued, barriers for women are eliminated, and the structure and its leaders do not permit the "strong" to prey on the "weak."[63]

Therefore, in order to "fix" organizations, it must first be recognized that equal opportunity does not necessarily yield equal outcomes in terms of gender diversity, and researchers have found that different cultures place different emphases on which is important.

Norway, a Scandinavian country known for its high-ranking on gender-equality indexes, struggled for many years with female recruitment into its military services. Real change began around 2013–2014 when structural changes to accommodate women began taking effect, and due to attitudes of acceptance in Norway, likely fostered by its societal and cultural acceptance of gender equality in general. A 2013 study compared Norwegian and American men's attitudes toward women in the military. While both were found generally positive, attitudes diverged regarding concepts of equality underlying those positive attitudes. Norwegian men supported the equal *treatment* of men and women, while American men more limited their support for equal *opportunities* for women in the military.[64] The American perspective furthers compliance with policy rather than inclusion. But inclusion rather than only integration is necessary for real positive change to occur, rather than merely expecting women to acclimate to a masculine culture.

In 2018, Pixar Animation Studios created an 8-minute short, called *Purl*, that is available to watch online. It is the story of a ball of yarn that literally knits herself into whatever she has to be in order to fit in with the "bro" office culture. Many women do that to survive and to get ahead; some men do too. Doing so, however, loses the advantages that diversity brings.

In discussions with women in the military, particularly in male-dominated jobs – including pilots, special forces, and submariners – I've asked whether they felt their units were integrated or inclusive, and their answers are generally the same: It depends on the leadership. Fully inclusive, harmoniously working units – where everyone feels that they "belong" – can change overnight if a leader bound to gender stereotyping takes charge. Similarly, integrated but not inclusive units can improve significantly with a leader who makes it clear that inclusivity is expected and follows through with that directive.

Inclusion would mean that women who are allowed the opportunity to serve in combat and other male-dominated fields would receive the same encouragement, training, equipment, and respect as men do. Inclusion would mean that when an equal number of women and men of all races enter a career field, they would get promoted at the same rate. Given that organizational culture is often determined by the worst behavior tolerated by leadership, leadership matters. Diversity can initially be uncomfortable for groups accustomed to, and comfortable with, homogeneity of any sort, including gender. But even that discomfort can be useful to spark more attentive decision-making and subsequent goal achievement if recognized by leadership.

Balancing Gender Strengths

Diverse leadership can increase the presence of traits like prudence in national security-related decision-making, prudence recognized by men like American Founding Father George Washington and many other great leaders as a key trait of leadership. Unfortunately, however, not all leaders are great leaders, and prudence can give way to other inclinations, from both sexes, including those associated with confidence, aggression, hubris, and ego.

In his 2019 book *Why Do So Many Incompetent Men Become Leaders?,* organizational psychologist Dr Tomas Chamorro-Premuzic argues that confidence is often mistaken for competence in men and allows them to excel. He goes on to say that "manifestations of hubris – often masked as charisma or charm – are commonly mistaken for leadership potential, and that these occur more frequently in men than women."[65] A junior female naval officer explained to me how this works in practice, based on her experience addressing taskers.

> When I receive a tasker or request for information regarding a topic on which I do not consider myself an expert, my first reaction is to try to find someone who is better qualified to answer than I am, rather than venturing my own, ill-informed and incomplete opinion. If I do feel that I am the most knowledgeable person on the subject, I don't hesitate to answer confidently, even forcefully if required. But I am much less willing than most of my male colleagues are to act like an expert when I'm not. Leaders should be aware that women may be less likely to volunteer themselves, though they are usually in reality equally competent to the men around them. Leaders should also be trained to view the humility indicated by this deferral as a strength, not a weakness.[66]

Her point about leadership needing to be aware that humility can be a strength demonstrates how "confidence" is too often confused with competence, regardless of the underlying substance.[67]

Psychologists have found that women tend to be more prudent than men.[68] Prudence is often assumed to mean risk-averse or fearful, personal traits thought to have no place in national security affairs or leadership. But prudence does not mean being risk-averse or fearful; it means discerning, being attentive to risks that potentially obstruct goal achievement. It is the ability to discipline oneself to avoid those risks, including ego and hubris, by the use of reason, and it is classically considered a virtue. Consequently, having more women in national security decision-making increases the probability of more prudence by tempering unhelpful and often counterproductive overconfidence, aggression, ego, and hubris more often linked to males – and groupthink – that can hinder goal achievement.

The relationship between ego, confidence, and hubris is a complicated one. Most simply, a healthy ego drives ambition, confidence, and resolve. However, an unchecked and consequently inflated ego can lead to toxic hubris and arrogance, unhealthy for either the leader or the organization he/she is leading. But confidence is an essential trait for all leaders and is shown to be more prominent among men than women. Asserting confidence is, however, particularly tricky for women, as the same actions perceived as assertive for men are often perceived as self-promotion or bossiness for women, leading to less acceptance rather than more, and thus personally counterproductive.[69] Multiple studies also reveal that organizational cultural and structural issues have played a significant role in holding back women's career advancements and created a broad-brush impression of women as lacking in confidence.[70] Nevertheless, cultural and structural issues have taken their toll on women's confidence.

Studies over many decades and in many fields show that women are often less confident about their capabilities than their male peers, supplemented by anecdotes such as those given by Coach Dorrance. A study published in 2023 looking at gender and student confidence in solving math problems showed men being more confident in their answers, though the gender gap decreased as the problem difficulty increased, with the researchers concluding that the women were better calibrated to judge problem difficulty.[71]

In that 2023 competence/confidence study, the research addressed the pros and cons of confidence.

> The benefits of being over-confident include increased ambition, morale, and persistence. Individuals who over-estimate their performance are more likely to challenge themselves with problems that are beyond their capability. This is beneficial for interest and learning, except when over-confidence becomes excessive...In certain situations, the benefits of being slightly over-confident may not be worth the risks. For example, over-confidence leads to a lower awareness of mistakes. In math-intense STEM fields, even slight mistakes could be catastrophic. For instance, in 1999, spacecraft engineers lost a $125-million space orbiter due to a simple mathematical error. Over-confidence can also lead to unexpected failures.

Individuals can learn from failure. Winston Churchill once said, "Success is the ability to move from failure to failure without losing enthusiasm."[72] Less productively, though, failure can trigger anger and, subsequently, aggression[73] among individuals driven by competition and winning, for self-affirmation.

Leadership demands assertiveness, but not aggression. Aggressive leaders tend to be dominant, forceful, and confrontational in their leadership style, even reckless, which is the opposite of prudent.[74] Assertive leaders can still be prudent. During the Revolutionary War, Washington made a prudent, strategic retreat through New Jersey to Pennsylvania to gather reinforcements and prepare for his famous crossing of the Delaware on Christmas Day 1776 to successfully attack British forces at Trenton. Aggression is often linked to ego and hubris, through anger, and can push leaders to prioritize their own needs and goals over those of others or larger strategic goals. The hyper-partisan Washington DC environment (and across the nation) has seen a lot of aggression lately, even physical aggression, evidenced by, for example, Senator Markwayne Mullin challenging a union president to a fistfight in a Senate hearing in November 2023.[75]

Too much ego and hubris allow actions to become personal, rather than goal-oriented. Niccolò Machiavelli once said, "I hold it to be a proof of great prudence for men to abstain from threats and insulting words toward anyone, for neither diminishes the strength of the enemy."[76] With regard to the attributes required to create a new, democratic form of government, Washington believed "much was to be done by prudence, much by conciliation, much by firmness."[77] Be it in either domestic policymaking or foreign affairs concerning national security, prudence helps keep efforts focused on goals.

International Monetary Fund (IMF) President Christine Lagarde famously declared regarding the 2008 banking crisis, "if it had been Lehman Sisters rather than Lehman Brothers, the world might well look a lot different today,"[78] suggesting that the male domination of the banking industry made the collapse more likely due to groupthink and hubris. Indeed, research from the IMF has shown a correlation between financial institutions with a higher proportion of women on their boards and institutional stability.[79]

Research in the leadership field also indicates that women are more likely to learn from mistakes than men, with men already confident in themselves and their abilities. A study presented in 2024 suggests, for example, that men "tend to focus more on control at work. In contrast, women focus on supporting learning (they accept mistakes as a source of knowledge and share knowledge gained from them)."[80] As long as leadership is male-dominated, however, the plethora of "lessons learned" garnered from feedback sought by organizations so as to be seen as "learning organizations" may go unheeded.

It is standard, for example, for organizations to conduct After Action Reports (AAR) on activities, especially in the military since it was the Army that developed them. But how much they are actually used is something different. A team of researchers writing in *Harvard Business Review* addressed that question in 2023.

> The truth is, most AARs are ineffective. Instead of producing a deep and honest analysis of error and oversight, they are reduced to a pro forma exercise. Leaders use them to duck accountability and cover up mistakes. Inconvenient

> opinions are ignored or silenced. Hard conversations and painful reflection are avoided. Superficial changes are grandly announced, and the organization pats itself on the back and rolls on.[81]

Several women leaders I interviewed mentioned exit interviews as another potential source of information to leadership that is often ignored. One flag officer who asked to retire early – partly due to working for a leader whom she believed clearly did not value her – assumed that someone would certainly ask why she was requesting to retire early, but nobody did. Similarly, when I retired after serving as the first woman department chair at the Naval War College, I assumed someone would be interested in an exit interview, but that too turned out not to be the case.

While all decision-making environments are riddled with situational factors, there are examples of why and how having more prudence in national security affairs could have benefitted the nation, including some related to differing masculine and feminine responses to threats.

"Fight or flight" has been traditionally thought of as the universal human response to stress. Based on both neuroendocrinal and behavioral evidence, however, "fight or flight" has more recently been found to be the typically masculine response to stress or threats.[82] This coincides with the predominantly masculine approaches to conflict resolution: compete or avoid. [83] When exposed to a threat, individuals assess the threat and decide to fight if they believe they have a realistic chance of overcoming it versus fleeing if the threat is assessed as too formidable.[84] Whether to fight or flight is subjective, depending on an individual's personal threat assessment and their individual male hormonal triggers. Assessing whether to fight or flee can also be prudent, but the only nonaggressive option is avoidance, rather than trying to de-escalate the threat.

Women, on the other hand, differ in their human stress response. Psychologists have recognized "tend and befriend" as a distinctly feminine physiological threat response. Researchers suggest that when facing a threat, females nurture and tend to their offspring while reducing behaviors, such as fighting, that would jeopardize the safety of their offspring ("tend") and affiliate with different social groups to reduce risk and receive increased resources and protection ("befriend"). This approach coincides with the predominantly feminine approaches to conflict resolution: accommodate, cooperate, and collaborate.[85] Female hormonal differences tamp down the instinct to "fight" and make it more likely that females will adopt a more cerebral approach to conflict resolution, to protect themselves and their offspring. They tend to favor nonaggressive options, though they will fight if need be, and fight ferociously. Indeed, anthropologist Margaret Mead once said, "I do not believe in using women in combat because women are too fierce."[86]

There's a quote on the wall at the Naval War College that reads: "Since wars begin in the minds of men, it is in the minds of men that the defenses of peace must be constructed." Fighting wars should be a last resort. Preventing wars is the better option, making non-kinetic options to threats highly desirable. Relating different stress responses to security-related decision-making and leadership, researchers have asserted, for example, application to contexts like strategic deterrence. The "tend and befriend" approach focuses on post-deterrence to "mitigate threat through de-escalation ('befriend'), and seek to bolster human security in situations of deterrence failure ('tend')" and that a "blended deterrence stance of 'fight and befriend,' coupled with post-deterrence planning of 'tend and flight' offers clear advantages over simple, conventionally masculinist 'fight or flight'" strategies.[87] Combining both the masculine and feminine approaches increases the potential for assertive but prudent decision-making.

Before the toxic partisanship that has lately overtaken American politics, for example, it took the bipartisan efforts of most of the 20 women serving in the Senate in 2013 to end the government shutdown crisis. Senator John McCain credited the women with the leadership needed to get the job done.[88] In 2023, in the hyper-partisan environment of Congress, a first-ever all-female bipartisan team of women led the congressional appropriations committees (those congressional positions are known as the "four corners") that control government spending. Senators Patty Murray (D) and Susan Collins (R), Representatives Kay Granger (R) and Rosa DeLauro (D), all veteran lawmakers who have climbed the leadership ladder over the years, went into the process stating that they wanted to break the gridlock that often characterizes budget battles and build consensus. Senator Collins, a veteran of the 2013 effort, said at the outset, "In my experience, women tend to bring a more collaborative approach to decision-making."[89]

The Rutgers Center for American Politics and Women affirms that research has shown women employ more inclusive, democratic, and collaborative styles of leadership in both public and private sector positions, and that in politics and government, women look to facilitate discussion – rather than control discussion – and approach policymaking in less confrontational ways than their male counterparts. This, in return, expands options for decision-makers. Research has also shown that women are more goal-oriented than men, though generally less interested in ego and power.[90]

A female general officer I interviewed provided an illustrative anecdote regarding goal orientation. She was working in a parallel position to a male leader, at her same rank, who was feared and loathed by most who worked for him. They both received an after-hours tasker needing immediate attention. Her counterpart had generally ignored her in the past, but she nevertheless went to his office to discuss it with him. She was stopped at his outer office by his cowering executive officer, both of them able to hear her counterpart yelling at a subordinate from his desk. So, she simply went back to her office and took care of the tasker. At a meeting the next day with their mutual boss, the boss congratulated him, ignoring her, for a job well done. Her counterpart turned tentatively to her, clearly for permission to accept the praise. Almost indiscernibly, she nodded her assent, and he proceeded to thank their boss for the recognition, not mentioning her. She said they weren't organizationally or personally competing with each other and the job had been done, so she was okay with him getting the credit. She added, however, that he acted like her best friend after that.

But in Congress, the women's "four corners" budget efforts were thwarted when taken to the congressional body at large, in a complex upheaval within the Republican party that left House Speaker Kevin McCarthy ousted, with analysts citing hubris among some individuals as an underlying cause.[91] Moreover, aggression again raised its ugly head as McCarthy reportedly shoved a fellow House Republican who voted to oust him.[92] The US government was left dependent on continuing resolutions to stay open and intra-party calls (again) for the ouster of McCarthy's successor Mike Johnson as those resolutions and others were being negotiated and passed.

Sadly, however, more women being in Congress has not translated into more bipartisanship.[93] In part, that is because the current hyper-partisan environment has not allowed transgression from party lines, and partly because some formerly moderate women have seen their fastest avenue for career advancement as being as, or more, combative than their male colleagues.[94] Women working as a unit often work well together, but as part of a male-dominated organization, competition all too often comes into play for a variety of historical and cultural reasons related to gender stereotyping.[95] But as the 2023 "four corners" example showed, there are still women trying to tamp down the worst instincts of the legislative body and women in security organizations urging prudence in decision-making toward goal achievement.

Regarding foreign affairs, had women been more involved and exercised prudence, the United States might not have invaded Iraq in 2003 without a better understanding of the Sunni–Shia conflict. Having a clear understanding of the environment is a key prerequisite to developing a successful strategy for goal achievement. After the terrorist attacks on the United States in September 2001, the United States declared a Global War on Terrorism, with President George W. Bush stating that the United States would not stop until terrorism was eradicated. The goal was set within a hyper-masculinized decision-making circle,[96] which included only one woman, National Security Advisor Condoleezza Rice. Terrorism, however, is a tactic, not a place or a specific enemy. The United States had set for itself an impossible goal and began aggressively striking out – including in Iraq – without a full understanding of the Sunni–Shia conflict there and subsequently found itself in an imbroglio, especially when US efforts evolved from a shock-and-awe military campaign to democratization and nation-building under Bremer.

Rice's involvement in the decision to invade Iraq has been the subject of much analysis, with conclusions being drawn, including that she was shut out of the decision by Secretary of Defense Donald Rumsfeld and Vice President Dick Cheney, played an honest broker to the president, and was simply a Bush loyalist. With some truth likely regarding all of these, analytic retrospection suggests that groupthink and hubris played a big role in the invasion decision.[97] More diversity might have allowed more prudence against a decision still wreaking havoc in the Middle East, including an increased potential that Iran will become a nuclear-armed state.

The value of prudence has been globally recognized by respected military leaders and politicians beyond Machiavelli and Washington through the ages, with quotes lauding the advantages it yields. "It is only by prudence, wisdom, and dexterity that great ends are attained and obstacles overcome. Without these qualities nothing succeeds,"[98] said Napoleon Bonaparte. "We must expect reverses, even defeats. They are sent to teach us wisdom and prudence, to call forth greater energies, and to prevent our falling into greater disaster,"[99] said General Robert E. Lee. President Abraham Lincoln saw "prudence in all respects as one of the cardinal virtues." He further promised, in the midst of the Civil War, that the war would proceed "consistently with the prudence...which out always to regulate public service" and not allow it to degenerate "into a violent and remorseless revolutionary struggle."[100] And Thomas Jefferson, certainly not Washington's biggest fan, said after Washington's death: "Perhaps the strongest feature in his character was prudence, never acting until every circumstance, every consideration was maturely weighed; refraining if he saw a doubt, but when once decided, going through with his purpose, whatever obstacles opposed."[101]

Conclusion

This is a book about leadership, but as Bremer's vignette demonstrated, the line between leadership and management can be blurred and dependent upon the perspective from which the position is viewed. Therefore, research and experiential anecdotes about both leadership and management will be considered relevant in the discussions within this book. To reiterate from the Introduction as well, while perspectives and people are not binary, research regarding traits and proclivities is most often generalized in binary terms and so is discussed as masculine and feminine, though in reality there is a spectrum among and between them.

Few, if any, great leaders come out of the womb fully formed. Even monarchs acclaimed as great leaders – Alexander the Great, Elizabeth I, Peter the Great, etc. – learned the skills and virtues needed to lead in their time and within their circumstances both before and after ascending to their positions of power. Learning leadership is possible with the desire to do so. A female retired US Ambassador succinctly expressed a view heard in many different ways in response to a question I posed regarding having a preference for working with one sex over another. She said,

> I did not have a preference related to gender. My preference always centered on: competence, personality, able to get along with me/others, attitude toward

work, ability to communicate and lead. These traits were not confined to one gender or another.[102]

Diversity simply expands the talent aperture.

The inclusion of women in national security-related leadership and decision-making further opens the apertures of options for conflict resolution, decreases the potential for groupthink, and increases the potential for decisions to be made prudently. There are no disadvantages to diversity that outweigh those outcomes. The leadership traits, characteristics, and propensities of one sex can balance those of the other. Recognizing that, and having each sex listen to and learn from the other, maximizes the potential for developing and implementing effective national security policies and strategies to address the complex environment facing every country in the future.

Notes

1 Interview with L. Paul Bremer, transcript from "The Lost Year in Iraq," produced by Michael Kirk, Frontline on PBS, aired October 17, 2006.
2 "L. Paul Bremer, Scapegoat," *The Wilson Quarterly*, Fall, 2009. https://www.wilson-quarterly.com/quarterly/fall-2009-the-future-of-the-book/l-paul-bremer-scapegoat based on: Dobbins, James. "Occupying Iraq: A Short History of the CPA," *Survival*, Vol. 51, No. 3. https://www.tandfonline.com/doi/pdf/10.1080/00396330903011537
3 Fetouri, Mustafa. "Paul Bremer's Legacy in Iraq Is Being Expanded across the Arab World," *Middle East Monitor*, May 23, 2019. https://www.middleeastmonitor.com/20190523-paul-bremers-legacy-in-iraq-is-being-expanded-across-the-arab-world/
4 Interview with Michael Gordon from *The New York Times*, "The Lost Year in Iraq."
5 Pfiffner, James. "U.S. Blunders in Iraq: De-Baathification and Disbanding the Army," *Intelligence and National Security,* Vol. 25, No. 1, February 2010, p. 80. https://pfiffner.gmu.edu/files/pdfs/Articles/CPA%20Orders,%20Iraq%20PDF.pdf
6 *The Wilson Quarterly*, 2009.
7 Graff, Garrett M. "Orders of Disorder," *Foreign Affairs*, July 14, 2024. https://www.foreignaffairs.com/middle-east/iraq-united-states-orders-disorder?utm_medium=newsletters&utm_source=summer_reads&utm_campaign=summer_reads_2024&utm_content=20240714&utm_term=EUZZZ003ZX
8 Pfiffner, 2010, p. 77.
9 Interview with Rajiv Chandrasekaran, author of *Imperial Life in the Emerald City*, Vintage Books, 2007, "The Lost Year in Iraq."
10 Chandrasekaran, 2007.
11 We Are Tech Women. https://wearetechwomen.com/inspirational-quotes-grace-hopper-computer-scientist-u-s-navy-rear-admiral/ (accessed March 11, 2024)
12 Popper, Micha. "Leadership in Military Combat Units and Business Organizations," *Journal of Managerial Psychology,* Vol. 11, No. 1, 1996, p. 15, citing Kotter, J. "What Do Leaders Really Do?" *Harvard Business Review*, May–June 1990.
13 Email correspondence with Amber Mitchell, July 1, 2024.
14 Popper, 1996.
15 Personal interview, April 15, 2024.
16 Dorrance, Anson. Speaking at Carolina Pharmacy LEAD program, Youtube, 2012. https://www.youtube.com/watch?v=_RUr8vMbtjo
17 Dorrance, 2012.
18 Dorrance, 2012.

19 Dorrance, 2012.
20 Schrage, Michael. "Daniel Kahneman: The Thought Leader Interview," *strategy+business,* Winter 2002, Issue 33. https://www.strategy-business.com/article/03409
21 Smith, Khalil. "How Diversity Defeats Groupthink," Rotman School of Management, Fall 2020. https://www.rotman.utoronto.ca/Connect/Rotman-MAG/Issues/2020/Back-Issues---2020/Fall2020-ToolkitforLeaders/Fall2020-FreeFeatureArticle-HowDiversityDefeatsGroupthink#:~:text=Instead%2C%20the%20group%20assesses%20information,precisely%20why%20it%20defeats%20groupthink
22 Material referenced was part of a guest lecture to my Harvard Summer School class on Women, Peace & Security, 31 July 2024.
23 Ayeb-Karlsson, Sonja. "When the Disaster Strikes: Gendered (im)mobility in Bangladesh," *Climate Risk Management*, Vol. 29, 2020, p. 100237.
24 Women's Environment and Development Organization (WEDO). "Gender, Climate Change and Human Security Lessons from Bangladesh, Ghana and Senegal," 2008.
25 International Organization for Migration (IOM). "A Boy Should Be a Fighter": Addressing Harmful Masculinities Driving Cattle-Related Violence. IOM, Geneva, 2021.
26 "Gender, Violence and Peace: A Post-2015 Development Agenda," 2015. Collaborative product of Saferworld and Conciliation Resources. https://www.c-r.org/resource/gender-violence-and-peace-post-2015-development-agenda
27 Anthony, Andrew. "The Bosnian War Baby Still Searching for Answers, 20 Years On," *The Guardian*, July 12, 2015. https://www.theguardian.com/world/2015/jul/12/alen-muhic-bosnia-war-baby
28 Email correspondence, June 28, 2024.
29 Caverly, Jonathan and Yanna Krupnikov. "Leaders but Not Authorities? Gender, Veterans, and Messages about National Security," *American Political Science Review*, April 15, 2024. https://www.cambridge.org/core/journals/american-political-science-review/article/abs/leaders-but-not-authorities-gender-veterans-and-messages-about-national-security/5F09302AB8C312AE427854D743ADFC96
30 Hudson, Valerie. "PPT Presentation Drawn from: Hudson, Donna Lee Bowen & Perpetua Lynne Neilsen," *The First Political Order: How Sex Shapes Governance and National Security Worldwide,* Columbia University Press, 2020. https://pdfs.semanticscholar.org/1a02/327babfb20be0982b5154e40c0ca5695cb3b.pdf
31 Caprioli, Mary. "Gender Equality and State Aggression: The Impact of Domestic Gender Equality on State First Use of Force," *International Interactions*, Vol. 29, No. 3, 2003, pp. 195–214.
32 Janis, Irving L. *Victims of Groupthink: A Psychological Study of Foreign-policy Decisions and Fiascoes*, Houghton Mifflin, 1972.
33 Fukuyama, Francis. "Women and the Evolution of World Politics," *Foreign Affairs*, September/October 1998, pp. 20–44.
34 Chang, Edward, et al. "Does Diversity Training Work the Way It's Supposed to?" *Harvard Business Review*, July 9, 2019. https://hbr.org/2019/07/does-diversity-training-work-the-way-its-supposed-to
35 Rivera, Lauren. *Pedigree: How Elite Students Get Elite Jobs*, Princeton University Press, 2016.
36 Winkie, Davis. "General Suspended for Alleged Meddling in Ex-Assistant's Command Board," *Army Times.* https://www.armytimes.com/news/your-army/2024/03/22/general-suspended-for-alleged-meddling-in-ex-assistants-command-board/; Reneau, Allyson. "Who's Your Sea Daddy," *USNI*, April 2, 2014. https://blog.usni.org/posts/2014/04/22/mentoring-in-the-military-whos-your-sea-daddy
37 "The DEI Rollback of 2023," *Wall Street Journal*, December 26, 2023. https://www.wsj.com/articles/dei-wisconsin-oklahoma-state-universities-88ecc684

38 "Under Attack, DEI Quietly Transforms," *The Washington Post*, May 5, 2024. https://www.washingtonpost.com/business/2024/05/05/dei-affirmative-action-rebrand-evolution/
39 Hunt, Vivian, Dennis Layton and Sara Prince. "Why Diversity Matters," McKinsey & Company, 2015. https://www.mckinsey.com/capabilities/people-and-organizational-performance/our-insights/why-diversity-matters; Tsusaka, Miki, Matt Krentz and Martin Reeves. "The Business Imperative of Diversity," Boston Consulting Group, June 20, 2019. https://www.bcg.com/publications/2019/winning-the-20s-business-imperative-of-diversity
40 Dong, Sarah. "The History and Growth of the Diversity, Equity, and Inclusion Profession," Global Research & Consulting Group Insights, June 2, 2021. https://thehill.com/policy/defense/3912262-republicans-grill-military-on-diversity-equity-goals-at-hearing-on-recruitment-challenges/
41 Office of Congressman Mike Gallagher. "Gallagher: Pentagon Should Focus on Lethality, Not Pronouns," September 1, 2023. https://gallagher.house.gov/media/press-releases/gallagher-pentagon-should-focus-lethality-not-pronouns (accessed March 8, 2023)
42 Dress, Brad. "Republicans Grill Military on Diversity, Equity Goals at Hearing on Recruitment," *The Hill*, March 22, 2023.https://thehill.com/policy/defense/3912262-republicans-grill-military-on-diversity-equity-goals-at-hearing-on-recruitment-challenges/
43 O'Brien, Mary F. *One Team, One Fight: Diversity and Inclusion in the Department of the Air Force,* Air University Press, ed. Matherly, C. and Greenlee, Jr. R., 2024, p. xx.
44 Dickstein, Corey. "No Longer Too Short to Fly," *Stars and Stripes*, May 22, 2020. https://www.stripes.com/no-longer-too-short-to-fly-air-force-lifts-height-restrictions-for-pilots-1.630941
45 Ruttenber, Jessica. "Invisible Women: Advancing the National Defense Strategy through Modernizing Human Systems Integration," Hidden Barriers, August 25, 2020. https://hidden-barriers.org/2020/08/25/invisible-women-advancing-nation-defense-strategy-through-modernizing-human-systems-integration/; Presentation by Jessica Ruttenber. "Failure to Adapt," Valkyrie Project Military Women's Symposium, March 7, 2024. https://www.google.com/search?q=valkyrie+project+ruttenber+video&oq=valkyrie+project+ruttenber+video&gs_lcrp=EgZjaHJvbWUyBggAEEUYOTIHCAEQIRigATIHCAIQIRigATIHCAMQIRigATIHCAQQIRigAdIBCTg3MThqMGoxNagCCLACAQ&sourceid=chrome&ie=UTF-8#fpstate=ive&vld=cid:744e05a6,vid:9ERhxfUL4Is,st:0
46 Ruttenber, 2024.
47 Garamone, Jim. "Chiefs Discuss Military Recruiting Challenges at Committee Hearing," *Defense Department News*, December 7, 2023. https://www.defense.gov/News/News-Stories/Article/Article/3610846/chiefs-discuss-military-recruiting-challenges-at-committee-hearing/
48 Mongilio, Heather. "Navy Set to Miss Recruiting Goals by 6700," *USNI News*, April 17, 2024. https://news.usni.org/2024/04/17/navy-set-to-miss-recruiting-goals-by-6700-chief-of-naval-personnel-tells-house
49 National Defense Strategy, 2022, p. 28. https://media.defense.gov/2022/Oct/27/2003103845/-1/-1/1/2022-NATIONAL-DEFENSE-STRATEGY-NPR-MDR.PDF
50 https://www3.weforum.org/docs/WEF_The_Global_Risks_Report_2024.pdf
51 https://etoolbox.cnrc.navy.mil/commercials.html (accessed April 23, 2024)
52 Coblemtz, Emilee. "US Navy Will Open Recruiting to Those Without High School Diplomas," *USA Today*, January 1, 2024. https://www.usatoday.com/story/news/nation/2024/01/29/us-navy-recruiting-diplomas/72402449007/
53 Annual Threat Assessment of the US Intelligence Community. 2024. https://www.dni.gov/files/ODNI/documents/assessments/ATA-2024-Unclassified-Report.pdf

54 Williams, Lauren C. "1/4 of DOD Cyber Jobs Are Vacant," *Defense One*, August 4, 2023. https://www.defenseone.com/defense-systems/2023/08/pentagon-lays-out-plan-boost-its-cyber-workforce/389123/
55 Warner, Lillian. "This is What the Air Force Can Do To Recruit and Retain Cyber Warriors," *Air Force Times*, December 3, 2020. https://www.airforcetimes.com/opinion/commentary/2020/12/03/this-is-what-the-air-force-can-do-to-recruit-and-retain-women-cyber-warriors/
56 "Women Soldiers Make History in First Gender-Integrated Ranger School," *NBC News*, April 23, 2015. https://www.nbcnews.com/news/us-news/women-soldiers-make-history-first-gender-integrated-ranger-school-n347366
57 UN Women. https://www.unwomen.org/en/what-we-do/leadership-and-political-participation/facts-and-figures
58 Buchholtz, Katharina. "Military Women Remain in the Minority," *Statista*, September 21, 2021. https://www.statista.com/chart/25840/women-as-share-of-active-duty-military-personnel/
59 Husseini, Halal. "The Most Senior Military Women across NATO Nations," *AirForce Technology*, June 2019. https://www.airforce-technology.com/features/nato-most-senior-military-women/?cf-view
60 European Institute for Gender Equality. "4 in 5 NATO Council Representatives are Men: The Need for More Femal Represenation," July 3, 2023. https://eige.europa.eu/newsroom/news/4-5-nato-council-representatives-are-men-need-more-female-representation?language_content_entity=en
61 General Accounting Office. *Female Active-Duty Personnel: Guidance and Plans Needed For Recruitment and Retention Efforts,* May 2020. https://www.gao.gov/assets/gao-20-61.pdf
62 Druskat, Vanessa. "Gender and Leadership Style: Transformational and Transactional Leadership in the Roman Catholic Church," *Leadership Quarterly*, Vol. 5, No. 2, 1994, p. 100.
63 Minnich, James M. "Politics of Belonging: Men as Allies in the Meaningful Inclusion of Women in the Security Sector," in *Women, Peace & Security in a Fragile World*, ed. Saira Yamin, Naval War College Press, 2023. https://digital-commons.usnwc.edu/wps/6/
64 Gustavsen, Elin. "Equal Treatment or Equal Opportunity? Male Attitudes Towards Women in the Norwegian and US Armed Forces," *Acta Sociologica*, March 28, 2013.
65 Chamarro-Premuzic, Tomas. "Why Do So Many Incompetent Men Become Leaders," *Harvard Business Review*, August 22, 2013. https://hbr.org/2013/08/why-do-so-many-incompetent-men
66 Email correspondence between Joan Johnson-Freese and Lieutenant Commander Elisabeth Erickson, March 17, 2017.
67 This anecdote was earlier conveyed in: Johnson-Freese, Joan. *Women, Peace & Security: An Introduction, 2nd edition*, Routledge Publishing, 2024, p. 67.
68 "Women More Than Twice as Likely to be Cautious About Risk Than Men," Psychological Consultancy (PCL), March 16, 2016.
69 Gourguechon, Prudy. "Women in the Workplace: The Myth of the Confidence Gap," *Forbes,* November 6, 2018. https://www.forbes.com/sites/prudygourguechon/2018/11/06/women-in-the-workplace-the-myth-of-the-confidence-gap/?sh=6ef638fc6fd0
70 O'Neil, Donna and Margaret Hopkins. "The Impact of Gendered Organizational Systems on Women's Career Advancement," *Frontiers in Psychology,* June 29, 2015. https://www.frontiersin.org/journals/psychology/articles/10.3389/fpsyg.2015.00905/full; Darren T. Baker and Juliet Bourke. "How Confidence is Weaponized Against Women," *Harvard Business Review*, October 2, 2022. https://hbr.org/2022/10/how-confidence-is-weaponized-against-women

71 McMurran, Meaghan, David Weisbart and Kinnari Atit. "The Relationship Between Student's Gender and Their Confidence in Correctness of Complex and Difficult Mathematical Problems," *Learning and Individual Differences*, August 24, 2023.
72 https://www.azquotes.com/author/2886-Winston_Churchill/tag/enthusiasm
73 Wang, W., X. Chen, G. Ning, G., et al. "The Relationship between Anger and Learning from Failure: The Moderating Effect of Resilience and Project Commitment," *Current Psychology*, Vol. 42, 2023, pp. 22726–22737. https://doi.org/10.1007/s12144-022-03330-5
74 Maloney, Mary and Patricia Moore. "From Aggressive to Assertive," *International Journal of Women's Dermatology,* Nov 7, 2019, pp. 46–49. https://www.ncbi.nlm.nih.gov/pmc/articles/PMC6997833/pdf/main.pdf
75 Thorp, Frank, Rebecca Shabad, Kyle Stewart and Rebecca Kaplan. "Fistfight Nearly Breaks Out in the Senate Until Bernie Sanders Steps In," *NBC News*, November 14, 2023. https://www.nbcnews.com/politics/congress/stand-butt-fistfight-nearly-breaks-senate-hearing-bernie-sanders-steps-rcna125140
76 https://www.forbes.com/quotes/7009/
77 https://founders.archives.gov/documents/Washington/05-04-02-0363#:~:text=Much%20was%20to%20be%20done,my%20situation%20had%20to%20act
78 Partington, Richard. "If It Was Lehman Sisters, It Would be a Different World – Christine Lagarde," *The Guardian*, September 5, 2018. https://www.theguardian.com/business/2018/sep/05/if-it-was-lehman-sisters-it-would-be-a-different-world-christine-lagarde#:~:text=5%20years%20old-,'If%20it%20was%20Lehman%20Sisters%2C%20it%20would%20be,a%20different%20world'%20%E2%80%93%20Christine%20Lagarde; Wray, Tim. "The Role of Leader Hubris in the Decline of RBS and Lehman Brothers," in *The Intoxication of Power*, eds. P. Garrard and G. Robinson, MacMillan, 2016.
79 Sahay, Ratna and Martin Cihak. "Women in Finance: A Case for Closing Gaps," IMF, September 17, 2018. https://www.imf.org/en/Publications/Staff-Discussion-Notes/Issues/2018/09/17/women-in-finance-a-case-for-closing-gaps-45136
80 Kucharska, Wioleta and Aleksandra Kopytko. "Gender as a Moderator of the Double Bias of Mistakes," *International Conference on Gender Research*, Vol. 7, No. 1, April 2024, p. 190.
81 Fletcher, Angus, Preston Cline and Matthew Hoffman. "A Better Approach to After-Action Reviews," *Harvard Business Review*, January 12, 2023. https://hbr.org/2023/01/a-better-approach-to-after-action-reviews
82 Taylor, Shelley E., et al. "Behavioral Responses to Stress in Females: Tend-and-Befriend, Not Fight-or-Flight," *Psychological Review,* Vol. 107, No. 3, 2000, pp. 411–429.
83 Klein, Roohia K. "The Role of Women in Mediation and Conflict Resolution: Lessons for UN Security Council Resolution 1325," Washington and Lee Journal of Civil Rights and Civil Justice, March 1, 2012. https://scholarlycommons.law.wlu.edu/cgi/viewcontent.cgi?article=1319&context=crsj
84 Taylor, 2000.
85 Klein, 2012.
86 https://www.goodreads.com/author/quotes/61107.Margaret_Mead#:~:text=I%20do%20not%20believe%20in,because%20females%20are%20too%20fierce
87 Centre for Feminist Foreign Policy. "Feminist Foreign Policy and Deterrence," July 7, 2021. https://centreforfeministforeignpolicy.org/2021/07/07/feministforeignpolicyanddeterrence/
88 Newton-Small, Jay. "In Shutdown Washington, Women Are the Only Adults Left," *Time*, October 16, 2013. https://swampland.time.com/2013/10/16/women-are-the-only-adults-left-in-washington/

89 Barkley, Mary Lenore. "Women Hold the Four Highest-Ranking Appropriator Roles in Congress," *19th,* January 11, 2023. https://19thnews.org/2023/01/women-house-senate-appropriations/
90 Wilmuth, Gino F. "Compared to Men, Women View Professional Advancement as Equally Attainable, but Less Desirable," *PNAS*, Vol. 112, No. 40, October 6, 2015, pp. 12354–12359. doi: 10.1073/pnas.1502567112. Epub 2015 Sep 21. PMID: 26392533; PMCID: PMC4603465.
91 Blow, Charles M. "Donald Trump, Kevin McCarthy and Ripples of Republican Chaos," *The New York Times*, October 4, 2023. https://www.nytimes.com/2023/10/04/opinion/trump-kevin-mccarthy.html
92 Schapiti, Lexie and Claudia Grisales. "GOP Rift Boils Over in Exchange Between Reps. McCarthy and Burchett," *National Public Radio*, November 14, 2023. https://www.npr.org/2023/11/14/1212912482/mccarthy-burchett-elbow-house-republicans
93 Johnson-Freese, Joan and Alexandra Nicole Islas. "Will More Women in Congress Mean More Bipartisanship?" *WIIS*, 2023. https://wiisglobal.org/will-more-women-in-congress-mean-more-bipartisanship/
94 Gronewold, Anna. "A Trumpist Star is Born," *Politico*, December 14, 2019. https://www.politico.com/news/magazine/2019/12/14/elise-stefanik-new-york-district-084853; Ladden-Hall, Dan. "Elise Stefanik Breaks Fundraising Record After College Antisemitism Hearing," *Daily Beast*, January 10, 2024. https://www.thedailybeast.com/elise-stefanik-breaks-fundraising-record-after-college-antisemitism-hearing; Cohen, David. "Shame, Shame, Shame: Nancy Mace Spars with George Stephanopoulos," *Politico,* March 10, 2024. https://www.politico.com/news/2024/03/10/shame-nancy-mace-spars-george-stephanopoulos-00146149
95 Johnson-Freese, Joan. *Women vs Women: The Case for Cooperation*, Routledge, 2022.
96 Mann, Bonnie. *Sovereign Masculinity: Gender Lessons From the War on Terror,* Oxford University Press, 2014.
97 Nakhleh, Emile. "The Iraq War Was Dominated by Groupthink and Absolutely no Humility," *Responsible Statecraft*, February 27, 2023. https://responsiblestatecraft.org/2023/02/27/two-decades-later-what-has-the-us-learned-from-the-iraq-invasion/
98 https://www.azquotes.com/quote/1377155
99 https://www.brainyquote.com/quotes/robert_e_lee_400168
100 Guelzo, Allen. "The Prudence of Abraham Lincoln," *First Things,* January 2006. https://www.firstthings.com/article/2006/01/the-prudence-of-abraham-lincoln
101 Thomas Jefferson to Walter Jones, Letter, January 2, 1814. https://founders.archives.gov/documents/Jefferson/03-07-02-0052#:~:text=perhaps%20the%20strongest%20feature%20in,his%20purpose%20whatever%20obstacles%20opposed
102 Email correspondence, June 28, 2024.

2

THEORIES AND THE CONTEXT OF LEADERSHIP

World War II US General George Patton is known and respected as a great battlefield commander. Military historian and author Stephen Moore describes him as: "Charismatic, irreverent, impulsive and inspiring, Patton possessed a massive ego and the ambition to match. But he could also motivate men to fight."[1] Patton, nicknamed "Old Blood and Guts," and his troops are credited with defeating his archnemesis, German General Erwin "the Desert Fox" Rommel. More than once, however, Allied Supreme Commander US General Dwight D. Eisenhower considered relieving Patton of command due to Patton's impulsive and often impolitic behavior, including insulting British allies.[2]

Conversely, Eisenhower was an outstanding strategic leader but never served in combat during World War I. He excelled at staff assignments, having served under Generals John J. Pershing, Douglas MacArthur, and Walter Krueger, thereby learning organizational skills and how to work with and for difficult people, all skills necessary to hold the allied forces together. British Field Marshal Bernard Montgomery said of him:

> His real strength lies in his human qualities. He has the power of drawing the hearts of men toward him as a magnet attracts the bit of metal. He merely has to smile at you, and you trust him at once.[3]

In the context of the battlefield during the war, Patton was needed and so his foibles were tolerated by Eisenhower. Once the battlefields were quieted, though, Eisenhower had to remove Patton as commander of the Third Army in 1945 postwar Germany, for making inopportune and inflammatory statements concerning denazification policies. Eisenhower and Patton were very different types of leaders, and the qualities that made each a great leader were largely context-specific.

DOI: 10.4324/9781003564065-3

Leadership Theories

There is an abundance of literature on institutional variations of leadership, including government, military, corporate, education, health care, non-profit, and more. There have also been crosscutting studies of these discipline-focused areas over the years, through different leadership theory lenses. Theories are intended to describe, explain, and predict behavior. Leadership theories have attempted to serve that function.

Trait-centered leadership theories prevailed into the 1940s but proved inadequate in identifying traits that predicted leadership under all conditions. From there, behavioral theories asserting that leaders are largely made, rather than born, then came into vogue, and so focused on what behaviors needed to be learned to be an effective leader. A contingency approach, which distinguished people-oriented from task-oriented leaders and attempted to relate their success to their degree of situational control, was popular in the late 1960s through the early 1980s. And more recently, leadership studies have focused on charismatic and transformational leadership.

Charismatic leadership uses verbal and nonverbal communication to attract, influence, and persuade others to see things as they do and fulfill their mandate. Wharton Business School Professor Robert House described the power of charismatic leaders in the 1970s, saying "by force of their personal abilities [they] are capable of having profound and extraordinary effects on followers" including "commanding loyalty and devotion" and "inspiring followers to accept and execute the will of the leader without hesitation or question or regard to one's self-interest."[4] Leaders including Ronald Reagan and Steve Jobs have been described as charismatic, but so too, negatively, have Adolf Hitler and Donald Trump.[5]

The potential pitfalls of charismatic leadership are several. Charismatic leaders can become "addicted" to the unwavering and unquestioning approval and support of their followers, and their followers "addicted to the leader's charisma, resulting in a 'reciprocal dependence' that then distorts reality for both."[6] Consequently, researchers have found that while charismatic leaders can achieve a great deal, charisma is effective in goal achievement only to a certain point. When leaders score too high in charismatic traits, their effectiveness begins to decline (though not surprisingly, the leader might not think so), as ego begins to interfere and potentially overtake other considerations.[7]

Transformational leadership influences, motivates, and provides intellectual stimulation and individual consideration to each person in the workforce to perform in ways that create meaningful change. It strives to create an engaged workforce that is empowered to innovate and have input into an organization's long-term and successful future. South African former President Nelson Mandela is considered transformational because he achieved significant positive and long-lasting change in his country. Steve Jobs is also considered transformational, evidenced by both that, with balance, leaders can be both charismatic and transformational.

Studies specifically looking at military leaders suggest that the emphasis placed on leadership training as individuals rise in their respective ranks, along with the significant responsibility and power granted to military leaders, makes them good leaders – more charismatic and transformational – compared to other leaders at the same level in other organizations.[8] Ideally, learning leadership would be part of broadly based educational curricula for everyone, through the study of civics (if it were still taught), toward a populace better prepared to be a responsible member of the body politic. This is particularly important given the increasingly volatile, uncertain, complex, and ambiguous (VUCA) environment due to globalization, the information revolution, and the consequent broadening of citizen participation in all matters political.

Academic theorists struggle to find useful methods of analysis for complex fields like international relations. An almost precursor step to theory development in that field is deciding what level of analysis to focus on: the international system, the national political system, or individual leadership. Looking at the international system considers the impact of a multipolar versus bipolar versus unipolar system, differences between democratic and nondemocratic states, economic gaps between states, etc. Focusing on national systems considers the internal workings of countries and how those workings affect their foreign affairs. Emphasizing individuals is the third level of analysis because leadership matters.

American diplomat and author John Stoessinger believed that leaders' personalities play pivotal roles in taking nations and their populations into war. His book, *Why Nations Go to War*,[9] was first published in 1974. Using case studies, including World War I, World War II, and Korea, he delved into the personalities of political and military leaders to analyze the root causes of conflicts. He considered German Kaiser Wilhelm a moody man with a mercurial temper, blinded by tragic attachment to the romanticism of Nibelungen, mystical German sagas peopled with heroes who see the world through a lens of honor, courage and loyalty rather than reality. Concurrently, Stoessinger analyzed Czar Nicholas II as unprepared and psychologically ill-equipped to be an autocratic leader as expected of him in Imperial Russia, being distracted by his son's hemophilia, his wife's obsession with Russian mystic Rasputin, and surrounded by arrogant, lazy, and entitled Russian generals, thereby allowing himself to be dragged into war.

Stoessinger recognized that as much can be learned from leadership failures and toxic leadership as from "the greats." He analyzed Adolf Hitler not as a father figure but that of a rebellious older brother who seduced the disgruntled post-World War I German public by presenting himself as their champion against a parent/government they saw as having abandoned them. His analysis of Hitler surrounding himself with sociopathic individuals selected for their loyalty to him, and their use of propaganda campaigns to get and maintain power, even before social media was available as an echo chamber for lies, misinformation, and outlandish claims scrubbed by the media and presented as if sane considerations, reads almost as a playbook adopted by modern autocrats and would-be autocrats. Stoessinger concluded that the character complexities of involved leadership served to fuel and even trigger decisions that might have gone otherwise had other individuals been in power. The 11th[h] edition, published in 2010, similarly analyzed leadership extending into the years of Vietnam, Lebanon, Bosnia, Afghanistan, and Iraq.

Whereas Stoessinger looked at how leaders' personalities affected external relations, others have chosen to take a holistic look at a leader's personality, often through biographies. As a graduate student, for example, American biographer and historian Doris Kearns Goodwin was personally selected by President Lyndon Johnson to help him write his memoirs. In that role, she spent considerable time with the Johnson family and with Lyndon Johnson individually. Eventually published in 1976 after his death, *Lyndon Johnson and the American Dream: The Most Revealing Portrait of a President and Presidential Power Ever Written* [10] became a psychological portrait of a well-intentioned but troubled man who unfortunately went down some very destructive, ego-driven paths. Goodwin subsequently has written several other political biographies of individuals, families, and individuals and families interacting with each other, including Abraham Lincoln, Franklin and Eleanor Roosevelt, and Theodore Roosevelt and William Howard Taft.

Other American presidential biographers, including journalist Bob Woodward, historian David McCullough, Georgetown Professor Stephen J. Wayne, and my former Naval War College colleague Steven Knott, have similarly examined different presidents and presidencies. Leadership styles of military leaders have also been subject to biographical considerations by individuals such as Sir B.H. Liddell Hart. Hart, who fought in World War I, was an early advocate of air power and mechanized tank warfare. His biographies examined and advocated those tactics and proved influential among strategists, which was his intent. He is famously quoted as saying, "The only thing harder than getting a new idea into the military mind is to get the old one out."[11] More contemporarily, American journalist Tom Ricks has focused his work on both individual leaders and leadership principles within military cultures and institutions.

Others have undertaken more comprehensive analyses of leadership by combining political psychology, history, and biography. Political scientist James David Barber's 1972 book, *The Presidential Character: Predicting Performance in the White House*,[12] attempted to categorize American presidents, beginning with William H. Taft, toward predicting the future performance of candidates based on factors placing them into the four categories he created. He looks at certain factors as the historical/biographical part of his analyses: personal character, world view, and style; the environmental power situation; and the political climate of expectations, positing that character, world view, and style are established before a person has enough power to run for president. From that analysis, individuals were categorized as active-positive, active-negative, passive-positive, and passive-negative. The active/passive categorization is based on how much energy a president invests in his presidency, and the positive/negative on whether or not the president enjoys his job and the exercise of power; these dimensions being associated with dimensions of dominance/submissiveness, extroversion/introversion, and optimism/pessimism.

He deems active-positive presidents to be those who are highly energetic and enjoy the job. They possess healthy personal self-esteem and are therefore able to be flexible and results-oriented with policy. Analysts have placed presidents including Franklin Roosevelt, John F. Kennedy, and George H.W. Bush in the active-positive category. Active-negative presidents, on the other hand, are those who devote considerable time to the job but get little enjoyment from it. They are characterized by low self-esteem, thereby compulsively seeking approval and power. Consequently, they are also unable to admit mistakes and are therefore rigid in decision-making, even when decisions prove demonstrably bad. Woodrow Wilson, Herbert Hoover, and Lyndon Johnson have been considered exemplary of active-negatives.

Passive-positive presidents are those likely to delegate decision-making to others, but enjoy being president. Rather than power, low self-esteem drives them to seek affection. They are agreeable and cooperative rather than assertive, with William Howard Taft and Ronald Reagan often placed into this category. Passive-negatives are presidents who don't spend much time on a job they don't really like. Many passive-negatives are said to have taken the job out of a sense of duty, drawing cheerless satisfaction from accepting what they see as a calling, with Calvin Coolidge and Dwight Eisenhower often placed in this category.

Criticisms of Barber's approach have included that its predictive value is limited because so much retrospection comes into play, and that character analysis that places individuals into categories is analyst dependent. Supporters of Ronald Reagan, for example, have argued he is an active-positive rather than a passive-positive. The approach also generated somewhat of an assumption that in complex modern times, only active-positive presidents could really be successful, while others have found that not to be the case. While some analyses of more recent presidents have attempted to use Barber's framework – characterizing Donald Trump, for example, as an active/negative[13] – other considerations have extended presidential leadership literature in different directions.

In his 2012 book, *Indispensable: When Leaders Really Matter*, author and Harvard Professor Gautam Mukunda presented what he called Leadership Filtration Theory. Specifically, he said that most leaders come to power through a filtering system within their organization – whether political parties, the military, a government department, or a corporation – and these leaders make choices that are predictable and incremental. A male military leader I interviewed, for example, said that a certain amount of assimilation was required of all military members, male and female, and the default has been to assimilate to masculine expectations. Predictable and incremental decisions and policies are often exactly what those within their organizations/populace want. In terms of the presidency, Dwight Eisenhower's passivity as president, for example, could be seen as exactly the "rest" that the country wanted after World War II; Eisenhower as a heroic, grandfather figure.

Some leaders, though often those minimally filtered through the usual vetting processes, are the ones capable of making sweeping changes, for good or ill. By profiling a mix of historic leaders, Mukunda reveals how a single individual in the right place at the right time – e.g., Hitler for ill in post-World War I Germany or Winston Churchill for good in England during World War II – can destroy or save the country they lead.

Joseph Nye's 2013 book, *Presidential Leadership and the Creation of the American Era*,[14] while specifically addressing American presidential leadership, focused on leaders' goals, styles, and skills more or less applicable to leadership generally. Similar to Mukunda, he suggests that leaders range from transformational to incremental in terms of their goals. To achieve those goals, they may use a transactional style, whereby leaders "manage their hard power resources for coercion and payment," or an inspirational style, whereby their leadership "rests more on soft power skills of attraction and persuasion."[15] The relationship between leaders and followers is essentially emotional. It was Nye who first popularized the concept of soft power in the late 1980s and brought it to the forefront of "winning hearts and minds" policy debates post 9/11. Illustrating differences in style, when Secretary of Defense Donald Rumsfeld was asked how he felt about "soft power" at a press conference in 2004, he snapped, "I don't know what that means."[16]

Nye then describes differing soft and hard power leadership skills. Soft power, including inspirational skills, encompasses emotional IQ, communication, and vision. Emotional IQ includes the ability to manage relationships, use personal charisma, and having emotional self-awareness and control. Eisenhower, for example, had a bad temper which he recognized was counterproductive, so personally strove throughout his life to control it. Communication skills are those which are persuasive to followers through words, symbols, and examples. Former actor Ronald Reagan excelled at communication. Vision requires the ability to balance ideals and capabilities.

Hard power, transactional skills are organizational capacity and Machiavellian skills. Organizational capacity means being able to use rewards and information systems for the benefit of inner and outer circles. Transactional leaders make others aware that there is a link between their efforts and personal support, and rewards. Machiavellian skills are those that allow the leader to bully, buy, and bargain to build winning coalitions.

Nye suggests that leaders who combine resources, such as through diversity, accrue smart power, which is accomplished through contextual intelligence. Specifically, they understand the evolving environment, capitalize on trends (thereby creating their own luck), and adjust their style to the situational context and followers' needs.[17] He goes on to say that, "Above all, effective leadership requires the skill of contextual intelligence and an intuitive diagnostic ability that helps a leader understand change, set objectives, and align strategies and tactics accordingly."[18] In the context of international relations, Nye describes contextual intelligence as both a capability to distinguish trends within a complex environment and adaptability while trying to shape events. He cites Prussian General and Statesman Otto von Bismarck as saying it is the "ability to intuit God's movements in history, and seize the hem of His garment as He sweeps past."[19] Nye goes on to relate contextual intelligence to contemporary foreign policy, saying an effective leader must understand both the culture and the power structures in other societies, and how they interact with the international system, providing an example.

> With years of experience in foreign affairs, George H. W. Bush had excellent contextual intelligence. With almost no experience in foreign affairs, "W" did not. That gap proved the difference between the success of the father and the failure of the son.[20]

Effective contextual intelligence demands the constant education and reeducation of leaders. While leadership studies have often focused on the tacit learning of skilled leaders, sometimes referred to as a leader's intuition or innate wisdom, tacit learning is considered difficult to teach because it is based on trial-and-error experiences.[21] Strategic leaders cannot be experts in all the fields encompassed in the broader, more complex environments they encounter. Consequently, they must be both willing and anxious to learn as situations evolve, including about and from internal followers and external stakeholders, and be comfortable with and skilled at handling unstructured situations.

Learning takes time and experience, which leads to an important consideration too often overlooked: age. Strictly speaking, age doesn't matter, competency does. But there can be a correlation between age and competency when education and experience are factored into competency. Many of the individuals (10:1 male/female) sent by the Bush Administration to "rebuild" Iraq were 20-something years old with little or no experience in the fields for which they were responsible. They were known as the "Brat Pack."

> It was a bunch of young kids – had no experience managing finances – who were given the task of running Iraq's budget. It turned out that this group of kids who had come over together couldn't quite figure out why they'd been chosen. They finally discovered that what had tied them together was that they had all applied for jobs at the Heritage Foundation, this conservative think tank in Washington.[22]

Not only were they ineffective in their jobs, but they also sometimes fouled civil–military relations when they treated seasoned soldiers as their errand boys.

Studies have also found, however, that as leaders age, they can be seen as more resistant to change and innovation but, nevertheless, older leaders are considered more reliable.[23] Overall, however, it is competency that matters, and competency is individual and must be judged as such. Unfortunately, but perhaps not surprisingly, research has also found that age is an especially tricky consideration for women in the workforce. Young women are less accepted as competent than young men, but they more quickly move to being considered too old for positions, rather than "seasoned" as are older men. US presidential hopeful Nikki Haley was dubbed "past her prime" by CNN host Don Lemon in 2023, with Haley then being 51 years old. There is no "good age" for professional women.[24]

Generally speaking, contextual intelligence involves the convergence of three abilities: "1) an intuitive grasp of relevant past events, 2) acute awareness of present contextual variables, and 3) awareness of the preferred future."[25] Then, these three abilities must interact so that the leader can exert influence and make appropriate decisions. But beyond that, the full environment of the event, situation, or policy – and those involved – that leadership is addressing must be considered as part of the contextual intelligence. Context can be real or perceived, psychological, social, physical, and metaphysical and includes such things as: "geography, genders, industries, job roles or titles, attitudes, beliefs, values, politics, cultures, symbols, organizational climate, the past, the preferred future, and personal ethics."[26] Further, leaders must recognize their own strengths, weaknesses, capabilities, and limitations, to be able to resist their weaknesses and to actively supplement their personal limitations by seeking knowledge and/or the help of others. Leadership diversity among groups adds to the potential that context will be accurately assessed and considered. Leadership diversity among individuals allows the strengths of one gender to be supplemented by the strengths of the other. Understanding prevalent masculine and feminine leadership traits and when they are best used is part of leadership growth and learning.

The Importance of Context

This book explicitly explores leadership in war and peace, though leadership in national security affairs is, in some ways, similar to leadership in business, health care, education, charitable organizations, etc., though in other ways it is different. Indeed, as the vignette regarding Eisenhower and Patton in this chapter illustrates, leadership within different contexts of national security, even within military circumstances during and post-conflict, can differ. Organizational cultures, resources, timetables, goals – and just luck or timing – and the traits and styles of leaders are all elements of what can make the difference between leadership success and failure. Context matters.

It is interesting in the United States, for example, that while civilian control of the government is foundational to US democracy, there is a tradition, indeed a presumption within the military community, that almost any high-ranking military officer can leave the military and successfully step into the shoes of a diplomat or a political position. In fact, former military personnel comprise about 20% of the

State Department's Foreign Service. Former GFOs have served as ambassadors, as Secretary of Defense, in the White House as advisors, and as president. The reverse premise, however, is considered untenable; that an ambassador or politician, even with extensive experience, could step into the role of a military officer.

The rationale is explained by a foreign service officer, formerly a military officer, as leadership training. "Military officers begin from the start of their basic training to read about and study principles of leadership from both military and civilian sources."[27] While certainly there are benefits yielded from that study, the value may be context-specific. In *The Hillary Doctrine: Sex and American Foreign Policy*, for example, Valerie Hudson and Patricia Leidl point out the sometimes counterproductive nature of hiring ex-military into certain positions of power in other countries, as contractors administering aid funds through the US Agency for International Development, for example. An assessment from a local in Colombia illustrates the issues that can arise.

> The contractors are very conservative, often retired military. They don't establish relationships with the communities in which they work. It's not an equal relationship; they think of themselves as gods: very hierarchical, very patriarchal, very pyramidal. They came in and wanted to do what they wanted to do.[28]

Similarly, the Bremer-led CPA in Iraq showed no interest in working with Iraqi women. Iraqi writer Zainab Salbi stated, "[The Americans'] patriarchy and chauvinism was harder on Iraqi culture than Iraqis themselves."[29] Leadership preparation for one organizational culture and mission, in these cases the masculine-dominant culture of the military, was less appropriate or useful in another.

There are (many) instances beyond the military of leaders more suited for one context than another, and individuals with or without the ability to transition from one leadership role to another. Aung San Suu Kyi was born in 1945 in the country then known as Burma, now known as Myanmar. Like several other women leaders in South Asia, including India's Indira Gandhi and Pakistan's Benazir Bhutto, she came from a prestigious political family. Her father was a key figure in Burma's struggle for independence from England and her mother a politician. Suu Kyi studied philosophy, politics, and economics in India and England, and became especially interested in the nonviolence philosophy of Mahatma Gandhi. She married, had two sons, and lived and worked in England and the United States for many years, including at the United Nations. She returned to Burma in 1988, Burma then a dictatorship, to tend to her ailing mother.

During her absence, Burma had become a one-party dictatorship under ruler General Ne Win consequent to a military coup in 1962. Coincidentally, however, Ne Win was forced to step down the same year Suu Kyi returned. General Saw Maung led the ouster and subsequently repealed the 1974 constitution and established a State Law and Order Council, an institution that gave the junta brutal, authoritarian power. The massive student-led pro-democracy demonstrations that had been going on were then violently suppressed on August 8, 1988 (known as the 8888 uprising). Suu Kyi made her first public pro-democracy address on August 24, and another – to a half million people – on August 26. In September 1988, a new military junta took power. Suu Kyi formed the National League for Democracy (NLD) shortly thereafter. Her popular appeal was such that she was placed under house arrest by the military government in July 1989.

The military government, which changed the country's name from Burma to Myanmar in 1989, agreed to hold elections in 1990, and NLD candidates easily dominated. But the military annulled the results and refused to cede power. Aung San Suu Kyi, as the leader of the country's democratic movement, became a symbol of the struggle for democracy, especially among the youth population. She spent almost 15 of the following 21 years under house arrest. She wrote books and became emblematic of the struggle for human rights and democracy in autocratic countries, for which she was awarded the 1991 Nobel Peace Prize and numerous other awards over the years of her imprisonment.

Eventually, in part due to international pressure, the rules of political participation in Myanmar were eased. In 2012, the NLD was officially reinstated as a political party, and Suu Kyi announced she intended to run for office. She won a government seat and was able to travel to Thailand in 2012, her first trip outside Burma since 1988. By 2015, the NLD had secured enough votes in both legislative chambers to allow it to form the next national government, but Suu Kyi could not stand for the presidency. The Myanmar constitution stated that the president could not be someone whose immediate family owed allegiance to a foreign power (both of Suu Kyi's sons were British citizens) and also stated that the president was required to have military experience (which Suu Kyi did not have). Consequently, a proxy ran in her place, won, and quickly created the position of state counselor, similar to that of a prime minister and more powerful than the president, and named Suu Kyi to that position.

However, the constitution reserved 25% of legislative seats for the military and reserved ultimate power in the country for the military, known as the Tatmadaw. The military was not pleased with what they considered Suu Kyi's power grab. Though Suu Kyi's administration officially held power, the Tatmadaw was still a force to be reckoned with in Myanmar. Over the next six years, the Tatmadaw embarked on a brutal, genocidal campaign against the Muslim Rohingya minority in Myanmar, first between October 2016 and January 2017, and a second that began in August 2017 and remains ongoing as of 2024.

The military action against the Rohingya people was condemned by the United Nations, human rights organizations, neighboring states, the international community generally, and the US State Department. Aung San Suu Kyi was criticized for her failure to speak out against the genocide, or attempt to stop it, during her administration. Amnesty International withdrew its human rights award from Suu Kyi, and there were calls for her Nobel Peace Prize to be revoked, though that was not done because it had been awarded based on her work until the time it was given. Other awards were stripped from her, though, including that from the City of London and the Elie Wiesel Award from the US Holocaust Museum, evidencing her fall from grace.

As a human rights and democracy activist for the Buddhist population of Myanmar, Aung San Suu Kyi was admired and lauded, but as a governmental leader, Suu Kyi failed to serve, represent, and protect all the people of her country. She was more successful as a symbolic leader than in governance. The military seized power again in February 2021 and brought multiple charges against Suu Kyi, who as of 2024 is serving a 27-year prison sentence for crimes alleged by the military. Certainly, her prison sentence is an attempt by the military government to discredit her among the Buddhist population, where she remains very popular, and to legitimize its own power grab. The international community, however, finds it difficult to support Suu Kyi given her role – inaction – relating to the Rohingya genocide, which has permanently tarnished her once-sterling international reputation.

Like Aung San Suu Kyi, Nelson Mandela in South Africa suffered personal hardship and separation from his family as a government opposition leader. As a member of the African National Congress (ANC) political party in South Africa opposing the sitting apartheid government, he was convicted of treason in 1964 and sentenced to life imprisonment, narrowly escaping the death penalty. He spent 18 of his 27 total years in prison on Robben Island. In those early years, he was considered an angry rebel, wearing a traditional Xhosa leopard-skin kaross at his 1963–1964 trial to emphasize his traditional roots and warrior persona.

Mandela was unconditionally released from prison in 1990 largely due to international condemnation and pressure, including economic sanctions, on the apartheid government. He emerged a different man, a man in a suit, a symbol of and diplomat fighting for freedom and democracy, though not an appeaser or accepter of apartheid by any means. Quite the contrary, he emerged from prison with his fist raised in an ANC salute, and in his first speech on the day of his release, he called on the international community to maintain its sanctions and proclaimed:

> I have carried the idea of a democratic and free society in which all persons live together in harmony and with equal opportunities. I hope to live to see the achievement of that ideal. But, if need be, it is an ideal for which I am prepared to die.[30]

Apartheid did not end with Mandela's release; in fact South Africa entered a dangerous chapter when it was tenuous regarding what would happen next politically, including potential violence.

Mandela spoke to the apartheid government soon after his release, calling for "a new South Africa." What that would look like, however, was unclear. The apartheid government eventually was forced to agree to national elections. Mandela, now an international symbol of freedom, was elected president in 1994, becoming its first black president and the first elected in a fully democratic election. In that new role, he was transformative.

The racial tension in South Africa could have boiled over into civil war. Mandela was intent on that not happening. He worked hard to bring white and black South Africans together, perhaps most famously through the South African rugby team. Mandela formed a friendship with white team captain Francois Pienaar. At the Rugby World Cup finals in 1995, he wore the team shirt that Pienaar had given him and walked with the team into the stadium. In doing so, he accomplished what has been called "a masterful act of statecraft conducted squarely in the international spotlight," orchestrating "a show of unity in one of the world's most bitterly divided nations, using the slogan "One Team, One Country."[31] While the circumstances in Myanmar and South Africa can certainly be argued as different, the ability of Mandela to transition from a rebel leader to a national leader is noteworthy.

Some leaders are effective in one role or context, but not in another. Some leaders are adaptable; others are not. But it cannot be assumed that a person who has shown strong leadership skills in one context will be effective in any position they are placed in or choose to place themselves in. Context matters.

Leadership theories offer a "lens" to analyze leadership. But even when the analyses are done by women, they primarily consider masculine examples of leadership, or women interacting with men. Feminist theory offers another lens.

Feminist Theory and Gender Equality

Feminist theory, like all theories, comes in many different varieties with nuances such that sometimes only theorists are interested and the nuances have little relevance to the actions of governments, organizations, or individuals. But as related to leadership, feminist theories generally begin with the premise that leadership is gendered because social interactions are gendered. A team of multidisciplinary researchers suggested in a 2008/2009 article in *International Security* that when individuals meet, the three primary characteristics noticed about each other are age, sex, and race, with stereotypical assumptions about sex making the strongest and most lasting impression, and the hardest to dispel.[32]

Feminist theories that stem from the assumption that social interactions are gendered have evolved, mostly through considerations of gender-related differences and similarities, context, and positive or negative views of feminine traits. French feminist Simone de Beauvoir, writing after World War II, authored *The Second Sex* (1949) and there referred to women as "the other" to men. She argued that women lacked the concrete means to organize themselves into any type of opposition to men's dominance because their lives were more tied to men – tied by homes, work, economic interests, and social conditions – than to other women. Women were dependent on men. She went on to say that though men may also depend on women in various ways, men didn't grasp these ways as dependence, and women didn't seem to be able to leverage men's dependence on them for their collective liberation. She stated that women who opposed suffrage believed that this "liberation" would reduce the special protections (American conservative activist and anti-feminist Phyllis Schlafly referred to them as "privileges" in the 1970s) and routes of influence available to women, destroy the family, and increase the number of socialist-leaning voters. Women were, as de Beauvoir stated, tied more closely to men than other women.

The idea that women who are dependent on men influences their outlook about and support of other women has been explored further as "linked fate theory." Linked fate addresses perceptions of how much an individual believes their fate is linked to that of a group, and consequently, how group linkage affects, for example, their politics and voting behavior. Linked fate theory has long been used to explain voting patterns of racial minority groups, where individuals feel that they will benefit more personally if their group does better, and so group support takes priority over individual preferences in voting.[33] Among women, perceptions of a gender-linked fate have been found contingent upon two factors, race and marital status. Heterosexual marriage has been shown to make white women feel less connected to other women, with the disconnect to other women increasing along with the duration of the marriage. For example, long-married, conservative, white married women have seen their fate more linked to men – if their spouse did better, they would do better – than to other women and therefore felt little or no reluctance to vote against issues that would benefit women as a group, or for misogynistic candidates.

Feminist theory as related to leadership largely focuses on different versions of gender equality.

One version of gender equality in feminist theory posits that men and women are essentially similar/the same and that if women were afforded the same opportunities and advantages as men, they would behave and achieve as men do. That view of gender equality was prevalent in the 1970s and represented in the misguided advice Coach Dorrance had access to, as discussed in Chapter 1. Taking the "everyone is the same" approach to gender equality – as the US military still too often does – equates to being "gender blind," by saying that all tools in the toolbox are the same and failing to recognize that some tools are better for some jobs than others. It focuses on compliance (policy allowing integration) rather than effectiveness.

Similarly, the term "gender neutral" also attempts to imply virtue. Ambassador Donald Steinberg has offered his experience regarding what he thought the term gender-neutral meant, and what it really meant when he was involved with the Lusaka Protocol negotiations, toward ending the Angolan Civil War in the 1990s. Asked in 1994 about the role of women in negotiating and implementing the protocol, Steinberg said he proudly proclaimed the document gender-neutral. That designation was intended to positively indicate that no gender was favored. In practice, however, both gender-neutral and gender-blind mean that gender will not be considered. Later, upon reflection, Ambassador Steinberg explained that those gender-neutral negotiations reverted to the status quo, which meant male-dominated. Women were not included in either the peace negotiation or implementation process. Gender-neutrality resulted in ignoring the issues of half the population,[34]and a resumption of fighting.

A second, more evolved approach posits that men and women are essentially equal, but different, and that feminine gender traits should be viewed as benefits rather than drawbacks, as they traditionally have been in relation to leadership. Employment of "gender value," sometimes called gender utilization or optimization (utilization in support of initial integration, optimization to move beyond integration), has been done in the military, but driven by mission rather than recognition of value.

The US Army began standing up temporary Cultural Support Teams (CSTs) in 2010, with the first units deployed in 2011. Members were comprised of American female soldiers to serve as enablers in support of Special Operations Command (SOC) units in Afghanistan. These SOC units conducted night missions, usually in search of weapons or specific individuals. Other CSTs were assigned as two-person teams to live in remote locations with SOC units as part of Village Stability Operations. The primary task of the CSTs was to engage Afghan females and children during missions and in villages, as contact by American male service members was considered culturally inappropriate by the Afghanis. Similarly, some 80 Afghan women served in a similar program called Female Tactical Platoons (FTP); their role of carrying weapons and working with US troops was considered so abhorrent by the Taliban that it placed a "shoot to kill" order on them. Besides their role in engaging women and children, CSTs also specialized in support activities including medical, civic-action programs, searches and seizures, humanitarian assistance, and civil–military operations.

The selection process for the CST program involved multiple steps. Interested women responded to a recruitment notice sent out by email and were initially screened for physical fitness scores. Though the requirement was for scores of 80/100, rarely was a woman selected who didn't have perfect or near-perfect scores. How well a candidate did on a "ruck march" – a 12-mile march carrying a 35-pound rucksack – was considered a key indicator of potential success.

> We were out there every might [with] 50 pounds of gear on [our] back, up and down Afghan mountains [at] very high elevation. That's where the physical fitness really came into play. If you slowed down your platoon, if you couldn't keep up or if you fell out on infil [infiltration, maneuvering undetected] or movement to target, you were a liability.[35]

But PT scores were only the first part of screening for selection; program leaders then looked for candidates who could align with SOC attributes, including resilience, being part of a team, and being willing to learn. And as the program matured, female managers increasingly looked for empathetic candidates who could interact with and connect with others, as a primary focus of their job was to collect information.

The women were highly successful in their roles, often able to gain information requisite to mission success that would have been otherwise unavailable. Said one CST,

> We could find the terrorists [that the Rangers] were going after much quicker, and we were much more accurate usually because the women and children knew what was going on in the community. I think [the Rangers] mindset very quickly shifted to us being an asset and not a liability.[36]

Initially, seeing the CSTs as a liability stemmed from male SOC teams having one of their own, who they had trained with and had pragmatic and valuable hard-power skills like room clearing, replaced by an unproven, new person who had yet to show value. Once value was demonstrated, though, the women were accepted as an integral part of the team while they were on missions.

A woman who served as a CST member in Afghanistan conveyed to me[37] that she used to stuff beanie babies sent from home in her pockets to take with her on missions, which initially drew teasing from her male teammates. The teasing stopped though when she gave a beanie baby to a scared young male child one night and he subsequently led her to where a cache of weapons was being hidden. That beanie baby proved critical in the team achieving its goal, without aggression or having to fire a shot.

When the US drawdown began in 2014, however, the CST program was abandoned. The rationale was that the Army and Special Forces were now fully integrated, so the CST program was no longer needed. At a gathering of the CST members in 2015, called the Women in Service Review, Army leadership asked how many former CSTs wanted to be considered for special operations programs, where they would specialize in combat arms training since the Rangers were by then open to integration. Of the approximately 80 women in attendance, only two raised their hands. The Army leaders were shocked, thinking that the women would all leap at the chance. But combat arms training was not, most of them felt, where they could most valuably contribute to unit success. Their value came from being able to do jobs that men didn't or couldn't do.

One of the hardest parts of CST recruitment was the requirement that a candidate get released by their command for a one-year temporary assignment to the CST program. These women were valuable members of units like military police, where they would not be replaced, and often serving in positions where they would, for example, respond to domestic violence or other incidents where, again, their sex often positioned them for a unique role. It is highly unlikely that the kind of missions where the CSTs and FTPs proved valuable because of their sex will not arise again, or that in a future conflict, an integrated female Squad Leader would have time to also search and tactically question women and children on target without increasing the risk to the mission. But the view that all tools in the toolbox are the same still largely prevails.

Further, this "everyone is the same" version of gender equality is too often achieved through what has sardonically become known as an "add women and stir" approach. That, however, fails to consider that "the right woman" is needed for a job, not just any woman. Even early in the CST program, women managers felt that heavy reliance on primarily PT scores for candidate acceptance – necessary because there was no time for physical training before deployment – was not optimal. Finding the right woman required further screening. The everyone-is-the-same approach is basically box-checking based on opportunities being opened to women, but not necessarily optimizing their use in the roles now open to them. Several of the former CSTs have formed an organization, AllTru, to continue to advance the lessons learned about operationalizing gender-value assets in the military.

Definitions of gender equality as applied to issues involving integration versus inclusion are not the only ones that remain contentious. In some cultures the notion of "gender equality" is considered counter to culture or religious norms such that it is replaced by considerations of "gender utilization" in discussions urging the integration of women into security affairs. Otherwise, the advantages of involving women might well be rejected out of hand.

It must also be acknowledged that there are feminists who believe that discussion of women as military leaders, even members, indeed even in relating gender equality to national security, is an abomination of the original premises of Women, Peace and Security principles. Their perspective argues that Women, Peace and Security principles are basically anti-militaristic and that applied otherwise distorts them as excuses for managing war rather than eliminating it.[38] In this view further, real Women, Peace and Security advocates would support human security rather than (merely) adding women to nationalistic premises related to war to do a better job of achieving nationalistic goals. In a political sense for this Women, Peace and Security interpretation, "sisterhood" would mean women rallying around candiddates who supported human security goals inclusing being pro-worker, anti-war and climate action. This perspective stems from civil societies' original push for UNSCR 1325 as an agenda to end conflict, through actions including disarmament and reducing military expenditures, not to make conflict safer for women.[39]

That position, however, has proven difficult for politicians running for office, policymakers, and those responsible for policy implementation to support, even in Nordic countries like Sweden that rank high in gender-equality indexes. Sweden's former Minister of Foreign Affairs, Margot Wallström, is credited with launching the first feminist foreign policy in 2014. Feminist foreign policy:

> seeks to address the reality that foreign policy has long been the domain of elite men – and that as a result, decision making on peace, security, trade and other

issues has often ignored women's interests and perspectives and perpetuated rather than addressed global gender inequities.[40]

More than a dozen countries have adopted feminist foreign policies of one sort or another, many of them focusing on assisting other countries with development.

Wallström faced difficulty, however, in reconciling feminist ideals internally, specifically in reconciling working toward global disarmament with the importance of lucrative Swedish arms sales to the Swedish economy.[41]

Alternatively, there is the argument that ending conflicts and creating a sustainable environment for human development, called positive peace, is an incremental process that must realistically start where we are, not where we want to be. That approach has become the focus of the Women, Peace, and Security frameworks in many countries, and subsequent feminist foreign policies that have focused on development and the inclusion of women in security affairs as a road to peace.[42] Though it is often assumed that a feminist foreign policy is inherently a pacifist policy, only one country has stated it as such, Colombia.[43]

But even for an incremental approach to work, WPS principles must actually be known, followed and implemented. Unfortunately, there has been considerable slow-rolling[44] and sometimes outright ignoring of its premises. For example, if the United States had been serious about inclusive diversity as WPS calls for, and the United States had its first WPS National Action Plan calling for inclusion in 2011, it would have insisted on women being included in later peace talks with the Taliban, but it did not. Ironically, the United States had pressed for a 25% women quota in the Afghan parliament, per the 2004 Afghan Constitution, though the United States had no such quota or that many women in the US Congress at the time. Do-as-we-say, not-as-we-do policies are rarely successful.

The view that Women, Peace, and Security requires women to be pacifist rests on the stereotype of women as inherently peaceful and caring oriented. Margaret Mead believed women fight less often but more fiercely than men because they fight only when cornered. But they will and do fight. Further, women are not part of a Borg, creatures with a single mind, but rather have differing ideas and identities.

Within feminist literature, the term "intersectionality" is key regarding identities. American attorney Kimberlé Crenshaw coined the term in 1989 in a judicial case where she was representing black women working at an auto factory. She argued that "treating black women as purely women or purely black, the courts, as they did in 1976, have repeatedly ignored specific challenges that face black women as a group."[45] The term has evolved (sometimes in distorted ways to generate fear-based opposition) to simply reference that not all women are alike, and they may have multiple identities that make them more vulnerable to bias than others: white women make less money than white men, but more money than black women, while black women make more money than Latina women.

But as many women in the military and professional positions have told me, their first hurdle in male-dominated environments is being seen as women, with race as a secondary discriminator. A female chaplain, a woman of color, told me[46] she focuses on commonalities among women, not differences, in trying to overcome hurdles to leadership. She further said she has also sometimes seen white women treated more harshly than women of color by white men in the military because the women were "expected" to "get along." When hiring women as faculty in Professional Military Education (PME), women veterans were preferred to civilian academics because, as a retired male officer I taught with years ago said, women in the military "know how to behave."

The military has had to address intersectionality in a number of areas, including hair. Recent changes in regulations allow women to wear their long hair in ways other than the tight buns required previously, buns not amenable to helmets but amenable instead to migraine headaches and alopecia. These changes "have arguably had the biggest impact on soldiers with textured hair – Black women, in particular – who struggled, emotionally and physically, to conform to the old rules."[47] Previous compliance with the military's strict grooming rules often required chemical hair relaxing and short – but not too short – hairstyles. Women were previously too often required to comply to rules set largely and arbitrarily by white men, and expected to conform to gender stereotypes.

Further, in practice, whether being more caring and relationship-oriented, or more competitive and controlling, helps or hurts an individual leader is, again, somewhat dependent on context. In direct elections, for example, leaders are beholden to the general public (or smaller samples of the public, as with the US Electoral College) often creating a context more prone to competition. In a parliamentary system such as in Britain, however, party leadership and being able to build coalitions seems to favor individuals who can work with others and build relationships. While coalitions can fail as well, that failure is most prevalent when members are wedded to extreme positions.

It is important to remember too that whether a man or a woman is elected, promoted, or appointed to a position of leadership, that leader's job is to advance organizational goals. A woman leader perceived as seeing her role as promoting feminism will quickly see her organizational credibility vanish. Hence, a woman leading an organization does not inherently signal that the organization has accepted that diversity yields benefits, that there is gender equality within the organization, that there is a healthy bench of women behind her, or even that the organization has moved beyond the integration of women to the inclusion of women. Indeed, women leaders must often be extra careful not to be perceived as favoring women or placing too much effort and attention on diversity, or face potential backlash from male colleagues.

A term was coined in the 1970s when women were entering the workforce in expanding numbers – "Queen Bee" – suggesting a propensity for a toxic form of feminism wherein once a woman got into power, she would actively try to keep other women at bay and even deliberately sabotage them. Interestingly, there is no male corollary to Queen Bees. Yet there certainly are men who don't support their male coworkers and sabotage those male coworkers for personal gain. Men just call it competition. Further, several tall or physically imposing men I interviewed said they were careful to sit down around shorter, or slightly-built men in authority in case the shorter man had a Napoleon complex. However, the idea that women deliberately hold others back and are inappropriately aggressive is exclusively female.

In 2015, researchers at Columbia University looked at top management teams at 1,500 companies over a 20-year period and found that when women were in leadership positions, other women were more likely to climb the corporate ladder as well, dispelling at least that aspect of the Queen Bee Syndrome. What the researchers found instead was that it is structural and cultural barriers that keep the numbers of women small.

> Women face an implicit quota, whereby firms seek to maintain a small number of women on their top management team, usually only one. While firms gain legitimacy from having women in top management, the value of this legitimacy declines with each woman.[48]

After the implicit quota was reached, women were again put into competition with both men and each other.

There are certainly women who are toxic leaders, just as there are men who are toxic leaders. The toxicity often stems from similar sources, such as a lack of self-confidence due to being put into a leadership role they are unprepared for in one way or another, including context. As a senior corporate woman executive conveyed, her female boss came from a background of being an outstanding engineer but had little experience working with a team or as a team leader. Subsequently, she was a poor communicator and had difficulties dealing with others.

But again, context matters, and different researchers in different fields and contexts have found different results and reached different conclusions regarding why women can appear, or be, harder on other women than men. A 2004 study of university faculty members found that women faculty members were harder on women students regarding how committed they felt the students were to their careers than their male faculty counterparts, or regarding male students.[49] The study was replicated in 2020,[50] and the same results were found. But looking further into the "why" part of the question, researchers concluded that women faculty members were not being catty or mean; they were projecting the bias and lack of organizational support they had experienced in their own careers, as well as the personal sacrifices required, onto the younger women and thereby expecting them not to be just committed, but super committed if they were to have a chance at success. The researchers concluded that "eliminating gender bias in our organizations is really the only way to eliminate this phenomenon," not "fixing the women."[51]

Women realize too that when one woman fails, women generally are often broad-brushed with that failure, while the converse is not true. When Jack falls down the hill, that's just Jack. But when Jill falls, all women are assumed clumsy. Conversely, however, when a woman succeeds, she is seen as a one-off or lucky, without any positive attribution given to women generally.

The "Queen Bee" conjecture has been examined in the context of the military as well. In 2013, the Norwegian military considered forming an all-female Special Reconnaissance Platoon but was reluctant to do so because allegedly too many women in one place would inherently result in "catfight" drama and high emotions. Researchers decided to examine that presumption. What they found was that "Queen Bee" behavior was "an act of recognition whereby women comply with misogynist gender stereotypes and evaluate women negatively but set themselves apart from the group/category of women as someone who fits better with the guys."[52] More simply, the:

> queen bee behavior is a response to the social-identity threat women experience when they enter a unit in which their gender has a low reputation and status, and where it is expected that a woman should fit seamlessly in as one of the guys, and accordingly have to make a symbolic "change of gender."[53]

Further, in order to "fit in with the guys," women will go so far as to disparage other women. That makes their Queen Bee behavior particularly problematic as women's complicity is powerful in the legitimization of gender discrimination.

Women are often reluctant to admit that patriarchies wouldn't last a day without their complicity. But both when women were first integrated into surface combatants in the 1990s and into submarines beginning in 2011, the greatest resistance came not from male crew members, but from their wives.[54] Women are taught from a young age that they are in competition with each other for male attention, harkening back to the traditional notion that women need a protector/provider.[55] Also, as most often the primary caregivers to children, beliefs women instill in their childedren - boys and girls - matter as well. An Afghani woman who had served as a Female Tactical Platoon member in Afghanistan told me that she believed it would have taken two generations of mothers raising sons "differently" – requiring the mothers to think and act differently – to change their sons' values, and thereby their definitions of masculinity. Both men and women are responsible for perpetuating negative gender patterns.

LGBTQ+

Gender (and race) boundaries affect men as well as women. Navy Chief Joe Anand-Obleton retired after 22 years serving his country. A black, gay man, he said he too tried to fit in, to no avail.

> I remember times in my life, especially in the military, when I tried to act more straight/manly or when I tried to act more "normal"/white so that others would include me. I remember times in the not-too-distant past when I flipped whichever inside switch I had to flip to act accordingly to my environment. I found that changing who I was to fit in usually resulted in the opposite. It resulted in people not knowing *me*. My being the person I thought others wanted me to be resulted in my never truly belonging.[56]

A sense of "belonging" – the "B" in DEI(B) – is the ultimate goal of inclusion, and the dignity to be oneself.

Expected gender boundaries are inherently pushed within the lesbian, gay, bisexual, transgender, queer or questioning, or other diverse gender identity (LGBTQ+) communities. Levels of violence and experienced biases among members of these communities are, unfortunately, very high. Structural barriers against openly gay, lesbian, and bisexual men and women serving in the military were lifted in 2011, and acceptance of LGBTQ+ individuals expanded with the lifting of the transgender ban in 2021. But issues remain, of both a structural and cultural nature.

Pete Buttigieg ran for president in 2020 and then went on to serve as Secretary of Transportation in the Biden Administration. Widely known as "Mayor Pete" since he served as mayor of South Bend, Indiana, from 2012 to 2020, he came close to being the Democratic nominee in 2020, vaulting past other experienced, higher-profile candidates with bigger war chests of money in voter popularity. What many voters seemed to like about Buttigieg was his normality.

Buttigieg, 37 when he ran for president, has been described as modest, a reasonable pragmatist, rather conservative, Christian, who also happens to be a married gay man. He is a veteran, having served a tour in Afghanistan as a naval reservist, though he is careful not to overstate his proximity to or experience with combat given he was an intelligence officer.[57] He and his husband have a load of student debt, which young voters could relate to, and he was lauded for his ability to relate to voters through storytelling. Perhaps Pete Buttigieg's most unusual trait is that he is fluent in eight languages, whereas most Americans know only one, English.

During his time as mayor of South Bend, the Rust Belt city made a comeback as Buttigieg, a former consultant for McKinsey and a self-professed data geek, listened, learned, and then took action, particularly focusing on improving city infrastructure,[58] gaining self-confidence in himself along the way. When he was elected mayor in 2012, South Bend had just been listed in *Newsweek* as one of America's dying cities. By 2020, unemployment was down, and the population was rising for the first time in decades. The city drew hundreds of millions of dollars in private investment in industry, commerce, and homes for the working class. He delivered on campaign promises.[59]

When Buttigieg ran for president, there was speculation that he might be a transformational candidate.[60] He, perhaps more than any presidential candidate of late, has demonstrated the ability to employ both masculine and feminine traits in leadership. But he was unable to broaden his appeal to include voters of color, both African American and Latino, eventually resulting in him dropping his campaign.[61]

Pete Buttigieg is an openly gay married man, but his sexuality did not negatively overshadow his politics. The same cannot be said about Arizona Senator Kyrsten Sinema, as an openly bisexual woman and only the second openly lesbian member of Congress (after Tammy Baldwin). Her sexuality became, partly through her own choices, a focus of her political life and not always in a positive way. She retired from the Senate in 2024.

Kyrsten Sinema was once a critic of capitalism and a vocal anti-war activist. A social worker, lawyer, triathlete, and openly bisexual, LGBTQ+ woman known for sometimes donning vibrantly hued wigs, she came to the Senate with a long history in politics. She was the most progressive member of her caucus while serving in the Arizona state legislature and a self-described "bomb-thrower." In 2011, the *Phoenix New Times* named her a "local lefty icon."[62] Once affiliated with the Arizona Green Party, Sinema began her political career as a Democrat in the Arizona legislature, where she gained a reputation for success in passing legislation by working with Republicans who then held a supermajority.

Sinema served three terms in the US House of Representatives, then defeated former Senator Martha McSally in the 2020 special election to replace Arizona Senator Jeff Flake. In the 2018 Senate race against Republican Martha McSally, McSally painted Sinema as insufficiently patriotic and even went so far as to accuse her of treason. But Sinema was elected largely by appealing to centrists, the all-important suburban women swing voters, and moderate Arizona Republicans.

As a Senator, Sinema was once considered an LGBTQ+ icon for being willing to stand up to the far right, but public opinion began to sour on Sinema just a few years into her tenure. Many individuals, including those among the LGBTQ+ community, began to consider her politically unpredictable, self-absorbed, and attention-seeking. Said another bisexual woman in an Op-ed: "Sinema seems to embody many of the nasty assumptions about bi women I've worked my whole life to avoid."[63]

For example, Sinema voted "no" in March 2021 on a minimum-wage hike as part of President Biden's $1.9 trillion coronavirus relief bill. That was not a surprise, as she had indicated that she wanted the wage hike considered separately and intended to work toward a bipartisan solution to make that happen. What drew the wrath of many of her own party members was showing up for the vote with a chocolate cake, walking to the front of the chamber, and then pausing, signaling an exaggerated, often-used thumbs down gesture, and then curtsying. While Sinema declined to explain her actions, a spokesperson told an Arizona newspaper that the cake was for Senate staffers who had worked through the night. Her office also told the *Huffington Post* that "commentary about a female senator's body language, clothing, or physical demeanor does not belong in a serious media outlet."[64] Whether a man or woman, however, being theatrical draws attention; that's often the point of being theatrical, especially in a public forum. There is a difference between effectively using and combining different masculine and feminine leadership traits and approaches, and just seeming confused, as Sinema did.

Conclusion

Leadership theories often prove inadequate because leadership is complex and individuals are even more complex. Humans are imperfect, but there are ways whereby individuals can strive to "be better," and those ways are especially important for those who aspire to leadership positions to understand and strive for. That often involves learning about oneself and the environment, and understanding the context of decision-making and implementation. As is so often the case, one size fits one, not all.

A first step toward diversified team leadership and individual leaders who understand and effectively utilize masculine and feminine, hard and soft traits toward "smart leadership" is moving away from the perspective that gender equality means everyone is the same. All men are not the same, all women are not the same, and men and women are not the same. One sex is not better than the other; rather, they balance the strengths and weaknesses of each other.

Without consideration of the implications of individual personalities and actions, biographies are merely narratives, and the learning potential from them is minimal. Similarly, without consideration of gender, there is an important piece missing from the leadership puzzle that will be highly determinative of future decisions regarding war and peace.

Notes

1 Moore, Stephen. *Patton's Payback*, Dutton Caliber, 2022.
2 Ambrose, Stephen E. "A Fateful Friendship," *American Heritage*, Vol. 20, No. 2, April 1969. https://www.americanheritage.com/fateful-friendship
3 "Character Above All: Dwight D. Eisenhower Essay," PBS. https://www.pbs.org/newshour/spc/character/essays/eisenhower.html#:~:text=%22His%20real%20strength%20lies%20in
4 House, Robert J. "A 1976 Theory of Charismatic Leadership," Working Paper, quoted in Shonk, Katie. "Charismatic Leadership: Weighing the Pros and Cons," Daily Blog, Project on Negotiation, Harvard Law School, December 14, 2023. https://www.pon.harvard.edu/daily/leadership-skills-daily/charismatic-leadership-weighing-the-pros-and-cons/
5 Slattery, Grahm and Helen Coster. "J.D. Vance Once Compared Trump to Hitler: Now They are Running Mates," *Reuters*, July 15, 2024. https://www.reuters.com/world/us/jd-vance-once-compared-trump-hitler-now-they-are-running-mates-2024-07-15/
6 Chamorro-Premuzic, Tomas. "The Dark Side of Charisma," *Harvard Business Review*, November 16, 2012. https://hbr.org/2012/11/the-dark-side-of-charisma
7 Shonk, 2023.

8 Hamad, Hamad Bakar. "Transformational Leadership Theory: Why Military Leaders are More Charismatic and Transformational?" *International Journal on Leadership*, April 2015. https://www.researchgate.net/publication/299562626_Transformational_Leadership_Theory_Why_Military_Leaders_are_More_Charismatic_and_Transformational
9 Stoessinger, John. *Why Nations Go to War, 11th edition*, Cengage Learning, 2010.
10 Goodwin, Doris Kearns. *Lyndon Johnson and the American Dream: The Most Revealing Portrait of a President and Presidential Power Ever Written, 8th edition*, St. Martin's Griffin, 1991.
11 https://www.military-quotes.com/forums/threads/sir-basil-h-liddell-hart-quote.120836/
12 Barber, James David. *The Presidential Character: Predicting Performance in the White House, 4th edition*, Pearson Publishing, 2008.
13 Dean, John. "Active-Negative Trump is Doomed to Follow Nixon," *Newsweek*, May 29, 2017. https://www.newsweek.com/activenegative-trump-doomed-follow-nixon-616641#:~:text=The%20active%2Fnegative%20lives%20in,tense%2C%20wary%20readiness%20for%20danger
14 Nye, Joseph Jr. *Presidential Leadership and the Creation of the American Era*, Princeton University Press, 2013.
15 Nye, 2013, p. 9.
16 Nye, Joseph Jr. "A Dollop of Deeper American Values," *Washington Post*, March 29, 2004. https://www.washingtonpost.com/archive/opinions/2004/03/30/a-dollop-of-deeper-american-values/acd1b194-2d1c-46ff-a7d2-baa1a15ab3a7/
17 Nye, 2013, p. 13.
18 Nye, Jr. Joseph S. "The Right Stuff in Foreign Policy," *Project Syndicate*, June 5, 2013. https://www.project-syndicate.org/commentary/contextual-intelligence-and-foreign-policy-leadership-by-joseph-s--nye
19 Nye, 2013.
20 Nye, 2013.
21 Kutz, Matthew R. and Anita Bamford-Wade. "Understanding Contextual Intelligence: A Critical Competency for Today's Leaders," *ECO Issue*, Vol. 15, No. 3, 2013. pp. 55–80.
22 Chandraskaran, Rajiv. "Inside the Green Zone: The Lost Year in Iraq," Frontline, PBS. 2006. https://www.pbs.org/wgbh/pages/frontline/yeariniraq/analysis/greenzone.html
23 "Younger Leaders Seen as More Innovation, Older Leaders More Reliable," Association for Psychological Science, November 4, 2014. https://www.psychologicalscience.org/news/minds-business/younger-leaders-seen-as-more-innovative-older-leaders-more-reliable.html
24 Diehl, Amy, et al. "Women in Leadership Face Ageism at Every Age," *Harvard Business Review*, June 16, 2023. https://hbr.org/2023/06/women-in-leadership-face-ageism-at-every-age
25 Kutz, Matthew R. "Toward a Conceptual Model of Contextual Intelligence: A Transferable Leadership Construct," Kravis Leadership Institute, *Leadership Review*, Vol. 8, Winter 2008, pp. 18–31.
26 Kutz, 2008.
27 Staples, George M. "The Value of Military Training for Diplomats," *The Foreign Service Journal*, October 2015. https://afsa.org/value-military-training-diplomats-personal-story
28 Hudson, Valerie and Patricia Leidl. *The Hillary Doctrine: Sex and American Foreign Policy*, Columbia University Press, 2015, pp. 201–202.
29 Hudson and Leidel, 2015, p. 43.

30 Smith, Alex Duval. "Why F.W. de Klerk let Nelson Mandela Out of Prison," *The Guardian*, January 30, 2010. https://www.theguardian.com/world/2010/jan/31/nelson-mandela-de-klerk-apartheid
31 Evans, Farrell. "How Nelson Mandela Used Rugby as a Symbol of South African Unity," *HISTORY*, October 5, 2023. https://www.history.com/news/nelson-mandela-1995-rugby-world-cup-south-african-unity
32 Hudson, Valerie, et al. "The Heart of the Matter," *International Security,* Winter 2008/09, p. 9.
33 Cox, Kiana. "Most US Adults Feel What Happens to Their Own Racial or Ethnic Group Affects Them Personally," Pew Research, July 11, 2019. https://www.pewresearch.org/short-reads/2019/07/11/linked-fate-connectedness-americans/
34 Steinberg, Donald. "Looking Through a Gender Lens," *Women at the Frontlines of Peace & Security*, National Defense University, 2014, pp. 14–15.
35 "The US Army Cultural Support Team Program: Historical Timeline." https://arsof-history.org/articles/v12n2_cst_timeline_page_1.html
36 "The US Army Cultural Support Team Program: Historical Timeline." https://arsof-history.org/articles/v12n2_cst_timeline_page_1.html
37 Personal interview, June 6, 2024.
38 Shepherd, Laura J. "The Paradox of Prevention in the Women, Peace and Security Agenda," European Journal of International Security, September 30, 2020, pp. 315–331; Mariaini, Laura. "The Women, Peace and Security Agenda: A Critic of Liberal Peace," Trinita Dei Monti Think Tank, April 30, 2021. https://trinitamonti.org/2021/04/30/the-women-peace-and-security-agenda-a-critique-of-liberal-peace/
39 UN Women. https://wps.unwomen.org/preventing/ (accessed April 3, 2024)
40 Brechenmacher, Saskia. "Germany has a New Feminist Foreign Policy. What Does it Mean in Practice?" Carnegie Endowment for International Peace, March 8, 2023. https://carnegieendowment.org/2023/03/08/germany-has-new-feminist-foreign-policy.-what-does-it-mean-in-practice-pub-89224
41 Vucetic, Srdjan. "The Uneasy Coexistence of Arms Exports and Feminist Foreign Policy," *The Conversation*. https://theconversation.com/the-uneasy-co-existence-of-arms-exports-and-feminist-foreign-policy-93930
42 Johnson-Freese, Joan and Susan Markham. "Reconciling Two Key Frameworks: Feminist Foreign Policy & Women, Peace and Security," WIIS Policy Brief, May, 2022. https://wiisglobal.org/wp-content/uploads/Reconciling-Two-Key-Frameworks-Policy-Brief.pdf; Foster, Stephenie and Susan Markham. *Feminist Foreign Policy in Theory and Practice,* Routledge, 2023.
43 The Gender Security Project. https://www.gendersecurityproject.com/feminist-foreign-policy-countries/colombia#:~:text=The%20event%20also%20affirmed%20that,democratic%20processes%2C%20while%20recognizing%20the (accessed April 3, 2024)
44 Johnson-Freese, Joan and Tahina Montoya. "From Exception to Norm: Closing the Women, Peace & Security Gap Through Joint Professional Military Education," *Modern War Institu*te, July 13, 2023. https://mwi.westpoint.edu/from-exception-to-norm-closing-the-women-peace-and-security-implementation-gap-through-joint-professional-military-education/; Johnson-Freese, Joan and Nalani Tyrell. "Getting Serious about Women, Peace & Security," *Strategy Bridge*, 2021. https://thestrategybridge.org/the-bridge/2021/4/13/getting-serious-about-women-peace-security
45 Coaston, Jane. "Intersectionality, Explained: Meet Kimberlé Crenshaw, Who Coined the Term," *Vox*. https://www.vox.com/the-highlight/2019/5/20/18542843/intersectionality-conservatism-law-race-gender-discrimination
46 Personal interview, June 26, 2024.
47 Mpinja, Baze. "The New Battle Braids of the US Military," *Allure*, June 1, 2022. https://www.allure.com/story/black-hairstyles-updated-military-guidelines

48 Groskop, V. "Queen Bee Syndrome Among Women is a Myth, Study Finds," *The Guardian*, June 7, 2015.
49 Ellemers, Naomi, et al. "The Underrepresentation of Women in Science: Differential Commitment or the Queen Bee Syndrome?" *British Journal of Social Psychology*, September 2004, pp. 315–338. https://bpspsychub.onlinelibrary.wiley.com/doi/abs/10.1348/0144666042037999
50 Ellemers, Naomi, et al. "The Queen Bee Phenomenon in Academia 15 Years After: Does it Still Exist and If So, Why?" *British Journal of Social Psychology*, April 2021, pp. 383–399. https://bpspsychub.onlinelibrary.wiley.com/doi/full/10.1111/bjso.12408
51 Elsesser, Kim. "Queen Bees Still Exist, But It's Not the Women We Need to Fix," *Forbes*, August 31, 2020.
52 Rones, Nina and Frank Brundtlander. "The Queen Bees and the Women's Team – A Contextual Examination of Enmity and Friendship Between Military Women," NATO Pub Ref NBR (STO-SAS-137), 2017, p. 13.
53 Rones and Brundtlander, 2017, p. 1.
54 Bynum, Russ. "Navy to Allow Women to Serve on Submarines," *NBC News*, April 29, 2010. https://www.nbcnews.com/id/wbna36854592
55 Johnson-Freese, Joan. Women vs. Women: The Case for Cooperation, Routledge, 2022.
56 Anand-Obelton, Joseph. Email to me on April 15, 2024.
57 Beaumont, Thomas. "Buttigieg Touts Military Service, Wary of Overstating Role," *AP News*, November 18, 2019. https://apnews.com/article/ap-top-news-elections-des-moines-in-state-wire-iowa-2acf65b0b1b948d68de10607f170a1b3
58 Seitz-Wald, Alex. "The Making of 'Mayor Pete': An 'Aha Moment' Changed Buttigieg from Data Geek to Leader with a Heart," *NBC News,* April 29, 2019. https://www.nbcnews.com/politics/2020-election/making-mayor-pete-how-data-geek-learned-govern-heart-n998696
59 Andersen, Erika. "Pete Buttigieg and the Longing for Good Leaders," *Forbes,* January 10, 2020. https://www.forbes.com/sites/erikaandersen/2020/01/10/pete-buttigieg-and-the-longing-for-good-leaders/?sh=5f6012424a42
60 Sullivan, Andrew. "Is Pete Buttigieg a Transformational Candidate?" April 5, 2019. https://nymag.com/intelligencer/2019/04/is-pete-buttigieg-a-transformational-candidate.html
61 Epstein, Reid J. and Trip Gabriel. "Pete Buttigieg Drops Out of Democratic Presidential Race," *New York Times*, March 1, 2020. https://www.nytimes.com/2020/03/01/us/politics/pete-buttigieg-drops-out.html#:~:text=Buttigieg's%20main%20challenge%20was%20his,to%20coalesce%20and%20challenge%20Mr
62 Chavez, Aida. "How Kyrsten Sinema Sold Out," *The Nation*, March 22, 2021. https://www.thenation.com/article/politics/kyrsten-sinema-conservative-democrat/
63 Alptraum, Lux. "Is Arizona's Kyrsten Sinema Bad for Bisexual Americans?" *NBC News*, October 26, 2021. https://www.nbcnews.com/think/opinion/arizona-s-kyrsten-sinema-bad-bisexual-americans-ncna1282401
64 Boboltz, Sara. "Sinema Slammed for Exaggerated Thumbs-Down on $15 Minimum Wage," *Huffington Post*, March 6, 2021. https://www.huffpost.com/entry/kyrsten-sinema-thumbs-down-minimum-wage_n_6042a4b2c5b613cec15d9f41

3

LEADERSHIP STYLES

Former Secretary of Defense Donald Rumsfeld was a champion wrestler in high school and captain of the wrestling team as an undergraduate at Princeton, Class of 1954. If you believe, as the preface to Roger Olesen's book *The Turning Point* about the 1953 collegiate wrestling season portends, that, "Wrestling is not, as some contend, *like* life. Wrestling *is* life – reduced to its essence,"[1] then Rumsfeld's wrestling style explains everything you want to know about Rumsfeld's later leadership style. He had a reputation for quick takedowns – commanding, relentless, a bulldog, and a plugger.

From a middle-class Midwestern family, Rumsfeld was an Eagle Scout in high school, thereby demonstrating early on his willingness to work hard and his ability to excel; he was known as serious and intense in college. He attended Princeton on academic and Navy Reserve Officer Training Corps (NROTC) scholarships. There, he was popular and a member of Cap and Gown, one of the school's top-tier eating clubs. He also made no attempt to hide his ambition at Princeton and openly mused to classmates about potentially becoming president of the United States.

Being ambitious is neither inherently a bad thing nor a distinctly male characteristic. A female Air Force Academy classmate of Senator Martha McSally remembers McSally as overtly ambitious. Harvard classmates of US Representative Elise Stefanik and Stanford classmates of Senator Josh Hawley similarly remember musings about presidential ambitions from them during their undergraduate years. Perhaps ironically, both Stefanik and Hawley have recently become champions of the populist movement by railing against the elite institutions and backgrounds from which they came and benefitted. Ambition drove Rumsfeld to Princeton, but he maintained a sense of economic and class divide while there and carried a "lingering disdain of Ivy Leaguers and the Eastern establishment elite"[2] throughout

DOI: 10.4324/9781003564065-4

his life. Ambition is good, but ambition indicates drive; it does not inherently equate to leadership.

Fast forward to Rumsfeld's many years in leadership positions, both in the business and government sectors. After fulfilling his scholarship commitment through service in the Navy, Rumsfeld began his political career assisting two Republican lawmakers in Washington. He parlayed those positions into his own seat in the House of Representatives in 1963, from Illinois, as the youngest Republican member and a rebel against the legislative status quo. In 1969, frustrated by being unable to rise in the House leadership ranks due to what he considered Old Guard obstructionism, Rumsfeld jumped to the Executive branch under President Richard Nixon, working in the Office of Economic Opportunity. Perhaps most importantly in that position, he hired another Young Turk named Richard Cheney as his assistant. Similar in personality, they remained lifelong friends, allies, and each other's defender, and a powerful combination during the Bush 43 Administration, with Cheney as Vice President and Rumsfeld as Secretary of Defense.

In late 1974, President Gerald Ford named Rumsfeld as his Chief of Staff, and in 1975 as Secretary of Defense, then the youngest-ever US Secretary of Defense. During his tenure as Defense Secretary, he oversaw the transition of the military to an all-volunteer force and a military build-up that either helped hasten the end of the Cold War or paved the road to militarism in the Middle East, depending on perspective. But he left with his reputation intact such that he would get called back into the same position for an encore later, the only person to do so in nonconsecutive presidential terms.

When the Ford Administration ended, Rumsfeld moved to the private sector, where his success made him a multimillionaire. He also made a short bid for the presidency in 1988, hoping to succeed Ronald Reagan. Over the years, he was also on several shortlists for the vice presidency, but having what many peers considered as many personality liabilities as strengths kept him an "also considered." Government service drew him back in 2001 when George W. Bush named him Secretary of Defense, then the oldest Secretary of Defense, where leadership characteristics evident throughout his life became glaring to those who worked both for and with him, and to the public.

Nixon was impressed by Rumsfeld, especially as a bureaucratic infighter, and once described him, admiringly, as a "ruthless little bastard."[3] Others in the Nixon Administration were not as enamored, put off by his ambition, self-promotion, and autocratic methods. Under Bush, he didn't lead the Pentagon; he ruled it with an iron fist. Having been charged with reforming the military bureaucracy and developing more agile, adaptable armed forces, he alienated many military officers, lawmakers, and administration peers. "Transformation" was his bumper sticker for how to accomplish his goal, heavily reliant on information and "leapfrogging" technologies, with subordinates quickly learning to insert the word transformation into everything they did or risk a memo, or "snowflake" as they were called, from Rumsfeld questioning or challenging their actions. I was a Department Chair at the Naval War College at the time, and his snowflakes even reached down into military education, in conjunction with his view that "capturing the schoolhouses" was necessary to make long-lasting change in the military.

After 9/11, Rumsfeld's leadership style at the Pentagon drew criticism from several perspectives. His often confrontational, gruff, and belittling manner of treating others, including subordinates and peers, was annoying and frequently counterproductive. Douglas Feith, Rumsfeld's senior civilian policy advisor at the Pentagon, explained the problem: "His leadership style did not always serve his own purposes: He bruised people and made personal enemies, who were eager to strike back at him and try to discredit his work."[4] Senator John McCain simply labeled Rumsfeld "one of the worst secretaries of defense in history."[5]

Regarding policy, Rumsfeld's previous stint as Defense Secretary was during the Cold War, an era in many ways easier to understand than post-globalization, as power had been more easily quantified and enemies more easily identifiable. On Afghanistan, Rumsfeld was honest, at least in private, about the problems those issues posed. "Help!" he jotted on one classified cable, apparently worried in 2002 about how the United States would extract itself from the conflict. "I have no visibility into who the bad guys are," he scribbled on another.[6] The situational context of Rumsfeld's second tour as Secretary of Defense was very different from the first, and one he was not necessarily as familiar or comfortable with as the Cold War and Soviet Union.

Rumsfeld felt more confident about handling Iraq, where Saddam Hussein was easily identified as the bad guy and a bad guy with whom the Bush Administration was generally obsessed,[7] than Afghanistan. Consequently, shortly after sending the military to Afghanistan to root out the terrorists responsible for 9/11, he employed a claim of Iraq having an active weapons of mass destruction program as an excuse to send in US troops. No stockpiles were ever found, though, and a Pentagon Inspector General (IG) report later stated that Rumsfeld's office had "developed, produced and then disseminated alternative intelligence assessment on Iraq and the al-Qaeda relationship, which included some conclusions that were inconsistent with the consensus of the intelligence community, to senior decision-makers."[8] Perhaps worst of all, Rumsfeld threatened to fire anyone who tried to plan for post-military conflict stabilization in Iraq,[9] as he was adamant that US troops would prevail quickly and not engage in nation building. Withholding contrary views was a means of survival for Rumsfeld's subordinates.

Even while it became increasingly clear that the United States had gotten itself into a Sunni-Shia quagmire in Iraq that initially had not been understood, Rumsfeld was inflexible and defiant in his hard power policies, though without a clear policy goal beyond the impossible "eradicating terrorism." That, added to the controversial use of torture generally and the Abu Ghraib torture and prisoner abuse scandal specifically, eroded Rumsfeld's public and political support, eventually even from President George W. Bush.

The public outcry over Abu Ghraib was such that Rumsfeld twice offered to resign in 2004, with Bush declining to accept his resignation both times. But the November 2006 elections were devastating for Republicans, with Democrats having big wins in both congressional and state races, evidencing the public's displeasure with White House war policy. Though Bush had stated just a week before the election that he expected Rumsfeld's tenure to end with his own in 2008, Bush accepted Rumsfeld's resignation the week after the elections in 2006.

Donald Rumsfeld was unrepentant about the post-9/11 decisions he made and policies he undertook until the end of his life. In contrast, former Defense Secretary Robert McNamara came to regret, but never apologized for, his decisions and policies in conjunction with America's long war in Vietnam. Perhaps repentance and apologies are not necessary, but hard, serious reflection about mistakes is necessary for leaders to grow. Donald Rumsfeld seemed unable to do that. His style of leadership served him personally in many instances, judging from his long and largely successful resume, but it failed him and the country in the end.

Emotional Intelligence

Leadership involves both making good decisions and dealing with people. The propensities that influence individuals in decision-making – flexibility, rigidity, innovativeness, communication skills, etc. – may or may not influence (to some degree) how they deal with people. Effectively dealing with people requires strong communication skills. Consequently, an individual may be an excellent strategist but not good with communicating his/her vision to others, or be an outstanding people person but not good with strategy or decision-making. Also, circumstances and larger issues can intervene even if an individual is an excellent strategist and a beloved leader of followers. Such has been said regarding "brilliant" military leaders who nevertheless ended up on the losing end of a war, such as Erwin Rommel and Robert E. Lee.

Rumsfeld's commitment to policies in Iraq in many ways parallels those of Johnson in Vietnam and Nixon regarding Watergate. Rumsfeld was commanding in decision-making and commanding in dealing with people. Relevant to the thesis of this book – that future leaders will need to utilize both masculine and feminine styles, traits, and skills, and understand when to use each, to maximize their personal effectiveness – is the consideration of leadership styles most likely to achieve results. Rumsfeld's one-dimensional leadership was not effective. Reinforcing the thesis of this book, psychologist and author Daniel Goleman stated in 2000 that, "new research suggests that the most effective executives use a collection of distinct leadership styles – each in the right measure, at just the right time."[10] Some of those styles require traits, or what he calls competencies, that are more masculine, while other competencies are more feminine.

Goleman has suggested that there are six leadership styles drawn from an individual's emotional intelligence.[11] He defines emotional intelligence as "the ability to manage ourselves and our relationships effectively" and consisting of four fundamental capabilities, with each of those capabilities then composed of a specific set of competencies.[12]

Self-Awareness

- Emotional self-awareness
- Accurate self-assessment
- Self-confidence

Self-Management

- Self-control
- Trustworthiness
- Conscientiousness
- Adaptability
- Achievement orientation
- Initiative

Social Awareness

- Empathy
- Organizational awareness
- Service orientation

Social Skills

- Visionary leadership
- Influence
- Developing others
- Communication
- Change catalyst
- Conflict management
- Building bonds
- Teamwork and collaboration

Goleman cites the work of Harvard psychologist David McClelland regarding how these competencies are relevant to leadership. McClelland "found that leaders with strengths in a critical mass of six or more emotional intelligence competencies were far more effective than peers who lacked such strengths."[13] The gendered nature of some of these capabilities, as Goleman refers to them, has already been discussed as traits, such as empathy being more feminine and self-confidence more masculine. Goleman's six styles of leadership[14] then draw further from McClelland's work.

Building on Abraham Maslow's Theory of Needs from the 1940s, McClelland proposed in the 1960s that there are three basic types of motivators that drive each individual, one of those being dominant: power, achievement, and the need for affiliation. He further argued that individuals will have different personality characteristics determined by their dominant motivator.

In the 1970s, American economist and Harvard Business School professor Rosebeth Moss Kanter opened the door to differentiated studies on leadership, power, and gender, and "blind spots" in organizational analysis.[15] Previously, a "gender neutral" tradition of examining power and leadership had prevailed, though organizational gender-differentiated positions were evident: (female) secretary, (male) boss; (female) nurse, (male) doctor; even (female) cook, (male) chef. With such obvious masculine-dominant subtexts in job titles and classifications, views of leadership began to be recognized as difficult to integrate with femininity.[16]

McClelland's later 1975 book, *Power: The Inner Experience,* began to differentiate between genders, specifically noting that gender played a major role in the way power was expressed as a result of cultural norms and stereotyping. He pointed out that women in the workplace were stereotyped as submissive, cooperative, and friendly, and highly valued interpersonal relationships and communication in the workplace. Hence, while women maintained a need for power, societal expectations inherently create dilemmas for female leaders whereby they feel pressured to succumb to society's gender expectations of them.

Later research by other scholars carried McClelland's proposition regarding the influence of gender stereotypes further. Specifically, it was found that:

> considering the historical nature of what female supervisors may have had to overcome, and assuming that stereotypes were somewhat true, female supervisors may have used coercive power in an attempt to maintain the respect of their subordinates. This is important as prior research suggested that supervisors attempting to motivate [employees] should not use coercive power.[17]

In other words, research confirmed that female leaders can struggle with both stereotypical expectations of them, and (over) compensate against stereotypical assumptions through the use of coercive power.

Vanessa Druskat surveyed over 6,000 individuals in all-female and all-male religious orders of the Roman Catholic Church to measure the frequency of transformational and transactional leadership behaviors in 1988. She found that both males and females tend more toward transformational leadership, and that female leaders were found "to exhibit significantly more transformational leadership behaviors and significantly fewer transactional leadership behaviors than male leaders."[18] She also found, however, that the environment was not conducive to allowing women to display transformational leadership. Male-dominant environments, deep with masculine culture, tamped down women leaders' ability to be transformational.

This is to say that in these studies and many more, research has confirmed that, due to stereotypes, female leaders face numerous complications in trying to effectively be seen as leaders and deal with subordinates. This is true in areas including motivating subordinates, supporting subordinates, and coaching subordinates. Subsequently, these complications can affect their leadership style and make it imperative that multiple styles are employed depending on different contexts and environments.

Clearly as well, hierarchical organizations like the military can struggle to incorporate multiple leadership styles, especially the democratic style, given its mission. In crisis or combat, the authoritative, or even coercive, leadership style will and should prevail. But in times of peace, it is necessary and appropriate to heal organizational wounds, grow people for the future, and take the time to work with people. George (Hal) McNair served 22 years in Army Special Forces, including command of Special Forces Operational Detachment 'Alpha.' His leadership style, he said, depended on context. In non-combat environments, he described his leadership style as "consciously aware" of both what was going on around him and the people who worked for him, including their family life. In combat though, where lives and mission success were at risk, he described his style as "confident" – "so damned confident" that others simply assumed he was right in his decision-making and followed without question. Whether leaders have the skills to do that, however, can depend on the emotional intelligence skills that they have, or that they learn.[19]

A Menu of Leadership Styles

Goleman's six leadership styles are likely familiar to most people who have workplace experience. "*Coercive leaders* demand immediate compliance. *Authoritative leaders* mobilize people toward a vision. *Affiliative leaders* create emotional bonds and harmony. *Democratic leaders* build consensus through participation. *Pacesetting leaders* expect excellence and self-direction. And *Coaching leaders* develop people for the future."[20] Which style, or even better, styles, a leader employs will subsequently affect the organizational climate, or working environment, which in turn affects employee performance. A positive climate is one that is *flexible*, where employees have a sense of *responsibility* to the organization, high *standards,* a sense of appropriateness regarding performance feedback and *rewards*, *clarity* of mission and values, and *commitment* to a common purpose. Researchers acknowledge that climate is not the only determinant of organizational performance, but it is a strong factor. Four of the six styles have a positive impact on climate. The two that do not are coercive and pacesetting.

Coercive leadership, sometimes known as autocratic or commanding leadership, is often pursued by individuals driven to achieve, as it demands immediate compliance to their authority. Because extreme urgency is always a critical part of a crisis, coercive leadership is most often deemed appropriate in a crisis and can be useful for short periods to change the culture of an organization quickly. Over prolonged periods, however, it is corrosive, grinding down employee pride and alienating individuals from their jobs. Further, it can push subordinates to lose their sense of responsibility as they do not want to help a leader they consider a bully and who rewards only sycophants. And it encourages groupthink. It is not difficult to conceive of Rumsfeld as a coercive leader.

Similarly, pacesetting leadership is also often motivated by a drive to achieve, and a sense of conscientiousness and initiative. The leader sets extremely high standards for himself/herself and expects others to meet those standards as well. Most frequently, employees working with a pacesetting boss feel overwhelmed and burn out quickly. Employees find themselves spending more time second-guessing what their boss personally wants of them than achieving the organizational goal. But in instances where all employees are self-motivated and highly competent, this approach can work.

Examples of pacesetting leadership are often found in the business world: Elon Musk, Jeff Bezos, Mark Zuckerberg, and Jack Welch have all been called pacesetting leaders. Welch was the Chief Executive Officer at General Electric (GE) from 1981 to 2001, and during that time, he was heralded as the first celebrity executive. But his single-minded focus on quarterly earnings was achieved through ruthless cost-cutting and forced employee rankings, where he fired the bottom 10% of performers and rewarded only the top 20% of performers annually. Retrospectively, his methods have been said to have hurt both GE and American capitalism.[21]

The most effective leadership style, according to Goleman, is authoritative (not to be confused with authoritarian), sometimes called "visionary" leadership because authoritative leaders marshal people toward a vision. From the business community, Bill Gates is often cited as an example of an authoritative leader as he had a vision for Microsoft – a computer on every desk and in every home – and achieved it. Within the public sphere, Martin Luther King Jr. rallied a large group of individuals behind his vision, or his "dream," as he so famously put it in his 1963 speech in Washington, DC.

These leaders take the time to convey "why" the work done by individuals is important to overall goal achievement. Doing so inspires followers and helps them feel that they are making a valuable contribution, which then keeps them motivated. They also encourage their team to experiment and engage in (prudent) risk-taking, to speak up with opinions, and so while providing a "why" to the team, they don't necessarily provide a "how." An authoritative leader can rally individuals to work together as a team, with confidence in themselves and empathy for others, and will avoid micromanagement.

Because they are not primarily ego- or power-driven, authoritative leaders also tend to be flexible on policies to achieve their goals. They accept experimentation and are willing to make adjustments to accommodate successes and failures. They set standards, encourage transparency, and create reward and recognition systems that allow individuals to grow as part of the team.

However, authoritative leadership demands clear communication and often works best with incremental, "nested" goals within the bigger vision. If there is only a "big vision" – go forth and conquer! – without clarification regarding steps to achieve the big vision, followers may end up frustrated, confused, or angry. Consequently, an authoritative approach can also be problematic when a leader is working with individuals or peers more knowledgeable and/or experienced than himself or herself, thereby opening the leadership style to be seen as pompous or out-of-touch.

An affiliative leader lives by the motto of "people first," to create harmony and emotional bonds within individuals in an organization before tasks and goals. Their focus is on building a positive, harmonious, and effective culture, teamwork, and social engagement, which in turn is useful for goal achievement. Affiliative leaders use ongoing positive feedback to employees, frequent rewards, and regular recognition of a job well done as approaches.

Jacinda Ardern, the former Prime Minister of New Zealand, embodied the affiliative leader style through her inclusivity, compassion, and empathy demonstrated during her time in office, particularly after the mass shooting at a Christchurch mosque in 2019. A newspaper article described her response as "Not robotic or platitudinous, not scripted or insincere."[22] She hugged Muslim men and women survivors and families of victims, symbolically wearing a hijab to show her respect for their religion, without self-consciousness or attention to who was or was not snapping pictures for the media. She was an empathetic leader. But she then swiftly followed up with new gun control legislation, showing she could be an authoritative leader when the situation called for it.

Though particularly popular after Goleman introduced it in 2000, in many business and government circles, affiliative leadership soon suffered from being associated with the buzzword "synergy," overused by leaders seeking to be seen as "caring" and stovepiped units being "connected." Though sincere affiliative leaders employ synergy to achieve greater team and community effectiveness than individuals could do on their own, performative use and overuse of the word quickly became off-putting. Sincere affiliative leadership is indicated by actions, not words.

While positive on a day-to-day basis, Goleman posits that affiliative leadership should not be used alone, but is best when used in conjunction with the authoritative style for balance. Otherwise, there is a potential downside to affiliative leadership because lines between leaders and followers can become blurred. That is, if leaders and followers become "too friendly," leaders may become conflict-averse and subsequently reluctant to offer criticism and address problems. Additionally, followers may become resentful of criticism from someone they consider a friend, with negative effects on the work environment.

The democratic leadership style is, as it sounds, inclusive. In this style of leadership, the leader becomes almost a first among equals rather than a top-down leader. Canadian Prime Minister Justin Trudeau, for example, regularly engages Canadians in decision-making processes. Trudeau introduced the use of town hall meetings, online consultation processes, and participatory platforms to engage Canadians in policy discussions. In spring 2023, for example, Trudeau engaged in 14 hour-long town hall meetings over an 11-week period, where he would begin with a speech, followed by a question-and-answer session in which individuals could voice their concerns and ask questions.

Wide input is useful when a leader wants (and perhaps needs) team input because of the breadth or complexity of the team's activity, and buy-in into a decision. Team morale is boosted because democratic leaders let team members know their perspectives and ideas matter. It requires, however, that there is time for the often-prolonged meetings that may be required to reach consensus. The time requirement means that the democratic style is not useful in times of crisis as it is not efficient. It also requires that the team members be knowledgeable about the subject under consideration.

The media is well known for asking the general public questions about public policy only to find individuals happy to provide an opinion – often a strong opinion – based on little, no, or mistaken knowledge. Public opinion on the Affordable Care Act passed in 2010, often referred to as "Obamacare," differed considerably depending on what wordage was used, though both referred to the same health care package.[23] Within organizations, leaders must take care to also make sure the team being asked for input is fully cognizant of the subject matter. At any level of analysis, professing a democratic approach and asking for input and then ignoring that input is demoralizing for those who have been asked, as they then feel the "ask" was merely performative, and they become distrustful. The Canadian media, for example, has pointed out regarding Trudeau's town hall meetings that some attendees "found themselves cynical about whether he and his government were actually listening."[24]

Finally, the coaching style also positively focuses on people, specifically on the development of people for the future. It is a leadership style that helps individuals improve their performance, often by trial and error. Coaching leaders are enthusiastic about working with their people, setting clear goals for themselves and others, demonstrating high levels of commitment, and working with individuals to help them become and see themselves as part of a team.

In some ways, coaching leaders can act as much as a counselor as a traditional boss.

Former German Chancellor Angela Merkel has often credited her mentor Helmut Kohl with providing the coaching she benefitted from, which allowed her to transition from being a scientist to a politician. Consequently, she is credited with mentoring other politicians who worked for and with her as well, fostering a culture of continuous leadership learning. The intent of coaching leadership is to ensure a pipeline of capable future leaders.

Clearly, however, coaching takes time, and there is no way to fast-track the results that might be sought for the team or the individual people on the team.

Attempting to fast-track coaching can be counterproductive, as individuals may not be able to keep up with expectations and become frustrated. As with the other styles, coaching is best used as part of a combination of styles appropriate for the circumstances, time line, and team makeup.

"Judging" or pigeonholing leaders by their style of leadership can be difficult and unfair. For example, Admiral Hyman Rickover, father of the nuclear Navy, is a complex leadership case study. Small in stature at about 5'6" and weighing around 125 pounds, Rickover was light on brawn but heavy in brain power. He did not "fit" the military's "warrior" culture, represented by a certain physicality, including strength, brawn, and endurance, monitored by mandatory physical training (PT) tests of all military personnel. But his contributions to the security and defense of the United States are unquestionable.

Rickover was born in Russian Poland in 1900 to Jewish parents, but his family soon immigrated to the United States, and he grew up in Chicago. An excellent student in high school, he received a commission to the US Naval Academy, where he was often confronted with anti-semitism.[25] He graduated 107th in his class of 540 midshipmen.

After being commissioned as an ensign, he worked on two ships before being sent to Columbia University for a degree in electrical engineering, graduating in 1929, and he prized that experience. "Columbia was the first institution that encouraged me to think rather than memorize. My teachers were notable in that many had gained practical engineering experience outside the university and were able to share their experience with their students."[26] Rickover was scornful of both education that was focused too much on theory taught by academics who had never been out of the classroom and on education by rote memorization or overuse of "gentlemen's b's" in grading, rather than thinking, a criticism regarding professional military educational institutions that is still heard.[27]

After Columbia, Rickover trained for and served on submarine duty. He advanced to Executive Officer on one submarine but continually clashed with his peers and superiors. Rickover applied for submarine command but was rejected by the Navy's Bureau of Navigation, with word of his unpopular demeanor already widespread. He commanded only one ship in his seagoing career, a decrepit minesweeper, a command that he considered an insult. In 1939, he moved to the Bureau of Engineering. In his position there, he was able to make the kind of contributions to the Navy and the nation – repairing and keeping ships running during World War II – that advanced his career and personal power.

His confrontational, bombastic, and unforgiving personality aside, Rickover's career accomplishments cannot be overstated. In five years during the height of the Cold War, between 1949 and 1954, Rickover and his hand-picked team – selected through interviews that often belittled and intimidated the candidates – developed a nuclear reactor small enough to fit and safely operate onboard the world's first nuclear-powered vessel, *Nautilus*. The conceptual design for *Nautilus* was approved in 1950, and *Nautilus* was launched in 1954. That accomplishment provided the United States with a capability unmatched at that time. He did so often without the support of his Navy peers and superiors; in fact there were multiple internal attempts to oust him. But support from Congress and the White House, because he achieved his and their goals, gave Rickover immense power and earned him four stars and two Congressional Medals of Honor.

Descriptions of Rickover differ in wordage but are nearly unanimous in the overall picture of his personality that the words paint. Rickover has variously been said to be a loner, a cutthroat, a bully, paranoid, having a ferocious will and a combative personality, displaying a disdain for naval regulations, showing an indifference to the chain of command, frequently used harsh, abrasive, and insulting language, worked his men to exhaustion, ripping through red tape, and driving contractors into rages.[28] President Jimmy Carter was hired by and worked for Admiral Hyman Rickover and said of him: "We feared and respected him and strove to please him...There were a few times, yeah, when I hated him."[29] But, I had the pleasure to work with a Navy submariner who was hired by and worked for Rickover. He agreed with this harsh characterization of Rickover but also admired Rickover's brilliance and work ethic and said he learned a great deal from him and believed that many, if not most others, who worked for Rickover felt the same way.

Rickover's naval colleagues were often the target of his acerbic and often barbed waggishness. Rear Admiral Chester Ward, the Navy's Judge Advocate General at the time, published an article on leadership in the Navy's *JAG Journal* in 1960. There he professed that "the great leader is one for whom his men will *CHEERFULLY* give up their lives. That is the real test of leadership." Rickover later, apparently out of the blue, sent a letter to Captain A. A. Kerr, Special Counsel in the Office of the Secretary of the Navy, in 1968, referencing that quote.

> Dear Andy,
>
> I have not been able to find a single person in my organization who would die for me, much less CHEERFULLY die for me. This definitely shows I am not a leader in accordance with Admiral Ward's definition.
>
> Incidentally, when Admiral Ward's article came out I telephoned him and asked how many people in his office had volunteered to cheerfully to die for him, whereupon he hung up on me.[30]

Rickover clearly felt no compunction regarding pointing out what he considered other individuals' foibles.

In a 1984 *60 Minutes* interview with Diane Sawyer, Sawyer confronted Rickover about what many of his peers saw as his unacceptable disregard for Navy regulations.

Rickover: We never had a book of Navy regulations in my office. I prohibited it. One time, some guy brought it in, and I told him to get the hell out and burn it.

Sawyer: Because you wanted them to think?

Rickover: I wanted them to think. If they knew what their job was, they didn't need a book of regulations.

Sawyer: How can you run a navy if everybody acts like you do? If everybody considers himself-

Rickover: Well, I don't – I – I never told the others how to act. I acted my own way, my own genius.

Sawyer: But you know they said that you were unaccountable.

Rickover: I was 100% accountable. If anything had ever gone wrong with a nuclear ship, to whom would they have pointed their finger at? What they mean is that I would not do all the things they asked me to do. I did the things I thought were right.

Sawyer: But that's not working within the system. Isn't that what the military is about, working within the system?

Rickover: I – my job was not to work within the system. My job was to get things done and make this country strong.[31]

Rickover was finally forced to retire in 1982 at the age of 82, after 63 years of service. That tenure made Rickover the longest-serving naval officer in history, having served under 13 presidents (Woodrow Wilson through Ronald Reagan). According to Rickover, he first learned of his retirement – firing – when his wife told him she had heard about it on the radio. Rickover was not a "typical" military warrior, yet his services to the security of the United States were equal to those of any battlefield commander.

Rickover managed to effectively utilize pacesetting leadership to achieve his, the Navy's, and the country's goals in a field where only zero failure was acceptable. He did it by hand-picking his team and keeping everyone focused on their critical national-security goal. It didn't happen, though, without considerable angst consistently swirling around him, and workers occasionally hating him. But was his leadership toxic? Some have certainly said that was the case. Is he a leader to be admired or a case study to avoid repetition? Both Rumsfeld and Rickover illustrate the dangers of one-dimensional leadership and the complexity of leadership generally, neither of which is limited to men.

Margaret Thatcher was Britain's first female Prime Minister, holding that position from 1979 to 1990; she was the longest-serving Prime Minister for over 150 years and the most influential British politician since Winston Churchill. Described by friends and enemies alike as steadfast, tenacious, and bulldoggish, those traits made her admired, scorned, and divisive. The stringent economic reforms she implemented in Britain, dubbed "Thatcherism," were aimed at lowering inflation, promoting the small state and free markets, encouraging privatization, and imposing constraints on unions and the British labor movement. While they were largely effective and much needed, they also inflicted significant economic pain on portions of the British working public. She accomplished what her male Conservative colleagues had been unwilling or unable to do. Thatcher's popularity soared among the general public, however, and her position as prime minister was cemented with her leadership of Britain's swift and decisive military victory in the 1982 74-day Falklands War. But her rise to power and her style in maintaining it were largely akin to that of Rumsfeld and Rickover.

Thatcher's family hailed from the small town of Grantham in eastern England, where her father was Mayor and the local greengrocer. She lived above his shop with her older sister and parents, sometimes working behind the counter after school. Growing up during and between the two world wars, there was hardship but also a great sense of patriotism, pride, and perhaps especially self-reliance, which shaped the conservative views that defined her later political life. Her father was very interested in politics and instilled a similar interest in his daughter, who began helping out at local elections at age 10.

Margaret Roberts, as she was known then, attended all local state schools, worked hard, and won a place at Oxford University, studying chemistry. She won her first election at Oxford as president of the university Conservative association. Though only a small club, famous politicians visited as guest speakers, and Thatcher began making useful friends for later life. After graduation, she worked briefly as a research chemist but had already set her sights on political office. Her background in chemistry was not inconsequential, as it required both hard work and established her methodical, fact-based thinking. Further, her support for linking the funding of scientific research (beyond "basic" science) to market demands provided an early indication of her conservative policies.[32]

Thatcher tried twice to become a Member of Parliament (MP) for a town called Dartford, on the southern edge of London, in 1950 and 1951. But the 1950s were not easy times for women in politics. While she didn't come close to winning either year, she was the youngest candidate in the country and considered very pretty, so consequently, her picture was frequently run in newspapers. It was in Dartford that she met and married businessman Denis Thatcher, several years her senior. They married in 1951 and had twins in 1953, a boy and a girl. Her quest to become an MP, however, was not to be thwarted by motherhood. She completed and mailed her application to become a lawyer from her hospital room after giving birth.

She trained as a lawyer to further her political career. She very much enjoyed the competition involved with both elections and politics in general. She remained focused on trying to find places where she could stand for Parliament but often found herself thwarted by fellow Conservatives who believed that women with young children should not have careers. Finally, she was chosen to be the Conservative candidate for Finchley, in north London, and became an MP in October 1959.

Her relationship with her children was, not surprisingly, complicated. According to her daughter Carol,

> All my childhood memories of my mother were just someone who was superwoman before the phrase had been invented. She was always flat out, she never relaxed, household chores were done at breakneck speed in order to get back to the parliamentary correspondence or get on with making up a speech.

Though both children attended boarding schools from relatively early ages, her daughter also remembers her mother as being "domestically involved" in their lives.[33] Like men, and especially women today, Thatcher struggled with work-life balance.

As Thatcher rose in positions of power, critics' personal critiques of her grew louder and more frequent. Her voice, in particular, drew sexist remarks, including that she spoke in a shrill voice and was patronizing. One critic compared her voice to "a cat sliding down a blackboard."[34] Subsequently, Thatcher was an early example of an outsider having to mold themselves to an organization or institution, in this case, British politics. She took voice lessons to sound more authoritative, specifically to raise the pitch at which she spoke, keep the pitch steady, and help her vary the volume of her voice which she was speaking.[35] Her perceived need to be authoritative in order to be accepted was evidenced in other ways as well.

As Prime Minister, Thatcher was early on accused of bullying colleagues and abusing her seniority. Thatcher's first Foreign Secretary, Lord Carrington, once described her as a "fucking stupid, petit bourgeois woman."[36] She was undoubtedly tough. She liked the tag of "Iron Lady," given to her by a Russian journalist. But she was also always the most prepared person in the room and intolerant of others who weren't equally prepared. So how much of her critics' complaints would have applied if she were Michael Thatcher rather than Margaret Thatcher can be questioned.

Her style of leadership was purely one-dimensional and masculine. Leadership gurus Robert Kaiser and Robert Kaplan have described her assertiveness and forcefulness as both her greatest strengths and weaknesses, for the same reasons I assert in the thesis of this book.

> Most leaders intellectually understand the complementary nature of forceful and enabling leadership. Nonetheless, we find over and over again that few leaders are able to integrate both sets of behaviors in their own repertoire. Instead, they gravitate to one side or the other and risk taking that approach to such an extreme that it reduces the complementary approach to a void.[37]

Though feminine in appearance in her famous royal blue "power suits," carefully coiffed hair, and always-present, soft-leather conservative handbags, she aspired to be – and was – "one of the boys" politically, even enjoying a special friendship with American President Ronald Reagan. This aspiration, perhaps necessary for her at that time, eventually brought her down, as it did for others. Thatcher resigned subsequent to a leadership challenge in 1990.

Building Emotional Intelligence

There are emotional intelligence "tests" available to initially gauge an individual's personal strengths and weaknesses. Research has shown that "top-performing leaders overestimate their strengths on, at most, one emotional intelligence ability, whereas poor performers overrate themselves on four or more,"[38] again evidencing the dangers of over-confidence. Psychologists have identified a cognitive bias called the Dunning-Kruger effect, where people with limited competence often vastly overestimate their abilities. If, however, individuals are open to self-improvement, these tests can be effectively used to help leaders expand the leadership skills that will benefit them personally and their organization. Being open to feedback and recognizing the need to improve is, however, necessary.

There has also been a cottage industry built in support of helping employees know themselves, including tests often initially developed and used by the business sector. The Myers–Briggs personality test, 360 performance assessment reviews, the Harvard Implicit Association Test, and a slew of others have been used at various times in different organizations, with varying degrees of effectiveness. These tools are available but primarily useful for those open to learning. Individuals lacking self-esteem and driven by likability for positive ego feedback, or with propensities for strong gender stereotyping, often lack the personal flexibility necessary for useful self-reflection or are simply comfortable with the status quo.

For effective organizational improvement to occur, leadership must be actually interested in the data these tests can yield. Leadership experts say that's not always the case.

> Too many companies don't take the 360-degree feedback process seriously enough. Often it goes like this: After shopping around and deciding on a 360-degree feedback instrument, talent professionals administer it to the colleagues of each participant. After aggregating the data, those same professionals send a summary report to the leaders, who then reads through the report with some interest and puts it away. Sometimes, it's never discussed again. The outcome? Little, if anything, changes.[39]

Whether in businesses, government organizations, or the military, as raised regarding the democratic leadership style, respondents to 360 assessments can quickly realize that the effort was for naught, that leadership doesn't really want or care about their input, and that the entire effort was performative. If morale is already bad, things can subsequently get worse.

In the military, institutional or unit assessments are called "command climate surveys." In my experience, which seems backed by statistics, the initial problem is response rates. The 2023 response rates from US Army Garrison Fort Riley, for example, ranged from 30% to 75% depending on the unit, with responses from women lower than men in most cases. Individuals, especially women who already feel less inclusion, fairness, and cohesion than the men they work with, are often reluctant to respond, fearing that, though the surveys are said to be anonymous, they could be identified and face retribution for negative responses, indicating a lack of trust in their organizational leadership. There is also sometimes an assumption that the surveys are performative only, as illustrated in part by the summary of the Fort Riley survey referencing passive leadership.

> The biggest increase was in Passive Leadership for Unit Leader (5%–15%) and NCO (4%–7%). The Presence of Sexist Behaviors (prejudicial, stereotypical, or negative attitudes and opinions) went up from 6% to 7%. Both of which are trending in the wrong direction. Females feel less inclusion, fair treatment, and cohesion in the workplace more than any other demographic. Which ties into Females feeling their morale is lower than any other demographic.[40]

The passive leadership aspect relates to individuals feeling that the goal of their leadership is primarily to show that "everything's fine," including whitewashing command climate survey results to advance their personal careers.

Whereas DEI efforts attempt to change the composition of organizations and the behavior of people, oftentimes it is the organization itself and the culture within that must be changed for more overall personal satisfaction of employees, and consequently organizational effectiveness. There are a number of companies that now focus on a more holistic approach and focus on, for example, aligning "culture with purpose," and it is utilized by organizations from sports teams to corporations. The approach is based on the science of organizational behavior,[41] but still relies on a willing leader cognizant of the benefits of a healthy culture and climate for effective implementation.

It takes an assertive, self-confident leader to make change, and it doesn't come without risk of misperception. A male GFO, new to a mixed-gender unit, led his first meeting to consider promotion files. All files had been reviewed in advance and they were all males. He began the meeting by noting that he found it difficult to believe that there wasn't one female in the unit merit-qualified to be in the group of files for consideration. His intent was to send a clear, potentially culture-changing message to others that he was paying attention to gender inclusion and they should to. Unfortunately, what some of the men heard was "find a woman to promote, merit optional." Perspective matters.

Conclusion

Every leader has their own style. Whether they adapt that style to a specific context, the individuals they are working with, and the needs of the institution they are part of to achieve the institutional goals, or whether they expect others to adapt to them, can mean the difference between success and failure. Further, the world is too complex for one-dimensional leadership anymore. To reiterate from earlier: one size doesn't fit all; one size fits one.

Consideration of Rickover as a possibly toxic leader who was honored and lauded by many individuals outside his organization raises several questions. Would you want to work for him? Would you want him to work for you? Was he an effective leader? Was he a good leader? What three words would you use to describe him as a person? What three words would you use to describe him as a leader? How much depends on context? What discussions addressing questions such as these point out is that the very concept of leadership depends on context and definitions.

A multidimensional, flexible approach to leadership takes knowledge, self-awareness, and a willingness to put collective goals over individual, personal power. That has become a problem of late. Both ethical leadership and leadership accountability seem to have simultaneously declined. Good leaders, committed leaders, too often find themselves fighting against the tide of personal entitlement – whether for power, money, sex, or something else – flowing from others. Ethics have too often become fungible.

Notes

1 McGrath, Ben. "Rummy Meets His Match," *The New Yorker*, April 6, 2003. https://www.newyorker.com/magazine/2003/04/14/rummy-meets-his-match
2 Grahm, Bradley. "Donald H. Rumsfeld, Influential but Controversial Bush Defense Secretary, Dies at 88," *The New York Times*, June 30, 2021.
3 Kaplan, Fred. "Donald Rumsfeld: A Master Bureaucratic Infighter Who Led American into the Abyss of Iraq," *Slate,* July 21, 2021. https://slate.com/news-and-politics/2021/07/donald-rumsfeld-obituary-iraq.html
4 Feith, Douglas. *War and Decision: Inside the Pentagon at the Dawn of the War on Terror*, Harper Publishing, 2009, cited by Scheffer, Ben in "Former Defense Secretary Donald Rumsfeld Dead at 88," *International Business Times*, June 30, 2021. https://www.ibtimes.com/former-defense-secretary-donald-rumsfeld-dead-88-3239818
5 Epstein, Jennifer. "McCain: 'Thank God' Rumsfeld Quit," *Politico,* February 3, 2011. https://www.politico.com/story/2011/02/mccain-thank-god-rumsfeld-quit-048765
6 Flitten, Daniel. "Donald Rumsfeld: Defiance Defined by Iraq," *The Interpreter*, July 1, 2021. https://www.lowyinstitute.org/the-interpreter/donald-rumsfeld-defiance-defined-iraq
7 Reidel, Bruce. "9/11 and Iraq: The Making of a Tragedy," *Brookings*, September 17, 2021. https://www.brookings.edu/articles/9-11-and-iraq-the-making-of-a-tragedy/
8 Landay, Jonathan. "Pentagon Office Produced 'Alternative' Intelligence on Iraq," *McClatchy Washington Bureau*, May 15, 2015. https://www.mcclatchydc.com/news/special-reports/iraq-intelligence/article24461020.html
9 Dickinson, Tim. "Rumsfeld Threatened to Fire Anyone Who Planned Iraq Nation Building," *Rolling Stone*, September 9, 2006. https://www.rollingstone.com/politics/

politics-news/rumsfeld-threatened-to-fire-anyone-who-planned-iraq-nation-building-90057/
10 Goleman, Daniel. "Leadership that Gets Results," *Harvard Business Review*, March–April 2000, p. 80.
11 Goleman, Daniel. *Emotional Intelligence*, Bantam, 1985; *Working with Emotional Intelligence*, Bantam, 1998.
12 Goleman, 2000, p. 80.
13 Goleman, 2000, p. 80.
14 Goleman, Daniel, Richard Boyatsis and Annie McKee. *Primal Leadership*, Harvard Business School Press, 2001.
15 Kanter, Rosebeth. *Men and Women of the Corporation*, Anchor Press, 1977.
16 Takala, Tuomo and Iiris Aaltio. "Charismatic Leadership and Ethics from a Gendered Perspective," *Electronic Journal of Business Ethics and Organizational Studies,* November 12, 2007. http://ejbo.jyu.fi/articles/0901_6.html
17 Kovach, Mary. "Conclusions: Female Leaders Using Coercive Power Motivate Subordinates," The Journal of Values based Leadership, 2021. https://scholar.valpo.edu/jvbl/vol14/iss2/3/ citing Randolph, W. Alan and Edward Kemery. "Managerial Uses of Power Bases in a Model of Managerial Empowerment Practices and Employee Psychological Empowerment," *Journal of Leadership and Organizational Studies,* Vol. 80, No. 1, pp. 95–106. https://journals.sagepub.com/doi/10.1177/1548051810379798
18 Druskat, Vanessa. "Gender and Leadership Style: Transformational and Transactional Leadership in the Roman Catholic Church," *The Leadership Quarterly,* Vol. 5, No. 2, p. 99. https://psycnet.apa.org/record/1995-09181-001
19 Personal interview, December 5, 2024.
20 Goleman, 2000, p. 80.
21 Gelles, David. *The Man Who Broke Capitalism*, Simon and Schuster, 2022.
22 "Christchurch Massacre: PM Confirms Children among Shooting Victims," *The Guardian*, March 15, 2019. https://www.theguardian.com/world/live/2019/mar/15/christchurch-shooting-injuries-reported-as-police-respond-to-critical-incident-live?page=with:block-5c8b7760e4b0cf92e5a578c6
23 Newport, Frank. "What's in a Name? Affordable Care Act versus Obamacare," Gallup, November 20, 2–13. https://news.gallup.com/opinion/polling-matters/169541/name-affordable-care-act-obamacare.aspx
24 Djuric, Mickey. "Justin Trudeau: Town Halls bring New Format and Skeptics," *CTV News*, April 15, 2023.
25 Jewish Virtual Library. entrée: Hyman George Rickover. https://www.jewishvirtuallibrary.org/hyman-rickover
26 Rickover, Hyman. "Doing a Job." https://www.validlab.com/administration/rickover.html (accessed March 19, 2024)
27 Johnson-Freese, J. *Educating America's Military,* Routledge, 2013; Joan Johnson-Freese, testimony before the House Armed Services Committee, Personnel Subcommittee, May 2022. https://democrats-armedservices.house.gov/_cache/files/1/2/123237b9-aaed-4614-be08-dcc6906867e1/E0826C6C1A3F6D6B25172F668F4C5D33.2022518-mlp-witness-statement-johnson-freese.pdf
28 Schratz, Paul R. "Admiral Rickover and the Cult of the Personality," *Air University Review*, July–August 1983. https://quietwarriors.files.wordpress.com/2014/04/admiral-rickover-and-the-cult-of-personality.pdf (accessed March 20, 2024); Wortman, Marc. *Admiral Hyman Rickover*, Yale University Press, 2022.
29 Matthews, 2023, p. 161.
30 Beshany, Philip A. "As I Recall…Selling the Los Angeles," *Proceedings*, October 1987, Vol.113/10/1,016, referencing Kerr, Andy. *A Journey Amongst the Good and the Great*, U.S. Naval Institute Press, 1987.

31 Transcript archived at Virginia Commonwealth University. https://nuclearstreet.com/pro_nuclear_power_blogs/b/science-history-nuclear/archive/2014/03/09/admiral-hyman-rickover-a-vintage-television-interview-and-some-thoughts(accessed March 20, 2024)

32 Lecher, Colin. "How Thatcher The Chemist Helped Thatcher the Politician," *Popular Science*, April 8, 2013. https://www.popsci.com/science/article/2013-04/margaret-thatcher-politician-and-chemist-has-died/

33 Hubbard, Lauren. "What Margaret Thatcher Was Like as a Mother," *Town and Country*, November 16, 2020. https://www.townandcountrymag.com/society/politics/a34551639/margaret-thatcher-children/

34 "Picard, Caroline. What Margaret Thatcher's Voice Sounded Like," *Yahoo News*, November 26, 2020. https://www.yahoo.com/lifestyle/margaret-thatchers-voice-really-sounded-000000564.html?guccounter=1&guce_referrer=aHR0cHM6Ly93d3cuZ29vZ2xlLmNvbS8&guce_referrer_sig=AQAAAD7CYz-xSFqXfR-Xzc5mXImBhquygsjAYiNyKXSedeydM3t_0RYzkglF2Mtt4yStzBHgqrXXUdbnnW1DrZgh_eZJMitwWprmDXQ4YWDNL2G6S_uksE04J1G8Tx4ABJEKrD8MIpvqC1Q4mX5k2nr9QrpvaBwjOcVozKft3wcY98xs

35 Adams, Susan. "How to Convey Power with Your Voice," *Forbes*, November 25, 2014. https://www.forbes.com/sites/susanadams/2014/11/25/how-to-convey-power-with-your-voice/

36 Watt, Nicholas and Patrick Wintour. "Thatcher Biography Reveals Adviser's Early Warnings," *The Guardian,* April 22, 2013. https://www.theguardian.com/politics/2013/apr/23/margaret-thatcher-biography-adviser-early-warning

37 Kaplan, Robert and Robert Kaiser. "Thatcher's Greatest Strength Was Her Greatest Weakness," *Harvard Business Review,* April 16, 2013. https://hbr.org/2013/04/thatchers-greatest-strength-was

38 Goleman, 2000, p. 88.

39 Zenger, Jack and Joseph Folkman. "What Makes a 360-Degree Review Successful?" *Harvard Business Review*, December 23, 2020. https://hbr.org/2020/12/what-makes-a-360-degree-review-successful

40 DEOCS Executive Summary. "FY 23 Executive Summary for EEO Page." https://home.army.mil/riley/application/files/6216/9650/9901/FY23_Executive_Summary_for_EEO_page.pdf (accessed April 15, 2024)

41 Houmanfar, Ramona, Mitch Fryling and Mark P. Alavosius. *Applied Behavior Science in Organizations,* Routledge, 2022.

4

ETHICS AND LEADERSHIP

Few of the military members I interviewed in connection with this book, active duty or retired, joined the military intending it as a career, but once in, many said they stayed because of the feeling of family. US Air Force Major General Sharon Bannister[1] told me of being at her first Dining In, a formal military dinner, as a young officer and being approached by Major General Billy McCoy, a renowned pilot. He had, he told her, served with her father, Captain Stephen Rusch, in Vietnam. McCoy recognized her from pictures he had seen years before. Her father was an Air Force aviator who for many years was missing, not declared killed in action until some years after this Dining In event. As the daughter of a dad who didn't come home from the war, General McCoy approaching her, remembering her father to her, and remembering her, touched Sharon Bannister immensely. She began to see the military as a family, and Billy McCoy as the kind of leader she wanted to be – one who would remember the names and faces of those she had served with, and their families.

Soldiers and commanders from combat units interviewed for research studies often describe their units as *families,* with commanders as resolute and somewhat paternalistic figures. That, as opposed to the environment of civilian business organizations as just a place to work. Describing a combat unit as a family with a paternalistic father carries significant and gendered implications for its leaders. The implication is that they are men, need to be battlefield wise, as well as part educator, part coach, and part protector.[2] But combat leaders are no longer only men, and not all individuals in the military see combat.

Though estimates vary, a high estimate says that (post-9/11) about 30% of individuals who join the military see combat, and most of those who do are in the Army[3] or Special Forces. Measured by those who receive combat action ribbons,

DOI: 10.4324/9781003564065-5

less than 15% of enlisted personnel see combat or are assigned a combat role.[4] The majority of those in the military serve in support roles. The differing demands of a combat unit leader versus a peacetime or noncombatant leader have created a dilemma for the military. With great power competition having replaced counterinsurgency as the anticipated "next war" scenario for the United States, politicians and military leaders alike have focused on "lethality" as the guiding principle, much as Rumsfeld focused on "transformation." But whether the military is training and educating for maximum lethality, and what that should look like, has been questioned. Further, given that the bulk of the military has not or may not see combat, leadership lessons, again, are not one-size-fits-all but rather context-specific.

In Chapter 1, the premise was raised that there are both similarities and differences between business organization leadership and military leadership, and it's been subsequently discussed that even within organizations, different contexts will matter in identifying appropriate, effective leadership styles. Psychologists have sometimes looked at these differences in theater terms, which then determine, for example, what roles individuals play and the rules that govern them. A business executive explained his perspective.

> In my work I know exactly where we all stand, where everything belongs, we have specific role descriptions, certain ways to dress every day, we have names and titles on our office doors, we have clear identities. I am a vice-president, 350 people who report to me all have a certain rank on the ladder. No personal relationship is close enough to blur the lines of authority. In fact, nothing is blurred by friendship or emotion. Everything is guided by doing business and making profits…if you learn your lines well you are all right.[5]

Psychologist Micha Popper, also formerly the commander of the Israel Defense Force's Leadership School, points out that the "stage" and "scenery" in combat units is very different from the business world. In combat units, the possibility of serious injury or even death is added. That raises overt and suppressed levels of anxiety within those units to extents often incomparable to most business organizations, significantly changing the role of the leader and training for leadership.

A retired Air Force Chief Master Sergeant explained the dilemma as he sees it – whether the Air Force, in particular, is preparing its future leaders for combat – in a blog post.

> You tell me. If training on sexual assault, human trafficking, suicide prevention, the Lautenberg Act, use of social media, yadda, yadda yadda, prepares leaders for combat then we are the most lethal fighting force in history. In an average year how much time is devoted to combat leadership training versus what would qualify as business management training?[6]

He goes on to cite the work of Richard Gabriel, professor of politics at St. Anselm College, regarding the dilemma, which can lead to some significant ethical problems.

> we have a giant career-enhancing machine that has defined the prerogatives of success, and that these prerogatives have nothing remotely to do with fighting and everything to do with budget battles and their ramifications...It seems that the main mode of operation of today's leaders is just to make sure nothing bad happens on their watch.

In other words, many (most?) career military leaders are climbing the corporate ladder much like someone in the civilian business world, narrowing the differences between them. Though Gabriel was writing in 1986, the same can be said of today: careerism – while on active duty and in anticipation of retirement – is a significant focus for many military and political leaders, with implications for ethics and ethical standards.

The military–industrial complex that President Eisenhower warned about in 1961 croons a siren song to many military and political leaders. Senator Elizabeth Warren compiled a report in 2023, titled "Pentagon Alchemy: How Defense Officials Pass Through the Revolving Door and Peddle Brass for Gold," that includes statistics on the sheer number of individuals involved.

> Warren found 672 cases in 2022 of "former government officials, military officers, Members of Congress, and senior legislative staff" working for top-20 American defense contractors. Some of the ex-officials have become board members or senior executives, but almost all – fully 91% – have taken jobs as registered lobbyist for the contractors, either working in-house of hired by the companies.
>
> The report indicates that the universe of ex-officials peddling influence might be larger than 672. That is because many former government employees are not registered as lobbyists but still perform advocacy work for defense corporations using titles such as a consultant.
>
> Nearly half of the contractor executives worked for the top five Pentagon defense contractors – those that build major weapons, military aircraft, warships, ground vehicles, rockets and satellites.[7]

Legislative efforts have been undertaken to slow, by waiting periods devaluing individuals' personal contacts that they are often hired to exploit, what many have come to see as a "revolving door" between government and lucrative industry jobs. The success of those efforts, however, has been limited, and wisdom questioned. Retired Air Force General Gregory "Speedy" Martin asserts that the practice of general officers moving to private sector jobs is both ethical and beneficial for American defense. "Access sounds sleazy, but it brings a value. I am interested in doing things that I think the Air Force might benefit from."[8]

The practice of exporting expertise from the government generally and the military specifically to the private sector is not inherently nefarious and can serve the country. Indeed, serious, well-respected government and military leaders are invited to join private sector boards and fill positions for their sterling reputations and the specialized knowledge and experience they bring. But the contacts and influence those general officers and government officials can offer may also better serve just the defense industry. Further, the lines between offering expertise and advice and persuasion are fine. That can be especially true when former general officers, turned industry executives, visit the Pentagon.

General officers' rank, even post-retirement, carries with it a sense of respect, indeed awe, from former subordinates whom they are now courting for contracts. "When a general-turned-businessman arrives at the Pentagon, he is often treated with extraordinary deference – as if still in uniform – which can greatly increase his effectiveness as a rainmaker for industry. The military even has a name for it – the 'bobblehead effect.'"[9] Retired generals and admirals with a seasoned command voice understand and utilize the persuasive effect their authoritative presence can have on former employees. For those on active duty and seeing retirement in their future, the desire to please in the hopes of securing a place for themselves in the future can be strong as well. Former Deputy Chief of Naval Operations, Admiral Robert Burke, was arrested and charged with federal bribery charges in 2024. Specifically, his indictment alleged that he steered training contracts to a particular company in return for a $500,000-a-year retirement job.[10]

The role of the media, specifically paying former members of the military to act as advisors for the media and spokespersons for Pentagon policy, must also be considered. Retired Army General Jack Keane, for example, appeared on *Fox News* nine times over a two-month period in 2014 to advocate for air strikes and special forces to defeat ISIS, declaring that a bolder strategy than the one employed by the Obama Administration was needed. He made similar calls for more military action before Congress. What was left unsaid by the media (and in congressional witness disclosure forms) was that Keane had a very personal interest in seeing military activity ramped up. At the time, Keane was a special advisor to Academi, the contractor formerly known as Blackwater; a board member of tank and aircraft manufacturer General Dynamics, where he was paid over $245,000 in 2013; a "venture partner" at SCP Partners, an investment firm that partners with defense contractors; and president of his own consulting firm, GSI LLC.[11] Dean Ed Wasserman of the US Berkeley Graduate School of Journalism was quoted in *The Nation* as saying, "I think an inclination to use military action a lot is something the defense industry subscribes to because it helps to perpetuate an overall climate of permissiveness toward military spending."[12] Those who profit from conflict weren't going to argue against it.

It would be difficult, indeed hypocritical, for Congress to point fingers at this problem as many members are on the "reaping financial gains from conflict" bandwagon as well. According to a review of financial disclosures, as of 2020, 51 Members of Congress and their spouses own between $2.3 and $5.8 million worth of stocks in companies that are among the top 30 defense contractors in the world. The numbers are estimated because Members of Congress are only required to report the value of their investments in ranges. On January 3, 2020, a missile strike killed Iranian General Qassem Soleimani. When stock markets opened the next day, defense contractors like Lockheed Martin and Raytheon saw a surge in the stock over the possibility of war and Members of Congress saw a nice bump in their stock portfolios.[13] As Speaker of the House, Nancy Pelosi defended the right of lawmakers to trade stocks. "We are a free market economy. They should be able to participate in that."[14] Money, however, can distort ethics.

Further, while the number of ethics investigations into Members of Congress has increased, the willingness of members to cooperate with the investigations has declined. While there is no requirement that lawmakers cooperate, in the past most have been anxious to do so to clear up issues. But the staff director of the Office of Congressional Ethics explained in 2021 that the ethics office now focuses on fewer cases but potentially more serious ones. Perhaps most troubling, "The fact that many [Members] will no longer even meet with ethics investigators reflects a troubling trend in American politics in which improper behavior is no longer a political liability."[15]

Military historian Jeffrey Matthews simply defines good and bad leadership in his 2023 book *Generals and Admirals, Criminals and Crooks: Dishonorable Leadership in the U.S. Military.*

"Good leadership is ethical, lawful and effective. Bad leadership is *either* unethical, criminal, or ineffective, or worse, all three."[16] He then addresses seven categorizations of criminal or unethical leadership by American generals and admirals: war crimes, insubordination, moral cowardice, toxic leadership, obstruction of justice, public corruption, and sex crimes.

War Crimes

War crimes include those of the sort committed at Abu Ghraib prison in Iraq that came to light in 2004 and the 1968 My Lai massacre in Vietnam. Twenty-six US soldiers were charged with criminal offenses in connection with My Lai, but only one, Army Lieutenant William Calley, Jr., an inexperienced platoon leader in Charlie Company, was convicted. He was found guilty of murdering 22 villagers and originally given a life sentence.

Charlie Company arrived in South Vietnam in December 1967. It was one of three companies charged with the destruction of the 48th Viet Cong (VC) Battalion, an especially effective VC unit operating in Quang Ngai province. Though their initial three months had been quiet, by mid-March 1968 Charlie Company had suffered heavy losses, including 28 casualties involving mines or booby traps. In connection with the Tet Offensive started in January 1968 by North Vietnamese and Viet Cong troops, US military intelligence concluded that some Viet Cong forces had retreated and were harboring in hamlets including My Lai.

Lieutenant Colonel Frank Barker was the officer in charge of the Task Force that included Charlie Company, deployed to secure the region, known as Pinkville by Barker's troops. The operation was to take place between March 16th and 18th. Colonel Oran Henderson, the Brigade Commander, urged his officers before the engagement to "go in there aggressively, close with the enemy and wipe them out for good."[17] In turn, LTC Barker reportedly ordered, though some witnesses contended with the potential for misunderstanding, the first Battalion commanders to burn the houses, kill the livestock, destroy food supplies, and destroy and/or poison the wells.[18]

At the attack pre-brief the night before, Captain Ernest Medina, nicknamed "Mad Dog" by his men, said that nearly all the civilian residents of the hamlets in the area of attack would have left for the market by 7:00 am, and that any who remained would most likely be VC or VC sympathizers. That information was incorrect. At Calley's trial, one defense witness testified that he remembered Medina instructing the soldiers to destroy everything in the village that was "walking, crawling or growling."[19] Varnado Simpson, a rifleman in Charlie Company, said, "We were told to leave nothing standing."[20]

After an artillery barrage that had begun around 7:30 am, Calley led his platoon into My Lai around 7:50 am. Though they encountered no resistance, the indiscriminate killing of women, children, and elderly men ensued. Numerous rapes were also committed by US troops. At approximately 9:00 am, Calley ordered the execution of as many as 150 Vietnamese civilians who had been herded into an irrigation ditch. By 11:00 am, as many as 500 Vietnamese civilians had been killed. Medina, from a nearby helicopter, ordered Charlie Company to break for lunch. The sole US casualty occurred when a soldier shot himself in the foot while trying to clear a jammed weapon.

Little of what had happened that morning with Charlie Company was reported to its task force headquarters. In fact, the morning's events were eventually "reported to the world's press as a significant victory."[21] Image and success were heralded externally.

But Warrant Officer Hugh Thompson was flying a scout helicopter at low altitude above My Lai as the massacre took place. He marked locations of wounded civilians with smoke grenades and radioed for ground troops to proceed to those locations and administer medical aid. Forced to leave the area to refuel, he returned to see that many of the wounded civilians had since been killed. Seeing a squad of soldiers approaching more than a dozen women and children, Thompson landed his helicopter between the groups and, with his door gunner and crew chief, manned their weapons as Thompson hailed other helicopters to join him in ferrying the civilians to safety. By noon of that day, Thompson had filed an action report with the company commander about the atrocities he had witnessed.

Initial investigations into Thompson's report involved all the immediate elements in the chain of command and "concluded (erroneously) that twenty civilians had inadvertently been killed by artillery and by heavy cross fire between American and Vietcong units during the battle."[22] The real events of the day would not become public until a New Orleans journalist, Seymour Hersh, published a story detailing his conversations with Ron Ridenhour, a Vietnam veteran who had not been at My Lai but had heard of the massacre from members of Charlie Company. Ridenhour had previously appealed to the Army, Congress, and the White House through letters about what he had heard. Consequently, investigations were initiated and witnesses were interviewed, but the Army steadfastly refused to reveal how many civilians had been killed at My Lai or what had actually happened there.

After the massacre was exposed, the Army eventually charged 25 officers and enlisted men with having taken part in the massacre or having covered it up. Nineteen had their charges dropped without facing trial. Of the six who came before courts-martial, including Oren Henderson and Ernest Medina, only William Calley was convicted.

Medina was acquitted and never spoke publicly about My Lai. After the trial, he did, however, admit that he "had not been completely candid to avoid disgracing the military [and] the United States."[23] Maintaining image was more important to him than the truth. President Richard Nixon commuted Calley's sentence after Calley had served three-and-a-half years under house arrest, as even many of his critics recognized him as only a scapegoat.

Initially, Hugh Thompson and his crew were spurned, even denounced as traitors by several US congressmen, including Mendel Rivers, Chairman of the House Armed Services Committee. Their disparaging version of what had happened was rejected as complete fiction. It was not until 30 years later, in 1998, that all three were awarded the Soldier's Medal for acts of extraordinary bravery not involving contact with the enemy.

Army photographer Sgt. Ron Haeberle was attached to Charlie Company and documented the day's events. His black and white imagery, shot for the Army, was used in Calley's trial. His personal color imagery was later sold to *Life* magazine and came to define the war for the American public and galvanized the anti-war movement.

William Calley was a scapegoat. In debacles such as My Lai, there always needs to be one. Similarly, after multiple investigations into the interrogations at Abu Ghraib prison in Iraq, the only individuals convicted of crimes were low-ranking enlisted military personnel who said they were only following orders. Matthews addressed the accountability problem for Abu Ghraib in his 2023 book.

> Not a single officer was judicially punished. The colonel in command of military intelligence and interrogations at the prison never faced criminal prosecution, although he was reprimanded and fined. His deputy, a lieutenant colonel who directed the prison's interrogation and debriefing center, was acquitted on charges connected to prisoner mistreatment. The one flag officer held accountable for the scandal was a reserve brigadier general, Janis Karpinski, who commanded the 800th Military Police Brigade. She was responsible for all detention facilities in Iraq, but *not* the interrogations at Abu Ghraib.[24]

Karpinski, demoted to the rank of colonel, was the scapegoat.

Karpinski and her unit of 3,400 soldiers were deployed to Iraq in 2003 to conduct the prisoner of war mission. That mission, like so many others, was considerably changed once in Iraq. Karpinski was put in charge of three large jails, and her reservists became responsible for handling suspected terrorists for interrogation, though none was trained for that mission. General Geoffrey Miller, who outranked Karpinski, initiated that mission change. Miller came from Guantanamo, bringing prisoner interrogation techniques already being used there with him. According to Karpinski in an interview, the military intelligence people working with Miller "removed Abu Ghraib from my command, yes, and turned it over to the command of military intelligence,"[25] thereby limiting her involvement and opportunity for oversight. Karpinski takes responsibility for her complicity regarding prisoner abuse at Abu Ghraib but has maintained that she believed everything going on there was with the implicit and explicit approval of her superiors, including Secretary of Defense Donald Rumsfeld.

Evidencing the often-perceived gendered nature of leadership, when initially appointed to her position in Iraq, Karpinski's sex was the subject of a number of media stories, positively portraying her as "caring" and "loves her soldiers"[26] in keeping with gender stereotyping. After the scandal broke, though, the media angle changed significantly, with those intent on focusing blame on Karpinski often doing so in very gendered terms. Karpinski was suddenly characterized as tough, masculine, even inhuman. Her sexual preference was questioned, including referring to her as a "bull dyke," though without any evidence of her sexual orientation. Her sexual preference, however, was not really the point of the changed portrayal. Rather, it was to suggest that Karpinski had deviated from traditional gender roles, so she must be dysfunctional and thereby punished.[27] Karpinski has maintained that she was scapegoated partly because she is a woman. "They made me a pox on our history."[28]

Insubordination

Insubordination is the willful disobeying of a legitimate order, threatening or insulting language, or behaving in a disrespectful manner toward a superior. Army General and World War II hero Douglas MacArthur was relieved of command in

Korea by President Harry Truman in 1951 for insubordination relating to statements MacArthur made in contradiction of administration policies regarding ending the Korean War.

Several general officers clashed with the George W. Bush administration. Admiral William "Fox" Fallon resigned as Central Command commander in 2008, and retired from the Navy, subsequent to an Esquire magazine interview with him regarding Iran, and in anticipation of being relieved of his position. The interview had resulted in an article flattering to Fallon and disparaging of the administration.

> So while Admiral Fallon's boss, President George W. Bush, regularly trash-talks his way to World War III and his administration casually casts Iranian president Mahmoud Ahmadinejad as this century's Hitler (a crown it has awarded once before, to deadly effect), it's left to Fallon – and apparently Fallon alone – to argue that, as he told Al Jazeera last fall: "This constant drumbeat of conflict...is not helpful and not useful. I expect that there will be no war, and that is what we ought to be working for. We ought to try to do our utmost to create different conditions."[29]

Then Defense Secretary Robert Gates claimed that the differences between the Bush Administration and Admiral Fallon were more of "perception" than reality.

Not long thereafter, General Stanley McChrystal, commander of US and NATO coalition troops in Afghanistan, was also forced to resign after he allowed a freelance reporter to embed himself with his staff officers, officers who regularly bad-mouthed President Barack Obama, Vice President Joe Biden, and others in the Obama administration. The resultant 8-page feature article in *Rolling Stone* was titled "The Runaway General." As military historian Andrew Bacevich characterized, "When it came to observing the formalities of civilian control the general turned out to be either spectacularly arrogant or stunning obtuse."[30]

Moral Cowardice

Matthews defines moral cowardice as "a fear-based failure to act responsibly in defense of moral values and ethical principles."[31] Much has been written about the moral cowardice of the many generals and admirals in the Pentagon during the George W. Bush administration who disagreed with Middle East policies and practices but failed to speak up, whether behind closed doors or publicly. The example of Admiral Fallon, however, certainly indicates why there might have been a reluctance to do so.

Retrospectively, there is an argument that speaking up, even resigning in protest of policies, would remove any influence individuals might have on the inside, though there is little evidence that influence contrary to support for Administration policy – privately or publicly – was sought or used. Matthews sums up the problem well: "The predominance of conformity and sycophancy also inhibited the moral courage of those generals closest to Rumsfeld – Myers, Pace and Franks. 'Secretary Rumsfeld wanted yes-men around him', observed Army Major General John Batiste, 'and that's what he got.'"[32]Batiste declined a promotion to Lieutenant General in 2006 and retired from the Army, concerned about Rumsfeld's failed war strategies.

Charges of moral cowardice have hung heavily over Congress since the 2020 election, especially the January 6 insurrection, regarding the perpetuation of false claims of the election being stolen, known as the "Big Lie," that the insurrection was just a group of tourists, and who was responsible for the violence that ensued. One person was shot by Capitol Police trying to enter the Speaker's Lobby of the House Chamber, another died of a drug overdose, and three died of natural causes, including a police officer. One hundred and seventy-four police officers were injured, and four, who responded to the attack, committed suicide shortly after. Those events are not typical of a normal day of tourists visiting the Capitol. Former Republican presidential candidate and Senator from Utah Mitt Romney stridently condemned what he considers the moral cowardice of many of his party colleagues in the 2023 book *Romney: A Reckoning* and in speeches with questions like "you sell yourself so cheap?"[33]

Less considered but certainly relevant to moral cowardice is the issue of institutional betrayal, where individuals put the institutional image above the truth. Women learn early on that the military too often cares more about itself as an institution than personal protections. From the Navy Tailhook cover-up in the 1990s to Operation Fouled Anchor, referencing the cover up of sexual assaults at the Coast Guard Academy from 1988 to 2006, there is evidence that the military has historically cared more about protecting its image than its members.[34] That lesson has intersectional implications for women while serving and as veterans, including in areas such as self-image and health care.[35] Male victims of sexual assault similarly suffer from institutional betrayal. Everyone suffers, at both the micro and macro levels, when institutions put the protection of toxic leadership and image above acknowledging and addressing its flaws.

Toxic Leadership

Matthews' case study for toxic leadership is Hyman Rickover, discussed in Chapter 3. Rickover's contributions to US security efforts are recognized as game-changing, but Matthews states, "For all his visionary brilliance and managerial and engineering competency, Rickover's leadership style amounted to a cult of toxic personality."[36] That toxicity, Matthews argues, created an unhelpful, unhealthy culture of "negativism." General Motors Chairman Roger Smith was once described by one of his employees as "brilliance unimpeded by humanity."[37] So too, Matthews appears to feel about Rickover.

Toxic leaders leave organizations worse off than when they joined, in terms of employee morale and effectiveness, or organizational effectiveness, or both, since they often go hand-in-hand, by abusing the leader–follower relationship. Army Doctrine 6-22 describes toxic leadership as a combination of self-centered attitudes, motivations, and behaviors that have adverse effects on subordinates, the organization, and mission performance. They consistently use dysfunctional behaviors to deceive, intimidate, coerce, or unfairly punish others to get what they want for themselves.[38] Some of these individuals may be hardworking, but their goal is often to promote personal goals, not organizational goals, even if at the expense of others.

Obstruction of Justice

Obstruction of justice consists of criminal acts toward interfering with the administration of the law. Matthews recalls the Watergate scandal during the Nixon years to illustrate, noting that Nixon administration officials John Mitchell, H.R. Haldeman, and John D. Ehrlichman were all convicted of lying to government investigators and conspiring to obstruct justice. George W. Bush administration official Lewis "Scooter" Libby was convicted of perjury and lying about his role in leaking the identity of former covert CIA agent Valerie Plame. Donald Trump pardoned him in 2018.

Plame was outed after her then-husband, former US Ambassador Joe Wilson, wrote an unflattering editorial about the Bush Administration, specifically that it had lied about the nuclear threat posed by Iraq, then used as an excuse to invade the country. Being exposed, Plame later wrote, "endangered my assets, ended my covert career, and unsettled my family…In those years, I was called a liar, a traitor, and – in the words of one Republican congressman – a 'glorified secretary.'"[39] Falsely gendering her role in the intelligence community was intended to belittle her service to the country.

The Trump administrations have perhaps been more plagued with obstruction charges than any since Nixon. The 2019 "Mueller Report" suggests ten times that Trump himself may have committed obstruction of justice,[40] and Donald Trump was convicted of 34 counts of falsifying business records in 2024. Trump's short-lived 2017 National Security Advisor, retired Army General Michael Flynn, pleaded guilty to twice making false statements to the FBI regarding his contact with Russian Ambassador Sergey Kislyak. Trump's initial 2024 nominee for the position of US Attorney General, Florida Congressman Matt Gaetz, has been investigated for obstruction of justice charges as well, in conjunction with Federal sex trafficking charges. Gaetz subsequently withdrew his nomination.

Public Corruption

Public corruption generally refers to a breach of public trust and abuse of position, most often specifically involving money. As Matthews points out, funds the size of those that the Defense Department receives (the Fiscal Year 2024 Defense Appropriations Act provides $825 billion in total funding)[41] make individuals susceptible to corruption. The Fat Leonard scandal began to surface in 2010, though whistleblowers had come forward as early as 2006 and were ignored. The scandal involved dozens of Navy personnel in the Pacific region taking bribes in the forms of cash, prostitutes, and gifts in return for classified information, which was then exploited for profit by the ringleader, Malaysian national Leonard Glenn Francis ("Fat Leonard"). He directed his "moles" – Navy personnel who had accepted the bribes – to send US Navy ships to ports he controlled so he could bilk the Navy for services and fuel. It was perhaps the costliest scandal of its kind since the Cold War in terms of dollars and personnel lost.

Consequent to a six-year-long investigation by the Department of Justice, the Fat Leonard scandal resulted in 33 federal indictments, 22 guilty pleas, and Glenn Francis admitting that his company had overbilled the Navy by $35 million for support charges in port visits by US warships.[42] But the damage to the Navy and the nation goes further due to the number of senior Navy officials involved, directly or peripherally, and taken out of the leadership pipeline. A Pacific Command staffer said in 2018, "China could never have dreamt up a way to do this much damage to the U.S. Navy's Pacific leadership."[43]

Sex Crimes

The categories of criminal and ethical violations that Matthews examines often overlap. Certainly, that has been the case with sex crimes and obstruction of justice. Not surprisingly, Matthews' case study for the sex crimes chapter is Tail Hook, the infamous scandal that followed the 1991 annual convention of naval aviators in Las Vegas, where 83 women and seven men were alleged to have been sexually assaulted. But the underlying problem behind that incident is important to the discussion of the need for and importance of diverse leadership inclusivity that is the thesis of this book. Sexual assault is a problem in every aspect of society, including college campuses and corporations. But the military includes principles in their core values and ethoses[44] intended to promote *esprit de corps* for all.

- Department of Defense: integrity, ethics, honor, courage, and loyalty.
- Air Force: integrity first, service before self, and excellence in all we do.
- Army: loyalty, duty, respect, selfless service, honor, integrity, and personal courage.
- Coast Guard: honor, respect, and devotion to duty.
- Navy: honor, courage, and commitment.

Sexual assault does not, however, promote *esprit de corps*, and for some women in the military, gender-based violence (GBV), especially sexual harassment and assault, is an occupational hazard. Young, enlisted women are especially at risk.

The Department of Defense FY 2023 annual report on sexual assault in the military estimated that 6.8% of female troops and 1.3% of male troops were assaulted while on duty during the past calendar year.[45] Those estimates, however, are known to be tempered by reluctance to report assaults for fear of retribution. A 2020 RAND study titled Prevalence of Sexual Assault in the Military included a survey of military members that evidenced both the underreporting and reasons for such. In response to the question "How many victims reported assault to DOD," only 30% of women and 17% of men answered affirmatively. In response to the question "How many women who reported the assault said they faced repercussions," 51% said they faced ostracism, 34% maltreatment, and 23% professional reprisal.[46] Victims know the chances of perpetrators being held responsible are low and chances of negative career blowback to them high, and so say nothing, leaving them to carry the weight of self-protection, harassment, and assault alone.

Young, enlisted personnel are the most vulnerable group. Individuals like Vanessa Guillén, the 20-year-old Latina enlisted soldier murdered by a fellow soldier at the Texas Army base where she was stationed, sometimes find their safety at risk from their comrades in arms. Before she disappeared, she had confided to her sister that she was being sexually harassed but was too afraid to report it, thinking that nobody would listen to her and instead she would face negative repercussions. An enlisted woman airman who served with only one other woman at a Forward Operating Base in Afghanistan told me of feeling "hunted" by some of her male brethren. She said some men kept track of the women's locations, seeking to catch one of them alone. The women felt strongly that reporting it would have only made things worse.

More recently, a young woman Army officer told me a horrifying story that occurred in October 2023 at a training event she attended with four enlisted women. While she was assigned a private room, the enlisted women were assigned bunkhouse-like base housing. The day after arriving, the enlisted women came to her, as an officer, asking for help in getting a key to their housing door lock. A key had not been provided, and a man had entered during the night and attempted to assault one of them. While the women had managed to drive him out, they were understandably afraid of a recurrence. When the officer asked for the key – assuming that not providing one had just been a mistake – she was told by the holder that he was not going to give it to the women, and that if the women were afraid, they could barricade the door. He also told this young woman officer that if she made trouble over this key, he would make trouble for her, and in fact, he did.

Women's underreporting of gender-based violence in general, not just in the military, often stems from fears of "victim blaming." One particularly insidious method of victim blaming with consequences for how women are perceived as leaders is dismissing them as simply unbalanced – crazy. Calling women some version of crazy – the hysterical woman trope – has long been a tactic to silence women, particularly subsequent to allegations of gender-based abuse or violence. Such was the case with presidential candidate Kamala Harris ("crazy"),[47] lawyer Anita Hill ("a little bit nutty, a little bit slutty"),[48] psychologist Christine Blasey Ford ("mixed up"),[49] retired Air Force Colonel and former Senator Martha

McSally ("nuts"),[50] and Army Colonel Kathryn Spletstoser ("toxic," "irrational," and "unstable"),[51] to name a few, and with little recourse on their part. Christine Blasey Ford published a book in 2024, *One Way Back*, that almost dares Brett Kavanaugh to sue her for defamation, perhaps as a matter of recourse.

Part of any discussion about sexual assault must also consider the long and prickly history regarding the prevalence of false rape charges, because the contention that false charges are widespread is often used as an excuse to dismiss allegations. The National Sexual Violence Resource Center puts the false reporting rate at 2–10%. Estimates vary widely, though, largely due to varying legal definitions of "false allegation" among legal jurisdictions and differences in gathering statistics. Sociologist Joanne Belknap has studied the belief (and panic) among many individuals that false allegations are frequent. "Although false allegations are 5% of all rapes reported to police, the fact that at least 90% of all rapes are never reported (not just including college samples) suggests that of all rapes, those reported and not reported to the police, only 0.005% are false allegations."

Although false rape claims are reprehensible, it is important to acknowledge that they are also incredibly rare, and that rape is reprehensible too. "Clearly, as a group, victims are very unlikely to report rapes to the police and even less likely to make false claims."[52] Writer Sandra Newman has explored the false rape charge consideration as well and found that: "Almost invariably, adult false accusers who persist in pursuing charges have a previous history of bizarre fabrications or criminal fraud."[53] Newman also found that it is rare for false allegations to result in charges being filed, thereby challenging the assertion that "lives are often ruined" by false rape charges. Further, anyone making a false allegation is subject to both civil and criminal laws.

But false allegations do happen, in many areas. In the Introduction of his book, Matthews mentions Rear Admiral Jeffrey Harley, whom I worked for, as having been removed as president of the Naval War College (NWC) in June 2019.[54] An anonymous letter of largely bogus and sensationalized complaints from disgruntled former and then-current faculty members and administrators[55] unhappy with reforms Harley instituted was sent to the Associated Press. The reforms included correcting a 12% gender pay gap among female faculty members (the NWC faculty is less than 10% female) and imposing academic standards for hiring and promotions, standards potentially negatively affecting military retirees hired as faculty and a burgeoning administrative structure. The anonymous complaints were published with little further investigation, triggering Harley's retirement within weeks of the publication due to the national attention it garnered.

After a detailed review of his actions, no serious allegations were substantiated, and Harley was fully exonerated in February 2020.[56] Further, in a January 2022 letter of endorsement for Harley from Admiral (ret.) John Richardson, who was Chief of Naval Operations when Harley left the Naval War College, Richardson noted Harley's "moral courage" in "resolving gender pay disparities and requiring minority representation on hiring and promotion committees."[57] Retired Admiral

Jeffrey Harley honorably continues his work on behalf of the Navy and education. He is a Senior Fellow for the Center for Maritime Strategy of the Navy League and served as the keynote speaker at the annual 2023 Naval Inspector General (IG) Symposium, speaking on the "Price of Leadership" and how the IG system was weaponized against him.

The individuals who made the false allegations remain publicly anonymous (though apparently known), unscathed, and collecting their paychecks, which in at least some cases subsequently included higher-than-average raises. A former Naval War College colleague has made a point of following up regarding why no effort has been made to expose and remove the perpetrators, for what he characterizes as textbook mutiny. In a 2024 Op-ed, he wrote that one of the perpetrators conveyed to him that Harley's educational reforms, including pushing for criteria-based hiring and promotions, "prompted an overt campaign led by a core group of long-time employees to remove him [Harley] from office… a few of whom were in his so-called inner circle and dozens more outside of it."[58] The perpetrators are strongly believed to be retired military.

Brigadier General Warren Wells, chief Army prosecutor for sexual assault cases, was relieved of his duties in December 2023 over concerns regarding whether he took sexual assault complaints seriously. Critics of his firing say it was unfair, given that the allegations were based on a single ten-year-old email, sent when he was a defense attorney to another defense attorney. Wells says he was simply encouraging another defense attorney to do his job. The email reads:

> Expect no commander to be able to make objective decisions involving [sexual assault] allegations as long [as] Congress and our political masters are dancing by the fire of misleading statistics and one-sided, repetitive misinformation by those with an agenda. Hopefully a soldier will be able to get a fair trial. You and your teams are now the ONLY line of defense against false allegations and sobriety regret. You literally are the personal defenders of those no one will now defend, even when all signs indicate innocence."

Defense attorneys are professionally responsible for representing their client's best interests and ensuring their legal rights are not violated. Whether the language of Wells' email goes beyond that is the question.

A female flag officer told me of reprimanding a male Tech Sergeant for inappropriate behavior toward a woman contractor at his base, over the objections of two other men in the chain of command, after she conducted a parallel review of all the available case evidence. One of those recommending against the reprimand asked her if what the perpetrator did was really worth potentially ruining his career, though he didn't refute the charges. While all branches of the US military have "zero tolerance" sexual assault/sexual harassment policies, clearly that "zero" is considered ambiguous by some individuals.

In 2024, the Coast Guard Academy was found to have deliberately withheld evidence (obstructing justice) from Congress regarding the mishandling of 102 sexual assault cases between 1990 and 2006.[59] A secret investigation of the mishandled cases completed in 2020, called Fouled Anchor, was kept secret until exposed by the media in 2023. Said the former Sexual Assault Response Coordinator upon her resignation in 2024,

> The whole thing was a cruel coverup at the expense of the victims, with the entire purpose being to preserve the image of the Coast Guard and avoid scandal. And the Coast Guard used me as part of their plan.[60]

A still-too-prevalent organizational culture still too often leaves women as penalty-free targets of abuse, putting organizational image above the safety of individuals.

Women in the military just want to do their jobs – serve their country – without harassment and fear for their physical safety. The Defense Advisory Council on Investigations, Prosecution, and Defense of Sexual Assault in the Armed Forces is striving to better procedures once a complaint is made, but more needs to be done to prevent the need for complaints. That job falls to leadership, which has largely failed in that regard to date.

Conclusions

Recall Matthews' simple definition of good and bad leadership from his 2023 book: "Good leadership is ethical, lawful and effective. Bad leadership is *either* unethical, criminal, or ineffective, or worse, all three."[61] While he then provides categories of ethical abuses, he doesn't define either ethics or any parameters within which ethics should be considered. That is likely at least partly because every person defines ethics and the morality upon which ethics are based differently, as do different organizations, leaving lots of room for questions and loopholes if they are sought.

Should leaders be held to different standards than others? Are they held to a higher standard? Has misconduct, once grounds for censure in Congress, now become a badge of political honor? Do ethics intended instilled in members of the military through core values over the course of a career become moot upon retirement? What about if that individual still receives military or governmental benefits, like a pension or a government job? The discussion regarding the official standard of zero tolerance for sexual assault in the military and instances of obstruction of justice certainly seems to indicate a tolerance for gray areas of ethical interpretations among leadership. How should that be addressed?

And what about cases of leaders – political or military – just "working the system?" Perhaps not doing anything illegal or technically unethical but rather simply repeatedly making choices that will better position them for future positions? Is that just human nature and therefore okay to be overlooked? Where is the line for that slippery slope? Former Supreme Court Justice Potter Stewart once said: "Ethics is knowing the difference between what you have a right to do and what is right to do."[62] Based on that standard, it is easy to see why leadership is in crisis.

Notes

1 Personal Interview, June 5, 2024.
2 Popper, 1996, p. 20.
3 Parker, Kim, et al. "How Veterans Feel about Deployment and Combat," Pew Research Center, September 10, 2019. https://www.pewresearch.org/social-trends/2019/09/10/deployment-combat-and-their-consequences/; Kratz, Jessie. "Contact, Brawls, and Chambering: The Combat Action Ribbon," March 10, 2022. https://prologue.blogs.archives.gov/2022/03/10/contact-brawls-and-chambering-the-combat-action-ribbon/#:~:text=Not%20all%20service%20members%20in,are%20assigned%20a%20combat%20role
4 Krantz, Jessie. "Contact, Brawls, and Chambering – The Combat Action Ribbon," Pieces of History, The National Archive, March 2022. https://prologue.blogs.archives.gov/2022/03/10/contact-brawls-and-chambering-the-combat-action-ribbon/#:~:text=Not%20all%20service%20members%20in,combat%20and%20who%20didn't%3F
5 Popper, Micha. "Leadership in Military Combat Units and Business Organizations," *Journal of Managerial Psychology*, Vol. 11, No. 1, 1996, p. 19, citing Rohrlich, J. *Work and Love*, New York, 1980, pp. 46–47.
6 Chamberlin, Dave. "Military Leader or Business Manager" (Part 2: Is There a Difference?), The Havoc Journal, August 18, 2020. https://havokjournal.com/writers/dave-chamberlin/, citing Gabriel, Richard. *Military Incompetence: Why the American Military Doesn't Win,* Hill and Wang, 1986, p. 1.
7 Donnelly, John M. "Warren: Hundreds of Former Feds Working for Defense Contractors," *Roll Call*, April 26, 2023. https://rollcall.com/2023/04/26/warren-hundreds-of-former-feds-working-for-defense-corporations/
8 Bender, Bryan. "From the Pentagon to the Private Sector," *Boston Globe*, December 26, 2010, cited in Johnson-Freese, Joan. *Space Warfare in the 21st Century,* Routledge, 2017, p. 113.
9 Bender, 2017, p. 113.
10 White, Matt. "Four Star Admiral's $500,000 Retirement Job was a Bribe, Feds Say," *Task and Purpose*, May 31, 2024. https://taskandpurpose.com/news/admiral-bribe-burke-half-million
11 Fang, Lee. "Who's Paying the Pro-War Pundits?" *The Nation*, September 16, 2014, cited in Johnson-Freese, Joan. *Space War in the 21st Century*, 2017, p. 116.
12 Fang, 2014.
13 Shaw, Donald and David Moore. "The Members of Congress Who Profit From War," *The American Project,* January 17, 2020. https://prospect.org/power/the-members-of-congress-who-profit-from-war/
14 Slodysko, Brian. "Pelosi Defends Lawmaker Stock Trades, Citing 'Free Market,'" *AP News*, December 15, 2021. https://apnews.com/article/business-nancy-pelosi-congress-8685e82eb6d6e5b42413417f3d5d6775
15 Broadwater, Luke. "Ethics Investigators in Congress Increasingly Run into Walls," *The New York Times,* December 28, 2021. https://www.nytimes.com/2021/12/28/us/politics/congress-ethics-investigations.html
16 Matthews, 2023, p. xx.
17 "Trials: My Lai: A Question of Orders," *Time*, January 25, 1971. https://time.com/archive/6838471/trials-my-lai-a-question-of-orders/

18 Kelman, Herbert and V. Lee Bailey. "The My Lai Massacre: A Crime of Military Obedience," *Crimes of Obedience: Toward a Social Psychology of Authority and Responsibility*, Yale University Press, 1989, p. 16.
19 Hughes, Russell. "My Lai Massacre," August 30, 2016. https://www.warhistoryonline.com/vietnam-war/my-lai-massacre-100s-of-vietnamese-were-murdered.html
20 Bakken, Tim. *The Cost of Loyalty, Dishonesty, Hubris and Failure in the US Military,* Bloomsbury Publishing, 2020, p. 230.
21 Hersh, Seymour. "The My Lai Massacre: A Mass Killing and its Cover-Up," *The New Yorker*, January 14, 1972. https://www.newyorker.com/magazine/1972/01/22/coverup-my-lai-vietnam-war-seymour-hersh
22 Hersh, 1972.
23 "Meet the Participants," PBS. https://www.pbs.org/wgbh/americanexperience/features/my-lai-selected-men-involved-my-lai/
24 Matthews, Jeffrey J. *Generals and Admirals, Criminals and Crooks: Dishonorable Leadership in the U.S. Military*, University of Notre Dame Press, 2023, pp. 43–44.
25 "Col. Janis Karpinski, the Former Head of Abu Ghraib, Admits She Broke the Geneva Conventions But Says the Blame 'Goes All the Way to the Top,'" *Democracy Now,* October 26, 2005.
26 Martin, Susan Taylor. "Her Job: Lock up Iraq's Bad Guys," *St. Petersburg Times,* December 14, 2003, p. A8.
27 Sjoberg, Laura and Caron Gentry. "Reduced to Bad Sex: Narratives of Violent Women from the Bible to the War on Terror," *International Relations*, Vol. 22, No. 1, 2008, p. 15.
28 Vlahos, 2008.
29 Barnett, Thomas, P.M. "The Man Between War and Peace," *Esquire,* June 23, 2010.
30 Bacevich, Andrew. *Breach of Trust*, Metropolitan Books, 2013, p. 153, cited in Matthews, 2023, p. 87.
31 Matthews, 2023, p. 89.
32 Matthews, 2023, p. 91.
33 Scriber, McKay. *Romney: A Reckoning*, Scribner, 2023; "Romney Starts Naming Names, Casting GOP Colleagues as Cowards," *The Washington Post*, September 14, 2023. https://www.washingtonpost.com/politics/2023/09/14/you-sell-yourself-so-cheap-romneys-stark-indictment-gop-cowardice/
34 Stone, Kristin M. "The Betrayal of the Red, White, and Blue: The Failures of Institutional Self-Regulation and the Military's #MeToo Movement," *Buffalo Law Review*, July 11, 2022. https://digitalcommons.law.buffalo.edu/cgi/viewcontent.cgi?article=4954&context=buffalolawreview
35 Meade, Vanessa. "Embracing Diverse Women Veteran Narratives: Intersectionality and Women Veteran's Identity," *Journal of Veteran's Studies*, Vol. 6, No. 3, 2020, pp. 47–53.
36 Matthews, 2023, p. 143.
37 Reich, Cary. "The Creative Mind: The Innovator," *The New York Times*, April 21, 1985. https://www.nytimes.com/1985/04/21/magazine/the-creative-mind-the-innovator.html
38 Army Doctrine 6–22, 2017. https://www.moore.army.mil/mssp/pdf/adrp6_22_new.pdf
39 Plame, Valerie. "'The Sisterhood' Review: Ex-Spy Valerie Plame on Women CIA Agents," *Foreign Policy,* January 6, 2024. https://foreignpolicy.com/2024/01/06/women-cia-spies-intelligence-espionage-us-government-history-valerie-plame/
40 Rahn, Will. "Mueller Testimony: 10 Times Trump May Have Obstructed Justice," *CBS News*, July 23, 2019. https://www.cbsnews.com/news/obstruction-of-justice-10-times-trump-may-have-obstructed-justice-mueller-report/
41 Bill Summary: Defense Fiscal Year 2024 Appropriations Bill, March 21, 2024. https://www.appropriations.senate.gov/news/majority/bill-summary-defense-fiscal-year-2024-appropriations-bill-conference

42 Lagrone, Sam. "Paying the Price: The Hidden Cost of the 'Fat Leonard' Investigation," *USNI News*, January 24, 2019. https://news.usni.org/2019/01/24/paying-price-hidden-cost-fat-leonard-investigation
43 Lagrone, 2019.
44 Military Leadership Diversity Commission. "DOD Core Values" Paper 06. https://diversity.defense.gov/Portals/51/Documents/Resources/Commission/docs/Issue%20Papers/Paper%2006%20-%20DOD%20Core%20Values.pdf (accessed November 4, 2023)
45 https://www.sapr.mil/sites/default/files/public/docs/reports/AR/FY23/FY23_Annual_Report_Fact_Sheet.pdf
46 https://www.rand.org/pubs/tools/TLA746-2/handbook/resources/data-on-sexual-assault-in-the-military.html
47 Haberman, Maggie and Jonathan Swann. "Trump's Race Against Harris May Bring Out His Harshest Instincts," *The New York Times*, July 23, 2024. https://www.nytimes.com/2024/07/23/us/politics/trump-harris-attack-lines.html
48 Brock, David. *The Real Anita Hill*, Free Press, 1993. The author later admitted he lied in the book. Ellison, Michael. "I Lied for Rightwing Court Judge," *The Guardian*, June 28, 2001. https://www.theguardian.com/world/2001/jun/28/michaelellison
49 Ruiz, Michelle. "Christine Blasey Ford isn't 'Mixed Up' But The Way We Talk About Sexual Assault Still Is," *Vogue*, September 18, 2018. https://www.vogue.com/article/christine-blasey-ford-brett-kavanaugh-excuses
50 Petersen, Christina. "Arizona Rep. Martha McSally Alleges Sexual Abuse by High-School Coach," *Wall Street Journal*, April 23, 2018. https://www.wsj.com/articles/arizona-rep-martha-mcsally-alleges-sexual-abuse-by-high-school-coach-1524518307
51 Weisgerber, Marcus and Kevin Baron. "General's Sexual Assault Accuser Was Deemed a Toxic, Self-Centered Abuser, New Docs Reveal," *Defense One*, August 16, 2019. https://www.wsj.com/articles/arizona-rep-martha-mcsally-alleges-sexual-abuse-by-high-school-coach-1524518307
52 Belknap, Joanne. "Rape: Too Hard to Report and Too Easy to Discredit Victims," *Violence Against Women*, Vol. 16, No. 12, 2010, p. 1335.
53 Newman, Sandra. "The Truth about False Rape Accusations," *Quartz,* May 11, 2017. https://qz.com/980766/the-truth-about-false-rape-accusations
54 Matthews, 2023, p. xviii.
55 Bogacz, Magdalena. "Enhancing National Security: Increasing Female Faculty in Professional Military Education Would Strengthen US National Security," *Joint Force Quarterly*, July 2023. https://ndupress.ndu.edu/JFQ/Joint-Force-Quarterly-110/Article/Article/3449965/enhancing-national-security-increasing-female-faculty-in-professional-military/
56 "Naval War College: Report Clears Jeffrey Harley on Most Allegations," *USA Today*, February 18, 2020. https://www.usatoday.com/story/news/nation/2020/02/18/ex-naval-war-college-president-jeffrey-harley-most-allegations-nixed/4794749002/
57 Letter from Admiral John M. Richardson (ret.), dated January 12, 2022.
58 Elleman, Bruce. *Newport Daily News*, "Letters: Time to Investigate the Naval War College Mutiny," June 8, 2024.
59 Matthews, Jeffrey J. "When Admirals Obstruct Justice," *Navy Times*, January 26, 2024. https://www.navytimes.com/opinion/2024/01/26/when-admirals-obstruct-justice/; Ellis, Blake and Melanie Hicken. "Coast Guard Leaders Made a List of Reasons Not to Tell Congress About Explosive Sexual Assault Investigation," New Records Show, *CNN*, January 16, 2024. https://www.cnn.com/2024/02/16/politics/coast-guard-sexual-assault-senate-records-invs/index.html

60 Hagen, Lisa. "Coast Guard Lied to Hide Sexual Assault, Whistleblower Says," *Hartford Courant*, June 11, 2014. https://www.courant.com/2024/06/11/coast-guard-lied-to-hide-sexual-assault-inquiry-whistleblower-says/
61 Matthews, 2023, p. xx.
62 https://www.azquotes.com/quotes/topics/ethics.html

5

MEN AND LEADERSHIP

Star Man, Striver, Golden Boy, Scholar, King

"The most competitive man on the planet." That's how one of his former aides described Army General David Petraeus. As a cadet at West Point, class of 1974, he was both in the top 5% of his class, a group known as "Star Men," and an intercollegiate athlete on both the ski and soccer teams. That rarified combination made him known to his peers (with equal parts envy and disdain) as a "striver." He also met his future wife Holly at West Point, as she was the Superintendent's daughter. A classmate described Petraeus as "the one who got the girl."[1]

As a cadet, Petraeus began a tradition he continued throughout his 37-year military career: being a winner, and equally important, being seen as a winner. Contradictions have defined Petraeus: being a lifelong team player, yet sometimes a rebel; being driven by palpable personal ambition and devoted to the institution of the Army; charming and cheerful at times, brusque, critical, and dismissive of those who failed to measure up to his standards at others. But he always stood out.

Physically, Petraeus stands relatively slight at 5'9". But his physical presence commanded every room he was in. A lifelong runner, he was unrelenting about maintaining and demonstrating physical strength, often challenging younger men to races. In 1991 he was accidentally shot in the chest at a live-fire range. Less than two weeks later, Petraeus, anxious to get back to his unit, did 50 push-ups for his doctors to convince them that he was well enough for an early post-surgical release.

Petraeus' Army career focused primarily on being a light infantry officer and included command positions usually held by more senior officers. He was "the golden boy" of the Army – a lieutenant colonel in 1991, a full colonel four years

DOI: 10.4324/9781003564065-6

later, and a one-star general in 2000 – all before he was 47.[2] His assignments also included intermittent schooling. Not surprisingly, at the Army Command and Staff College he won the annual "White Briefcase" award as the best student. More surprisingly, however, at least to Petraeus, was his initial time at Princeton, where the Army sent him to earn a doctorate.

Petraeus received a "D" on his first exam in advanced economics, and on a second-semester paper, the professor wrote, "Though the paper is reasonably well written and has some merit, it is relatively simplistic and I am left feeling that the whole is less than the sum of the parts." His grade for the paper was a "B."[3] Uncharacteristically humbled by Princeton's raised academic expectations, Petraeus asked to write a new paper and subsequently worked up to the new standards required of him. His dissertation was titled, "The American Military and Lessons of Vietnam: A Study of Military Influence and the Use of Force in the Post-Vietnam Era." It served as the basis for his strategy in Iraq.

Petraeus served in Iraq twice. The first time was soon after the 2003 US invasion, commanding the 101st Airborne's occupation of Mosul. He succeeded where others had failed by ignoring Jerry Bremer's order to ban former Baath Party officials from governmental roles. Petraeus saw the need for experienced, capable locals who knew the terrain and understood local issues that needed fixing to restore order, and so he used those locals, regardless of their political affiliation. When he and his unit left in 2004, things went bad quickly, but Petraeus had been dubbed "King David" by the people of Mosul. When he came back to Iraq, it was to head all US forces in the Middle East, having been promoted to that position ahead of many officers senior to him.

Petraeus was a rock-star general by 2008 when both presidential candidates, Barack Obama and John McCain, sought photo-ops with him. *Newsweek, Time, The Daily Beast, GQ, The Christian Science Monitor*...the media couldn't get enough of him, in text and on their covers. *Vanity Fair* called him "the Most Important General in America."[4] He authored the *Winning Hearts and Minds*, nuanced-use-of-force strategy in Iraq, countering the "overwhelming force" strategy used by his predecessors that had only created more anger among the population and fueled the insurgency. His assistant chief of staff in Afghanistan attributed his success to his leadership skills: leading from the front operationally and stemming from "his vision of the army as a flexible, intelligent, essentially human institution"[5] strategically.

Consequent to his success in Iraq, he was offered the job of commanding forces in Afghanistan, technically a step down from command of Central Command in the Middle East, but instead he left the Army in 2011, after serving 37 years, having achieved the lofty position of a four-star general.[6] He was subsequently unanimously confirmed by the Senate to become Director of the Central Intelligence Agency (CIA). Doing it all, having it all, fit in with what a childhood friend described as Petraeus' determined quest for what he called a high "Whole Man Score," whereby

> you got points for all the different things you did. It included sports, grades, extracurricular activities, Scouts, church, and there were all these physical fitness goals attached to it. He was always very concerned about having a very high Whole Man Score.[7]

Petraeus was forced to resign from his CIA position in 2012 after an affair with biographer Paula Broadwell was revealed, during which he shared classified documents with her. He pleaded guilty to a federal misdemeanor charge of mishandling classified information and was sentenced to two years of probation and a $100,000 fine. How that "moral lapse," as the press often called it, occurred, by a man obsessed with his Whole Man Score, has been the subject of considerable analysis.

Under Pressure

A man in the process of transitioning to a woman once told me that the hardest part of the decision to transition was the idea of giving up "male privilege." Privilege stems from tradition and custom. Recently, twice in one week, I heard stories from women regarding being questioned about why they were doing things – one teaching a class on Women in Government, the other hanging a photograph of Women in Aviation on a ship[8] – that excluded men. Why not a class, one was asked, on Men in Government? Her answer was simple: that's called "history." Why a photograph of only women aviators on a ship? Because traditionally they have been only men. Structures, institutions, policies, and laws have been built by men, for men, thereby assuring male privilege, hence the recent emphasis on women edging their way into and forward in nontraditional ways and fields.

Men have traditionally been considered protectors and providers for their families, their communities, and their nations, while women were considered child-bearers and caregivers in the home (though many poor women have worked outside the home throughout history). But, with the rate growing since the 1990s, almost half of all US households are now headed by women,[9] most of whom are never married or divorced. In other developed countries, employment statistics are roughly the same, with two-income families also increasingly becoming the norm. Stay-at-home wives and mothers are increasingly the exception rather than the rule. Consequently, while women are striving to find their place in this post-Cold War world, men are facing changes as well, though in very different ways.

However, while society has spent almost 60 years trying to figure out and accommodate women's new place in the world, little attention has been spent on thinking about or accommodating a positive, or healthy, new place for men in the world. A change in societal roles by one sex but not the other not only makes no sense but can and has caused strife among and between the sexes. Noted author Richard Reeves posits in his 2022 book, *Of Boys and Men: Why the Modern Male is Struggling, Why It Matters, and What to Do About It*, that a positive version of masculinity, compatible with gender equality, is needed.

Further, there are no more woolly mammoths requiring men to protect women and children from. The dangers facing women today are likely to be perceived by women as stemming *from men* – intimate partner violence, violence related to warfare, and femicide – as well as from disease and poverty-related issues. In 2024, an online discussion among women erupted regarding who a woman alone would most fear meeting in the woods, a man or a bear. One of the more thoughtful voices in the discussion was from a woman bike-packer who sometimes travels for months alone. Her words express how many women feel about being alone with a man, but perhaps few men recognize. I raise this discussion here, in a chapter on masculinity, as it evidences both the need and the difficulties of redefining masculinity, and because the feelings she expresses are experienced by women in a breadth of environments where this same basic scenario occurs, including a marriage, an office, a parking lot, a car, a ship, a park, a sidewalk, workplaces, and places where women might not even want to be, but must be to provide for themselves and their families.

> Men are lovable people with the same capacity for empathy, agency, and growth as any other human on the gender spectrum. But when men are socialized to identify their humanness as masculinity and to associate masculinity with power, we get some real problems...When I'm alone in the backcountry and come across a man, I feel a very low level of vigilance. Depending on the situation, I might even be happy to see him. He's a fellow human! Maybe we'll be friends! I'm likely to smile genuinely and say hello.
>
> I don't feel afraid, but I am aware. As we chat, my intuition absorbs a thousand things at once. His body language. His tone. How he looks at me and interacts. Most of the time, this produces an increased sense of security. Most men are friendly, respect my boundaries, and don't want to hurt me. Most of the time, I feel very safe around men.
>
> But not all the time. Sometimes, my intuition absorbs things that increase my level of vigilance. My awareness shifts into closer observation, and I look for signs of danger. Nothing is wrong, but it could go wrong very quickly.
>
> It could be something he says. Maybe he makes a comment about my body or my appearance. Or he asks if I'm carrying a weapon and then presses for details about where I'm camping that night. Sometimes, it's a shift in his tone, a leer, the way he puts his body in my space. But, usually, it's a combination of things, a totality of behaviors that add up to a singular reality: this man is either not aware that he's making me uncomfortable, or he doesn't care. Either way, this is a danger zone. Even if he has no intention of harming me, the outcome of that intention is no longer possible for me to assess or predict.
>
> In this moment, my mind snaps into a single, crystalline point of focus. My intuition rises to the surface of my skin. I become a creature of exquisite perception. The world is a matrix of emotional data: visceral, clear, direct. I need to get away from this man. But I need to do it in a way that doesn't anger

> him. This is the tricky bit. Men who lack social awareness or empathy often also lack other skills in emotional management. And usually, what men in these situations want is closeness. They're trying to get closer to me, physically or emotionally, in the only way they know how. That combination of poor emotional skillsets and a desire to get closer is exactly what puts me in danger.
>
> If I deny his attempts at closeness by leaving or setting a boundary, he could feel frustrated, rejected or ashamed. If he doesn't know how to recognize or manage those feelings, he's likely to experience them as anger. And then I'm a solo woman stuck in the forest with an angry man, which is exactly what most women are most afraid of. There's no time to think, so I operate on instinct. My task is ridiculously complex. I need to deescalate any signs of aggression, guide the man into a safe emotional balance, and exit the situation safely, all at once. This process requires all of my attention, energy and intellect. It's really hard.
>
> I've been in this position so many times that it exhausts me just to write about it. Sometimes it's not that I'm afraid of men; I'm just really, really tired.[10]

Men have in many cases gone from being considered by women as protectors to predators. The psychological ramifications for men – including both shame and anger – of being generally broad-brushed as dangerous and predatory have not been healthy, and in some cases, the anger both perpetuates and exacerbates women's fears. But, as Reeves points out, simply writing off men's issues as "toxic masculinity" does little to address the problem.

Men in democratic, developed, non-patriarchal countries have been confronted with two broken bargains that have turned their economic and social status upside down, leaving many of them rightly alarmed, worried, and indeed, in too many cases, angry. The first involves the evolutionary nature of capitalism from "Fordism" to globalization. During Fordism, a man could be hired into and retain a manufacturing job forever, a job that could support a family but was limited in potential advancement. That was the bargain. Automation and manufacturers' realization that there's always cheaper labor to be found elsewhere around the globe broke that bargain. Furthermore, "creative destruction" – the abolishment of some fields but the opening of others – was accelerated by the influx of information technology that accompanied the wave of globalization that swept the globe at the turn of the millennium. Goodbye mining sector, hello information technology.[11]

Second, both ambition and economic need during the second wave of feminism drove more women into the workforce, including married women, to compete for what had been considered "men's jobs." As a senior male leader pointed out to me, though, men have no exclusive "right" to certain jobs; they have simply always claimed them. But that neither means that men are best at doing those jobs nor that women can't do those jobs.

Harvard professor Claudia Goldin won the 2023 Nobel Prize in economics for her work explaining the gender gap in the labor market and pay.[12] Looking back to the 1970s, she said a "quiet revolution" began, centered on increased investment in education and delaying the age of first marriage. Women could plan an independent future and form their identities before marriage and a family.

Consequently, this "quiet revolution" also reduced women's economic dependence on men. As such, the nuclear family model with working-class men as providers has become the exception rather than the rule. Further, some analysts suggest that the nuclear family was an anomaly in the first place.[13] Yet masculinity has traditionally centered on the belief that men are and should be the head of the household, the breadwinner, the provider, and protector of the family. These mammoth economic and societal changes have spawned questions regarding what it is to be a "good" or successful person. A clergy friend refers to the differences in answering those questions as differences between what he calls "eulogy" virtues and "resume" attributes. For men within the general populace, and for those who lead or aspire to lead, those differences have been shown impactful.

Good Men vs. Real Men

Heather Huhtanen and I explored these impacts in a 2024 *Orbis* article where we looked at two versions of masculinity – real men and good men – in relation to national security.[14] An anecdote included there illustrates the difference between those two versions of masculinity.

In December 2017, Michael Kimmel, then Distinguished Professor of Sociology and Gender Studies at Stony Brook University, delivered the annual sexual assault awareness lecture at West Point. He described a plenary interaction with the cadets, summarized below:[15]

> *I asked, "What does it mean to be a Good Man? Imagine your funeral, and you want it to be said of you, 'He was a Good Man.' So, what does that mean?"*
>
> The West Point cadets said, "Honor, duty, integrity, sacrifice, do the right thing, stand up for the little guy, be a provider, be a protector, give to others, be generous, responsible."
>
> I would say, that's what it means to be a good person; however, those guys experienced it as gendered.
>
> I asked, "Where did you learn that?"
>
> They said, "Well, it's everywhere. It's our culture, it's Homeric, it's Shakespearean, it's the Judeo-Christian heritage."
>
> Then I asked, "Do all of those traits – integrity and honor and responsibility and sacrifice – do they show up for you when I say this: 'Man the F*ck up, be a Real Man.'"
>
> And they told me it's completely different. So, I asked why.

> The cadets said, "Tough, strong, never show weakness, win at all costs, suck it up, play through pain, be competitive, get rich, get laid" – that's what it means to be a Real Man.
>
> They told me they learned it, in order, from "My father, my coach, my guy friends, my older brother."
>
> I think they were telling me that the Real Man is the part that must be performed for others, in order to validate their masculinity. The Real Man interacts with and relates to other men. In contrast, the Good Man is abstract or conceptual, not necessarily interactive.
>
> I told them, "There's going to be a time in your life, if there hasn't already, when you are going to be asked to betray your own values, your own ethics, your own idea of what it means to be a Good Man, to prove to others that you're a Real Man. You're going to be asked to not see what you see. You're going to be able to not do anything about what you see even if you know it's wrong. You're going to be asked to not speak about something that you see. You are going to be asked to betray your own values."

This anecdote reveals the conflicting and competing values, attitudes, and beliefs surrounding masculinity in the military, and clearly within the broader population as well.

A 2007 Norwegian study presents a summary of the academic literature on the relationship between militarism and masculinity, beginning with a quote from British sociologist John Hopton.

> Historically, there is a reciprocal relationship between militarism and masculinity. On the one hand, politicians have utilized ideologies of idealized masculinity that valorize the notion of strong active males collectively risking their personal safety for the greater good of their wider community, gaining support for the state's use of violence, such as wars in the international arena and aggressive policing in the domestic situation. On the other hand, militarism feeds into ideologies of masculinity through the eroticization of stoicism, risk taking and even lethal violence.[16]

The environment subsequently created is referred to as hegemonic masculinity, where practices are normalized by consent to legitimize men's dominance and justify the subordination of women and other marginalized and feminized ways of being a man.[17] Consequently, the argument is that the military does not seek just any kind of male, but rather one characterized by a propensity toward violence, aggression, and a sense of invulnerability.

Tony Porter's 2016 book *Breaking Out of the Man Box: The Next Generation of Manhood* encourages men to reject the constraining real men mentality often drummed into them since childhood. It's fathers telling sons, as I've personally overheard, to "always be aggressive." That version of masculinity, as Kimmel points out, is largely aimed at men validating themselves to other men. It can lead to not just disrespect, mistreatment, and abuse of women, but also to mistreatment of each other through in-group competition. Conflict among men can be driven, amplified, and strategically employed among groups as well as between groups.

Osama bin Laden ordered his lieutenants to marry each other's women kin to quell competition between them that might have turned disruptive. Patriarchies are not just about men having power over women, but also some men having power over other men as well. There is often, for example, a cost to men, from other men, when they try to be allies to women. A Navy Captain, an aviator, told me about being at a military aviation conference and hearing another active-duty male Captain booed by the largely male audience when he gave a talk from the stage on the benefits of integrating (not even inclusion) and mentoring women in their units.

Just as there are lots of books, articles, and pundits ready to give advice on how to "fix" women, there are an increasing number of ideas on how to "fix" men. Josh Hawley, the senior US senator from Missouri, published a book in 2023 titled *Manhood: The Masculine Virtues America Needs.* In it he employs biblical influences to build a case in support of his thesis that American men need to "start families and build homes and leave legacies of character that will span generations," toward becoming "free men, as your fathers and grandfathers were."[18] Americans scoffed at radical Muslims who professed wanting to go back to the imagined, glorified time of the Caliphate as an excuse for terrorism, but some seem willing, indeed eager, to see going back to a glorified 1950s and 1960s in the United States – a time that included lynchings, backroom abortions, and domestic abuse not being considered a crime – as an excuse for domestic terrorism a la January 6, 2021. Carlos Lozada pointed out in his 2023 *New York Times* review of Hawley's book that:

> Hawley spends chapter upon chapter telling young men to stop blaming others for their troubles, urging them to take personal responsibility for their lives and failings...and then he proceeds to give those same young men someone to blame for their fate.[19]

The "Real Man" version of masculinity has significant implications regarding politics and elections. Author Jackson Katz's 2020 film The Man Card, examines the right's five-decade mastery of white, "real man" identify politics in US Presidential elections. Consequently, there are also implications for war and peace. Adherence to that version of masculinity and the supporting belief in the primacy of men over women, has correlated with mass violence, violent extremism, and mobilized violence. Indeed, misogyny has been called "the glue" that binds together right-wing extremists.[20] Research, for example, concerning a 2018 shooting in Florida where the attacker's background included decades of prior concerning criminal behavior directed primarily at women despite his participation in higher education, military service, and highly regarded professional positions of trust.[21]

Mass violence correlated with an adherence to the "Real Man" value is not limited to those who explicitly target women. The 2017 Las Vegas shooter, who killed 58 people and injured approximately 500 others at a music festival, was status driven by and felt entitled to demonstrations of social respect. Research shows that when such expectations or entitlements are challenged or ignored, the individual may experience a threat to their idea of being a "Real Man" and, as such, double down to demonstrate their masculinity.[22] Indeed, those who adhere to the "Real Man" version of masculinity are also more likely to support violence,[23] and generally be more supportive of war as a solution to national disputes.[24]

Similarly, attacks at two gay nightclubs in Colorado (2022) and Orlando (2016), where more than 50 people were killed, are generally understood to be driven by belief in the primacy of heterosexism, and homophobic sentiment rooted in the belief that the worst thing a man can be is feminine – in other words, "gay." Bonnie Mann's 2013 book, *Sovereign Masculinity*,[25] cites examples of prisoners being tortured at Abu Ghraib deliberately being made to feel "not a man" to create an existential crisis within them. In the case of Orlando, the shooter was abusive to women and openly homophobic – he directed violence at forms of masculinity not consistent with a "Real Man" narrative.[26]

The threat of the "Real Man" version of masculinity can also be seen in the planned 2020 kidnapping of Michigan Governor Gretchen Whitmer. In response to Covid-19 lockdown measures, the self-described "Wolverine Watchmen" made a targeted plan to kidnap Whitmer, a so-called "tyrant bitch" who, as a woman, had no right to tell people what to do. Two of the 13 men originally arrested were Marine veterans, one was convicted of providing material support for a terrorist act and handed a sentence of 10–20 years in prison.[27]

White supremacist violence is also correlated with support for the "Real Man" version of masculinity. The 2015 shooter who killed nine parishioners at the Emanuel AME Church in Charleston, South Carolina, wrote, "I have noticed a great disdain for race mixing White women within the White nationalist community...These women are victims, and they can be saved."[28] The quote reveals a competing vision of women's status and subordination in the context of the "Real Man" narrative and the white nationalist community. Women are either the subject of a protective patriarchal strategy to prevent sexual access to non-white men, protect genetic purity, and maintain social hierarchy between white men and white women.[29] Or in contrast, women are viewed as a primary enemy of men for not providing sexual access, attempting to gain and maintain socio-economic independence, and enjoy reproductive autonomy.[30]

Similarly, the 2022 shooter who killed ten black shoppers in Buffalo noted his belief that organized efforts are made to "weaken" the existing white race by promoting sexual and gender diversity that discourages white people from settling into a family structure that is focused on producing children.[31] F. Roger Devlin, a longtime white nationalist, argues that "women's liberation" has actively hurt (white) men's ability to procreate, because when white women have choices, they are less likely to get married, have children, and perpetuate the white race, succinctly evidencing the connection between racism and the subordination of women.[32]

The "Real Man" version of masculinity is also correlated with mobilized violence. This term is used to generally refer to violence committed by a group as a show of force in protest of or support for something. As such, mobilized violence includes violent extremism to the extent that the violence is committed by a group of mobilized extremists wishing to demonstrate power and force.

Political, economic, and cultural changes in the US landscape have amplified "Real Man" security risks. Mann's 2013 book argues that nations can take on a gendered identity and that the 9/11 attacks on the US mainland challenged America's manhood, thereby requiring America to "man up." Imagery, included President George W. Bush - wearing a flight suit - landing on an aircraft carrier and striding Top Gun style to address the waiting troops played into that. More recently, the United States has been engaged in Great Power Competition, specifically with countries with leaders like Vladimir Putin and Xi Jinping. As such, the "Real Man" version of masculinity is correlated with violent extremism and mobilized violence alongside national security policy and practice.

The "Real Man" belief, attitude, and value system is well evidenced within violent extremism, particularly right-wing extremism. This is perhaps most readily identified in the context of Al Qaeda, ISIS, and the Taliban. In these cases, women (among other groups) have an explicitly lower status in the society. They are subject to sanctioned violence and limited in their *de jure* and *de facto* rights, whether that is walking on the street, accessing an education, having a job, choosing who they marry, or controlling their own reproduction. These versions of violent extremism are centered around a "Real Man" narrative where men always have primacy over women, and gender roles are strictly enforced for both women and men.

To be clear, support for the "Real Man" narrative did not cause the January 6 attack on the Capitol. However, the "Real Man" narrative did provide the necessary conditions to mobilize a broad group of protestors to initiate violence. Roger Eatwell and Matthew Goodwin, in their book, *National Populism: The Revolt Against Liberal Democracy*, note that, "[t]hose who felt that the hierarchy was being upended – with whites discriminated against more than blacks, Christians discriminated against more than Muslims, and men discriminated against more than women" were more significant factors in support for Trump than the economy.[33] Thus, the "Real Man" narrative represented a unifying value that was called on to mobilize action.

The events of January 6, 2021, in the United States and notable similar events in Brazil in 2023[34] both featured rhetoric intended to mobilize intersecting groups of protestors using "Real Man" and nationalist narratives amplified by lies and propaganda about the stolen election. In the United States this included imploring tens of thousands of protestors to "be strong," "fight like hell," and "take back your country." The January 6 attack reinforces the connection between the "Real Man" version of masculinity and a variety of right-wing groups in the United States. This includes anti-government militias that are not necessarily ideologically anti-Semitic or racist, alongside expressly racist groups within the white nationalist and alt-right movements. Research documents how "hypermasculine posturing and appealing to male anxieties [i]s integral to the wider purchase of...narratives that fuel anti-democratic sentiments and demand a radical transformation of politics and society" – or a return to a time when women and minorities had limited rights.[35] Indeed,

> far-right extremism in the United States has tapped into misogyny, encouraging, generally white men, to demonstrate their masculinity by engaging in violent confrontations with those institutions, movements, and people that would dislodge them from their position in the social, political, and economic hierarchy.[36]

More generally, when the "Real Man" version of masculinity prevails, more feminine approaches to problem-solving, including communication and diplomacy, are more often ignored. In a discussion with a woman military leader about the ramifications of often being the only woman in the room, she conveyed an anecdote relevant here. A meeting was called to discuss potential responses to a modest hostile act against the United States, responses which very quickly escalated to consideration of kinetic options. Her response to that escalation was to interrupt and ask how they got there so quickly, with little discussion between "what are appropriate options" to planning a kinetic response, thereby tamping down ill-considered over-reaction. This was not, she told me, a one-time situation but happened multiple times. When I followed up by asking other women if they had similar experiences, the answer was often some version of "of course."

Further, the Real Man version of masculinity is bad for men personally due to both societal and economic costs. A 2017 study by Equimundo, an applied research organization focused on developing healthy manhood programs, highlighted the damage to young men 18-30 years of age in the United States, United Kingdom and Mexico. The study found a strong empirical correlation between harmful masculine stereotypes and traffic accidents, suicide, depression, sexual violence, bullying and violence, and binge drinking.[37] Stereotypical expectations can impact leadership as well. Male leaders have been found particularly reactive to financial stress, viewing financial success as an expected part of male protector/provider stereotyping, and consequently "likely to engage in abusive supervision because of it."[38]

"Further, men's continuing decline in life expectancy in the United States is correlated with the Real Man version of masculinity (among other factors like greater exposure to occupational risks/hazards). This trend includes avoiding health care interventions in lieu of stoicism and strength and not addressing mental health needs as a result of difficulty confiding in others or an explicit desire to be an "independent guy" or Real Man.[39] As such, it should not be surprising that many more men than women continue to die of suicide and substance abuse or "deaths of despair." We should be alarmed too that there has been a progressive increase in deaths of despair, particularly among men, since the 2000s.

Similarly, support for the Real Man narrative has profoundly negative consequences within the realities of the labor market, where traditionally male-dominated jobs have significantly contracted while the demand for work typically held by women has increased. This reality is well summarized by the *Economist* in an article entitled, *Men Adrift: Badly Educated Men in Rich Countries Have Not Adapted Well to Trade, Technology or Feminism.* The article's title highlights how one of the problems is that men have not been very interested in or successful at entering female-dominated areas of work due to experiencing "challenges to their masculine identity."[40] The 2017 Equimundo study concluded that $20.9 Billion "could be saved by the US, UK and Mexican economy if there were no Man Box."[41] Men are struggling for the approval of other men.

In remedy, Reeves suggests, for example, that boys need an extra year for brain development before starting school so that they can keep up with the girls, and that more male teachers are needed in early childhood as positive role models. That, however, would require men to be more amenable to career fields traditionally thought more appropriate for women. Positive, or "healthy," masculinity also requires recognition that the Real Man version of masculinity scapegoats women (and minorities) and positions men as victims of feminist (and minority) usurpers – thereby demanding a return to rigid gender roles, such as Josh Hawley advocates. It further requires leaders to be "strong" enough not to betray their own values, ethics, and ideas of what it means to be a Good Man in order to prove to others that they're a Real Man. A struggle between those two models has been glaringly obvious among male leaders over the past decade.

The Political Landscape

Jimmy Carter in the United States, Justin Trudeau in Canada, and John McCain in the United States have all exemplified the "Good Man" version of masculinity. Jair Bolsonaro in Brazil and Rodrigo Duterte in the Philippines have both exemplified the "Real Man" version of masculinity. As leaders, they have provided and will provide a model for others in society to follow. Whether that is, in fact, what is best for the countries they lead, in peace and potentially into war, is the question relevant here.

James Earl Carter served as the 39th president of the United States, from 1977 to 1981. He was a one-term president, failing to win reelection due to, in part, too much honesty. Stagflation (high unemployment and inflation) led to a severe economic downturn in the United States in the 1970s, resulting in many American families experiencing a decline in their quality of life. Early morning lines at gas stations before fuel ran out were uncomfortable, indeed unthinkable, for Americans who were increasingly seeing American exceptionalism as entitlement rather than having to do with responsibility.[42]

In July of 1979, Carter gave a televised speech that was supposed to be about energy, but after serious reflection and consultation with a variety of political, economic, and spiritual leaders and ordinary citizens, it developed into almost a sermon from this Evangelical president. It became known as the "malaise" speech, though he never used that word. Carter encouraged Americans to tighten their belts and live within their means, a theme he had spoken to earlier in 1977, telling people to turn down their thermostats and drive within the speed limits to conserve energy. Perhaps most importantly, he spoke to the American public about a "crisis of confidence," referring to a loss of meaning in their lives and a loss of American unity of purpose, as a hangover of sorts from the US failure in Vietnam. He told the American people some hard truths.

Critics charged that Carter was blaming the American people for his own shortcomings. Soon after the speech, his administration became embroiled in the Iranian hostage crisis and the Soviet invasion of Afghanistan. Perhaps even more importantly to voters, Republican candidate Ronald Reagan, a master communicator, provided American voters with a much more optimistic, appealing view of the future of America and their own futures. Reagan commenced his campaign with the quip: "A recession is when your neighbor loses his job. A depression is when you lose yours, and recovery is when Jimmy Carter loses his."[43] While the malaise speech alone didn't cost Carter a second term, it didn't help him and allowed his challenges to overshadow his successes, which included the Panama Canal Treaty and the Camp David Accords that provided a long-term peace agreement between Egypt and Israel. It also clearly taught American political candidates to never tell the American electorate anything they don't want to hear, a lesson now regularly heeded.

Jimmy Carter graduated from Annapolis as part of the class of 1946 with distinction and served in Rickover's nuclear Navy. He left the Navy in 1953 and returned to his home state of Georgia to manage his family business, a peanut farm, entering politics as a Georgia state senator in 1963, and becoming governor in 1971. He was married to his wife Rosalynn for 77 years, had four children, and spent his later years building Habitat for Humanity homes with her. Jimmy Carter lived his life as a Good Man.

At age 28 in 2000, Justin Trudeau came to national prominence in the Liberal Party after giving the funeral eulogy for former Canadian Prime Minister Pierre Trudeau, his father, leading to his first election to federal office in 2008. He became Prime Minister in 2015 and suggested in 2023 that he might run again, given that Canada does not have term limits on the Prime Minister's position. But his tenure has not been without difficulty, and even within his own party, critics suggest that his administration has become "long in the tooth."[44] For many years, however, Trudeau was seen as a Gen-X political breath of fresh air, poised to replace the

Cold War Baby Boomer leaders who had dominated politics – the "North Star" and "the free world's best hope"[45] – and therefore perhaps a harbinger of future national leadership.

Canadian Prime Minister Justin Trudeau grew up in a world of privilege. His father served as Prime Minister from 1968 to 1979, and then again from 1980 to 1984, and personally dominated Canadian politics for almost two decades. As the eldest son of Pierre, Justin was considered Canadian royalty. Married to Canadian television personality Sophie Grégoire from 2005 until their separation in 2023, Trudeau is the father of two sons and a daughter and considers himself somewhere between agnostic and a lapsed Catholic in terms of religion. A (very) handsome man, he somehow manages to simultaneously exude energy, positivity, approachability, calmness, intelligence, class, and a boy-next-door demeanor.

In terms of policy, Trudeau describes himself as a progressive and feminist. Women and minorities at times have made up more than half of his cabinet. Domestically, he has advocated for women's reproductive rights, made significant strides to reconcile with Canada's indigenous population, introduced a bill making conversion therapy illegal, legalized cannabis for recreational use, supported the right to medically assisted dying, developed a plan to reduce day-care costs for parents to $10 a day per child, and is strongly committed to environmental protection. In November 2022, his government announced that Canada would admit 500,000 immigrants by 2025. Trudeau has pushed "a kind but muscular" Canada in foreign policy circles, including strongly supporting Ukraine. He made significant national and international bona fides by navigating the tricky waters of staying on good terms with the United States during the Trump Administration and with Donald Trump (the antithesis of Trudeau) specifically.

About that relationship, Trudeau said in 2017:

> Obviously, I disagree [with Trump] on a whole bunch, but Canadians expect me to accomplish two things at the same time, which is emphasize where we disagree and stand up firmly for Canadian interests…But we also have a constructive working relationship, and me going out of my way to insult the guy or overreact or jump at everything he says [that] we might disagree with is not having a constructive relationship.[46]

Trudeau managed to successfully renegotiate NAFTA with the Trump Administration, not a minor feat. His approach was and has been very rational, very adult, and very "tend and befriend" when appropriate. The viability of his style of leadership, however, has been questioned.

An April 2024 Op-ed in *The New York Times* titled "Justin Trudeau is No Match for the Polarized World" stated that Trudeau's eventual failure was not questioned, only "how soon and how deep his failure will be when he goes."[47] While the author lauds Trudeau as one of "the most competent and transformative" politicians

Canada has ever produced, he sees Trudeau as "increasingly out of touch with the new world of division and extremism."[48] Trudeau is described as exhausted. That's understandable. Professing and supporting liberalism in an environment where the echo chamber of hate and division is in full operating mode 24/7 must become a bit like tilting at windmills. Donald Trump stoked political turmoil with and in Canada with threats of a 25% tarriff on Canadian goods even before being sworn back in to the presidency, and disparaging Trudeau as the governor of the 51st state and suggesting Canadian hockey legend Wayne Gretsky to replace him. Harkening back to Fukuyama's doubts about whether women's leadership would be strong enough for a world governed in an increasing number of countries by junkyard-dog autocrats, the leadership of rational, adult, competent – good – men is being questioned as "enough" as well.

John McCain, the son of a Navy Admiral, was also a Navy pilot, war hero, six-term Republican US Senator from Arizona, and Republican presidential contender in 2008. His 2018 obituary in the *New York Times* conveyed both his human frailty and his military heroism.

> Because his father was the commander of all American forces in the Pacific during most of his five and a half years of captivity, Mr. McCain, a Navy lieutenant commander, became the most famous prisoner of the war, a victim of horrendous torture and a tool of enemy propagandists.
>
> Shot down over Hanoi, suffering broken arms and a shattered leg, he was subjected to solitary confinement for two years and beaten frequently. Often he was suspended by ropes lashing his arms behind him. He attempted suicide twice. His weight fell to 105 pounds. He rejected early release to keep his honor and to avoid an enemy propaganda coup or risk demoralizing his fellow prisoners.
>
> He finally cracked under torture and signed a "confession." No one believed it, although he felt the burden of betraying his country. To millions of Americans, Mr. McCain was the embodiment of courage: a war hero who came home on crutches, psychologically scarred and broken in body, but not in spirit. He underwent long medical treatments and rehabilitation, but was left permanently disabled, unable to raise his arms over his head. Someone had to comb his hair.

Donald Trump, who never served in the military, referred to John McCain as a "loser."[49]

McCain was a maverick in many ways, but he never put personal gain above principles. At a political rally a month before the 2008 election, a woman in the audience referred to McCain's challenger Barack Obama as "an Arab" at the height of the Trump-inspired conspiracy movement to claim Obama was not a US-born citizen and thereby ineligible for the presidency. In what has come to be known as McCain's defining moment as a person, he didn't take the opportunity to gain an advantage over an opponent by dishonorable means. Instead, he replied evenly, to applause,

"No ma'am, he's a decent family man, citizen, that I just happen to have disagreements with on fundamental issues, and that's what this campaign is all about."[50]

His loss to Barack Obama in the 2008 election has been analyzed and attributed to a number of factors: a hostile economic environment, suspending his campaign in the middle of a financial crisis and thus appearing weak, not being able to shake his association with George W. Bush, who by that time was highly unpopular with many voters due to his war policies, and the selection of inexperienced female Alaska Governor Sarah Palin, who many people, especially liberal women, didn't like and who seemed to have an agenda of her own, all of which weighed him down. Fundamentally, however, it seemed all those factors related to him too often giving in to advisors who didn't allow McCain to be McCain. His reputation as a free-thinking maverick had been tarnished, but not beyond repair.

When Donald Trump became the 2016 Republican nominee, McCain stood by him, through gritted teeth, until the *Access Hollywood* tape was released. Then he said he could not offer even "conditional support." He further said he would not vote for Hillary Clinton but instead would write in the name of "some good conservative Republican who is qualified to be president."[51]

Showing his grit until the end, John McCain was the tie-breaking vote in the 2017 Senate vote to repeal Obama's health care law, a priority for the Trump Administration. McCain, then 80 years old and battling brain cancer, came to the vote as a man with a purpose. He:

> raised his right arm, paused for dramatic effect and flashed a determined thumbs-down, drawing gasps from both sides of the aisle. Trump's health care bill was dead. McCain's lifelong reputation as free thinker, never to be intimidated, was very much alive.[52]

His dislike of Obama's health care law was legendary, but he saved it. He did so because he disagreed with the stealth strategy taken by Republicans to kill it (by avoiding debate and discussion), because he always championed the little guy and health care behemoths certainly were beating them down (his empathy there perhaps heightened as a result of his brain cancer diagnosis), and because Republicans hadn't come up with an alternative, as they had promised to do.

Both former Presidents George W. Bush and Barack Obama spoke at McCain's funeral. Among both Republican and Democratic leaders, and the public, he was largely well-liked and viewed as an honorable man.[53] There are other types of leaders, though, including those who deliberately want to be seen as tough, real men. New York University professor and scholar on authoritarianism and fascism Ruth Ben-Ghiat calls them "strongmen" and notes that they explicitly use their masculinity as a symbol of strength and as a political weapon – and also use, to varying degrees, propaganda, corruption, and violence to stay in power.[54]

Former Philippine President Rodrigo Duterte exhibited anger issues from an early age. Twice expelled from elementary school for misbehavior, he controlled it sufficiently to graduate from college and attend law school, though he bragged about shooting a classmate while there.[55] Digong, as he is called in the Philippines, may have shot his classmate in a gun handling accident, but he likes to claim otherwise as part of his tough guy image. Besides Digong, Duterte has several nicknames, including "The Punisher." That name dates back to his time as mayor of Davao City in the 1980s when he cracked down on criminal activity through the use of vigilante "death squads" estimated to have killed some 7,000 individuals, mainly among the poor.[56]

Duterte was successful in reducing crime. His popularity was further boosted by a smoking ban, LGBT-friendly measures – Duterte claims he "used to be gay" but "cured" himself[57] – and huge ratings from a weekly television show, thereby granting him seven terms as mayor. Duterte announced he would run for president in 2015. His campaign originally focused on substantive policy issues, including government reforms and reviving the sluggish Philippine economy, but quickly derailed into the politics of anger through his expressly and frequently used incendiary language, which then came to characterize his presidency. As a candidate, he said criminals would be exterminated (comparing himself to Hitler as though that was a positive comparison), admitted that he had sexually assaulted a maid as a teenager, and refused to apologize for joking about the rape of an Australian missionary. He won the presidency in May 2016 by a landslide, promising both a war on drugs and a war on corruption domestically, and in July 2016 had an approval rating of 91%. He was viewed as a tough but effective leader.

As president, Duterte acted as a strongman in both foreign and domestic policy. Dictating Philippine foreign relations, he was erratic at best. No fan of US President Obama, who criticized him for supporting extrajudicial killings, Duterte announced in 2016 that the Philippines was "separating" from the United States to align closer to China. He later thought better of that, especially after Donald Trump was elected to office, who ignored Duterte's trampling of human rights and said instead, "we have a great relationship."[58] Domestically, he told his soldiers in 2017 that they could each rape up to three women with impunity on the island of Mindanao, where he had declared martial law in response to a long-running insurgency there, and followed that in 2018 with directions to soldiers to shoot female rebels "in the vagina" to render them useless.[59] A mid-term analysis of the Philippines under Duterte concluded that the country was experiencing a full "assault on human rights and democracy."[60]

Like other populist strongman leaders who have depended on "us versus them" anger-fueled rhetoric for power, that narrative was weakened by COVID-19. His administration strained against the health crisis even though it had dictated one of the most heavy-handed lockdowns in the world. In his final State of the Union, which lasted over two hours, he touted his war on drugs, but admitted he had failed in his war on corruption. The Philippines ranked 115/180 nations in Transparency International's 2020 Corruption Perception Index. Duterte's admission was shortly before a corruption scandal in his administration was revealed, involving financial misuse in relation to COVID-related pharmaceutical supplies.

Nevertheless, Duterte's popularity has remained relatively high and his resilience remarkable. Analysis suggests two viable explanations for both.

> The first…is the "fear factor," or how much is motivated by the fear of expressing dissatisfaction, such that what is observed is not genuine satisfaction. The second is social desirability bias, which makes survey respondents fudge their responses. A list experiment conducted…found that Filipinos who believed their neighbors supported Duterte were more susceptible to this social desirability bias…But for most diehard Duterte supporters, he continued to embody their *tatay* (daddy): the strict father of the nation, with only the interests of the Filipino people at heart.[61]

Philippine term limits allow a president to serve for only one six-year term. Duterte's daughter Sara announced her candidacy in 2022, with many analysts seeing her as a proxy for her father, but then withdrew and ran instead as the vice-presidential candidate of Bongbong Marcos, son of former president Ferdinand Marcos Sr. Marcos subsequently won the election. A feud between the Marcos and Duterte families, however, made headlines in 2024, including for the vitriolic language used in public exchanges by both families.

When Jair Bolsonaro was elected as Brazil's president in 2019, he sometimes referred to himself as the "Trump of the tropics." Analysts have suggested, however, that he was actually more akin to Duterte in that they are both "emerging market populists" rather than "right-wing" populists as in the United States and other countries where anger stems from the broken bargains discussed earlier in the chapter. In Brazil and the Philippines, weak democratic structures facilitate corruption that inhibits economic growth and tolerates violence, including gender-based violence.

Jair Bolsonaro told a female Brazilian lawmaker that he would not rape her because she was not worthy of it. He also dedicated his vote to impeach Brazil's first woman president, Dilma Rousseff, who was tortured as a political prisoner in the 1970s, to one of her torturers.[62] Women haven't been the only ones targeted by Bolsonaro though. He calls himself a "proud homophobe" and once said he could never love a gay son and would prefer his son to die rather than be gay.[63]

Bolsonaro was born in an Atlantic rainforest town, attended all military schools, and then went directly into the Army, serving between 1977 and 1988. Though he served for 11 years, he never rose above the rank of Captain, primarily due to a mercurial temper and open disdain for views and institutions he didn't agree with, including Army bureaucracy. In 1985 he gave an interview to the very popular Brazilian magazine *Veja*, including denouncing low salaries for the military's lower ranks. The initial *Veja* article got him in trouble with his commanders such that he spent 15 days in the penitentiary for insubordination. *Veja* then published further details of the interview, including Bolsonaro suggesting plans to disrupt the water supply in Rio with explosives, again in protest over low military wages, for which he was court-martialed. Though acquitted for lack of evidence, General Ernesto Geisel, the head of the military dictatorship at the time, publicly referred to him as a "bad soldier" and an "abnormal case."[64]

Bolsonaro left the Army in 1988 but has often expressed admiration for the military government that ruled Brazil between 1964 and 1985, and Brazil's military has sometimes continued to play a unique and complicated role in governance. Bolsonaro rose to national prominence from Brazil's legislature as a populist following the massive Petrobras oil scandal that tainted many of Brazil's sitting politicians in 2014–2015. He was elected president in 2019 and served until 2023.

Already known as erratic and temperamental, Bolsonaro offered General Carlos Alberto dos Santos Cruz, a decorated Brazilian Army officer who had commanded UN forces in both Haiti and the Democratic Republic of the Congo, a senior position in his administration, to the relief of many politicians, bankers, and investors. Ideally, it was thought he and other retired officers, including Vice President Hamilton Mourão, would tamp down Bolsonaro's notoriously mercurial and ill-conceived instincts. That optimism, however, didn't last. Within months Santa Cruz and others were out and subject to a barrage of explicit trashing on social media from Bolsonaro's friends and family. "A rupture had formed between the more pragmatic 'military wing' of Bolsonaro's government and 'movement conservatives,' many of them Evangelical Christians, who wanted more radical action on issues like gun laws and so-called gender ideology."[65] In response to Bolsonaro's attack-by-proxy, Santos Cruz said: "You can't even control a child after the age of 16. Good luck trying to control a 60-year-old president."[66]

Santos Cruz was proved prescient. Bolsonaro lost his 2022 reelection bid to former President Luiz Inácio Lula da Silva, though by the narrowest election margin in Brazil's history. His popularity had begun to decline after his first year in office as a result of domestic economics and a campaign finance-related scandal in his administration. His administration's handling of COVID-19, however, strongly contributed to his election loss. Bolsonaro downplayed the virus, use of masks and vaccines, which initially drew support from some of the machismo-oriented population. Bolsonaro told those who complained about his policy to "stop whining."[67] In Real Man terms, to "man up." But when Brazil surpassed Russia as the country with the most cumulative COVID-related deaths,[68] widespread riots erupted.

After his election loss, Bolsonaro refused to concede. His supporters stormed government buildings on January 8, 2023, allegedly to restore Bolsonaro to office. Since then, Bolsonaro has faced a number of legal investigations, including a possible coup attempt that subsequently resulted in his having to surrender his passport so he couldn't flee legal action.

Duterte and Bolsonaro are among a relatively new breed of strongmen leaders. But in frail democracies in other parts of the world, strongmen have long prevailed, bringing with them high levels of corruption known to threaten peace and security.[69] Nor does authoritarianism benefit long-term economic development.[70] African countries have long been known to suffer under strongmen rulers. Placing personal power and wealth above national benefit has been the curse of Africa. The devastation through wars among competing strongmen, rampant with gender-based violence and the use of child soldiers, has been such that healing measures for men have been developed and used to break the syndrome of anger and hate that accompanies these environments.

Working Toward More Positive Masculinity

The Democratic Republic of Congo (DRC) is one of the most dangerous countries in the world for men, women, boys, and girls. Conflict there since 1996 has led to approximately six million deaths. It ranks 162/180 countries in corruption, and 151/179 in gender equality. Physical and sexual violence among women is prevalent, and 3/4 of women and 3/5 of men believe that wife beating is justified for at least one specified reason, with intimate partner violence even more prevalent among younger age groups.[71] Children as young as six are recruited into militia groups, mostly as spies and messengers, though most commonly between ages eight and sixteen for frontline fighting.[72]

The World Bank and other organizations have invested significant time, energy, and resources in efforts to abate the violence in the country by changing the way men think about masculinity through programs such as the Fatherhood Program. That program and its founder, Jackson Mbakulirahi, were the focus of a 2018 documentary called *Baba Bora*. Producer Arild Kumar describes Mbakulirahi's approach.

> Toxic masculinity…has deformed and destroyed the men," he says in the film. Evidently, not beyond repair. According to Mbakulirahi, many of the men who enter this program do so with masculine pride and a commitment to traditional customs and values – "Here the men would say, 'If you eat with your wife, you are sharing with a witch,'" Mbakulirahi explains in the film, that the Fatherhood Program encourages them to reconsider what it means to be a man. Toward the end of the film, one of the program's participants says that of those who received training in his class, "only a few are still putting their wives in terrible situations.[73]

In countries like the DRC, questions about masculinity are not based around broken bargains, but traditional definitions of masculinity. How does a man be the family provider in one of the poorest countries in the world? How does a man protect his family in an environment of constant conflict? How do the answers to those questions drive and amplify expressions of masculinity that lead to violence in the home and in the country?

In other areas of conflict, research has been conducted that relates to problematic, constraining definitions of masculinity. In Indonesia, for example, research reported in 2023 discussed hegemonic masculinity. The term is commonly used in masculinity studies "to describe the most dominant and socially desirable way to be a man in a given context," usually hierarchical. In Indonesia, men said being strong, married, religious, a provider, and protector defined a "good" man. But, having only one acceptable way of being a man limited their ability to seek different paths: e.g., not being married or not being a father. Further, the pressure to conform and the social stigma of not conforming, or failing, affected men's mental health and social well-being such that it could lead to the perpetration of violence in the home or elsewhere.[74]

Local organizations have picked up the mantle as well. In the small US state of Rhode Island, where I live, for example, the organization Ten Men has focused efforts to redefine manhood on eliminating domestic violence.

> This groundbreaking group – poets, campers, golfers, dads – is made up of diverse Rhode Island men with a common vision: a world without domestic violence. Some have children. Some work with survivors. Some are survivors themselves. All of them want to say NO MORE. They know that true manhood doesn't include violence, power, or aggression, and they're here to spread the word to other men and boys. They know that many everyday men want to stop the cycle but don't just know how.[75]

Finding effective ways to move from unhealthy to healthy models of masculinity requires discussion among men.

During the run-up to the 2024 presidential election in the United States, columnist David French wrote about different ways to be a man, comparing professional wrestler Hulk Hogan as one version, representing anger and grievance, and Adm. (ret) William McRaven – a Navy SEAL and former commander of US Special Operations Command – as another, representing honor, principles, and courage.[76] The comparison presents two men of comparable physicality, often very important in considerations of masculinity, but worlds apart in emotional intelligence.

McRaven gave the commencement speech at the University of Texas at Austin in 2014 based on, he said, lessons he had learned in SEAL basic training. There he said:

> Start each day with a task completed. Find someone to help you through life. Respect everyone. Know that life is not fair and you will fail often. But if you take some risks, step up when the times are the toughest, face down the bullies, lift up the downtrodden and never give up – if you do these things, the next generation and the generations that follow will live in a world far better than the one we have today.[77]

That quote provides a roadmap to a version of masculinity positive to leadership in war and peace.

British writer Caitlin Moran's 2023 book *What About Men?* argues that there are too few and too limited discussions about modern masculinity. I agree and suggest that those discussions can be positive, based on roadmaps like those provided by McRaven. Misogynist influencer Andrew Tate's screeds regarding male victimization should not prevail. Further, those discussions should be in conjunction with leadership. Male leaders are strong role models for acceptable and desirable masculinity models. Further, to reiterate prior points, evidence directly links certain masculinity models to domestic violence, the first political order, and that once established as acceptable there, it breeds violence at higher political levels as the de facto method of problem-solving.[78] Those discussions likely won't be easy, but they are important.

Conclusion

All evidence suggests that David Petraeus was an outstanding military leader. His later failing has been characterized as a "moral lapse" which should not tarnish his leadership bona fides. Certainly, Petraeus wasn't the first leader to have such a lapse: perhaps Dwight Eisenhower and Kay Summersby? Franklin Roosevelt and Lucy Mercer? But is there a point, though, when "too many" lapses affect overall considerations of character and therefore leadership, or are personal character traits separate from professional character traits? When are character considerations holistic, especially given that women are often held to higher moral standards than men?

In considerations of masculinities, the role that women play in setting gendered expectations for men must also be remembered. In Ethiopia a few years ago, I spoke with a USAID worker who conveyed that women in some regions goaded their husbands into violence against alleged poachers, as the women received jewelry for their husbands' bravery. In countries where female genital mutilation is traditional, it is often the women who support the practice, as a rite of passage, so their daughters will be considered "marriageable." In the United States, in 2024, women in the Southern Baptist church voted to "support an amendment that would keep them out of the pulpit and restrict their full bodily autonomy."[79] Women contribute to the patriarchy, thereby maintaining a system shown to be neither secure nor stable.

In developed countries where broken bargains are sources of masculinity crises, the question of whether leaders who promote the politics of anger and fear will prevail looms large. While evidence clearly shows their tactics and politics are counterproductive in the long term, it is not evident that rationality is driving voters. With men still predominant as leaders, the question is whether "Good Men" can still be accepted as leaders in the current environment. If the answer is "no," evidence indicates that it does not bode well for national security.[80]

Notes

1 Strochlic, Nina. "Holly Petraeus: The Woman Behind the General," *Daily Beast*, July 17, 2017. https://www.thedailybeast.com/holly-petraeus-the-woman-behind-the-general
2 Bowden, Mark. "The Professor War," *Vanity Fair*, March 30, 2012. https://www.vanityfair.com/news/2010/05/petraeus-201005
3 Jaffee, Greg and David Cloud. *The Fourth Star: Four Generals and the Epic Struggle for the Future of the US Army,* Crown Publishing, 2010, p. 61.
4 Bowden, 2012.
5 Wyler, Grace. "General Petraeus: Bringing Myth Back to the Military," *Business Insider*, May 19, 2011. https://www.businessinsider.com/how-general-david-petraeus-brought-myth-back-to-the-military-2011-5
6 Jaffee and Cloud, 2010.
7 Bowden, 2012.
8 Anecdote provided as part of her paper presentation. Lecaroz, Melanie. "Allyship and Masculinity." Presentation for the *Cultivating Allyship in Defense and Security Sectors Panel* at the 10th Annual Naval War College Women, Peace, and Security Symposium, Newport, RI, May 2, 2024.
9 Goodman, Laurie, Jung Hyun Choi and Jun Zhu. "More Women Have Become Homeowners. Could the Pandemic Undo That Progress?" The Urban Institute, March 16, 2021. https://www.urban.org/urban-wire/more-women-have-become-homeowners-and-heads-household-could-pandemic-undo-progress#:~:text=Half%20of%20all%20households%20are%20now%20headed%20by%20women&text=Even%20among%20married%20two%2Dearner,to%2046.1%20percent%20in%202019
10 Killingbeck, Laura. "A Woman Who Left Society to Live With Bears Weighs in on 'Man or Bear,'" Bikepacking.com. May 22, 2024. https://bikepacking.com/plog/man-or-bear-debate/
11 Friedman, Thomas. *The Lexus and the Olive Tree: Understanding Globalization*, Anchor Books, 2000.
12 Beattie, John. "Why are Dual-Income Families on the Rise," *The Economics Review*, December 2023. https://theeconreview.com/2023/12/05/why-are-dual-income-families-on-the-rise/
13 Brooks, David. "The Nuclear Family was a Mistake," *The Atlantic*, March 2020. https://www.theatlantic.com/magazine/archive/2020/03/the-nuclear-family-was-a-mistake/605536/
14 Huhtanen, Heather and Joan Johnson-Freese. "The 'Real Man' and National Security," Orbis, Spring 2024, 276–293.
15 Kimmel, Michael. "Ask a Feminist: Michael Kimmel and Lisa Wade Discuss Toxic Masculinity," Lisa Wade, *Signs*, 2018, The University of Chicago. http://signsjournal.org/kimmel-wade-toxic-masculinity/
16 Skjelsbaek, Inger. *Gender Aspects of International Military Interventions: National and International Perspectives*, Report to the Norwegian Ministry of Defense, International Peace Research Institute, 2007, p. 13.
17 Jewkes, Rachel, et al. "Hegemonic Masculinity: Combining Theory and Practice in Gender Interventions," *Culture, Health and Sexuality*, October 2015, pp. 96–111.
18 Cited by Lozada, Carlos. "Men Have Lost Their Way. Josh Hawley Has Thoughts About How to Save Them," *The New York Times,* June 1, 2023. https://www.nytimes.com/2023/06/01/opinion/hawley-reeves-bly-men-mascculinity.html
19 Lozada, 2023.
20 U.S. Secret Service Media Relations, 2022-03-15. https://www.secretservice.gov/newsroom/releases/2022/03/secret-services-latest-research-highlights-mass-violence-motived-misogyny

21 National Threat Assessment Center. *Hot Yoga Tallahassee: A Case Study of Misogynistic Extremism*, U.S. Secret Service, Department of Homeland Security, 2021. https://www.secretservice.gov/sites/default/files/reports/2022-03/NTAC%20Case%20Study%20-%20Hot%20Yoga%20Tallahassee_0.pdf

22 Willer, Rob, Christabel L. Rogalin, Bridget Conlon and Michael T. Wojnowicz. "Overdoing Gender: A Test of the Masculine Overcompensation Thesis," *American Journal of Sociology*, Vol. 118, No. 4, 2013, pp. 980–1022. https://www.journals.uchicago.edu/doi/epdf/10.1086/668417

23 Munsch, C. L. and R. Willer. "The Role of Gender Identity Threat in Perceptions of Date Rape and Sexual Coercion," *Violence Against Women*, Vol. 18, No. 10, 2012, pp. 1125–1146. <https://journals.sagepub.com/doi/full/10.1177/1077801212465151>; and Willer, R., C. Rogalin, B. Conlon and M. Wojnowicz. "Overdoing Gender: A Test of the Masculine Overcompensation Thesis," *American Journal of Sociology*, Vol. 118, No. 4, 2013, pp. 980–1022. <https://www.journals.uchicago.edu/action/showCitFormats?doi=10.1086%2F668417>

24 Willer et al., 2013.

25 Mann, Bonnie. *Sovereign Masculinity*, Oxford University Press, 2014, pp. 2–3.

26 Chang, Stewart. "Our National Psychosis: Guns, Terror, and Hegemonic Masculinity," 2018, *Scholarly Works*. 1137. https://scholars.law.unlv.edu/facpub/1137

27 Cappelletti, J. and E. White. "Lengthy Prison Terms for Marine Vet, 2 Others in Whitmer Kidnapping Plat," *Marine Times*, December 16, 2022. https://www.marinecorpstimes.com/veterans/2022/12/16/lengthy-prison-terms-for-marine-vet-2-others-in-whitmer-kidnap-plot/

28 Chang, 2018.

29 Oh, Reginald. "Regulating White Desire," *Wisconsin Law Review*, 2007, No. 2. https://core.ac.uk/download/pdf/225557803.pdf

30 Sunderland, J. "Fighting for Masculine Hegemony: Contestation Between Alt-Right and White Nationalist Masculinities on Stormfront.org," *Men and Masculinities*, 2022. https://journals.sagepub.com/doi/full/10.1177/1097184X221120664

31 Abbas, T., I. B. Somoano, J. Cook, I. Frens, G. R. Klein and R. McNeil-Willson. "The Buffalo Attack – An Analysis of the Manifesto," International Centre for Counter-Terrorism, May 18, 2022. https://icct.nl/publication/the-buffalo-attack-an-analysis-of-the-manifesto/

32 Anti-Defamation League Center on Extremism. *When Women are the Enemy: The Intersection of Misogyny and White Supremacy*. 2018, V:4_7.26. https://www.adl.org/resources/report/when-women-are-enemy-intersection-misogyny-and-white-supremacy

33 Eatwell, Roger and Matthew Goodwin. *National Populism: The Revolt Against Liberal Democracy*, Pelican Books, 2018, pp. 4–5.

34 Jeantet, Diane and Diarlei Rodrigues. "Brazil Observes Anniversary of the Anti-democratic Uprising in the Capital," *AP News*, January 8, 2024. https://apnews.com/article/brazil-riots-anniversary-bolsonaro-lula-41c7e872916ca88ffdb8c27409726dd9

35 Homolar, Alexandra and Georg Löfflmann. "Weaponizing Masculinity: Populism and Gendered Stories of Victimhood," *Journal for the Study of Radicalism*, Vol. 16, No. 2, 2022, pp. 131–148. https://scholarlypublishingcollective.org/msup/jsr/article-abstract/16/2/131/319824/Weaponizing-MasculinityPopulism-and-Gendered

36 Matfes, Hilary and Devorah Margolin. "The Women of January 6th: A Gendered Analysis of the 21st Century American Far-Right," Program on Extremism, George Washington University, April 2022, 9. https://extremism.gwu.edu/sites/g/files/zaxdzs2191/f/Women-of-Jan6_Matfess-and-Margolin.pdf

37 Equimundo, The Cost of the Man Box, Research Report, 2017. https://www.equimundo.org/resources/the-cost-of-the-man-box-a-study-on-the-economic-impacts-of-harmful-masculine-stereotypes-in-the-us-uk-and-mexico-executive-summary/

38 Wascher, Dani Lee. "Financial stress in leaders harms team performance and morale," Phys.Org. 19 December 2024. https://phys.org/news/2024-12-financial-stress-leaders-team-morale.html#:~:text=%22Male%20leaders%20are%20more%20likely,abusive%20supervision%20because%20of%20it.%22
39 Marmot, M., J. Allen, R. Bell, E. Bloomer and Goldblatt. "WHO European Review of Social Determinants of Health and the Health Divide," *Lancet*, Vol. 380, 2012, pp. 1011–1029. https://www.thelancet.com/journals/lancet/article/PIIS0140-6736(12)61228-8/fulltext; McKenzie, S. K., S. Collings, G. Jenkin and J. River. "Masculinity, Social Connectedness, and Mental Health: Men's Diverse Patterns of Practice," *American Journal of Men's Health*, Vol. 12, No. 5, 2018, pp. 1247–1261. https://journals.sagepub.com/doi/full/10.1177/1557988318772732; and Yasuhiro, K., G. Pauline and S. David. "Mental Health Shame of UK Construction Workers: Relationship with Masculinity, Work Motivation, and Self-Compassion," *Revista de Psicología del Trabajo y de las Organizaciones,* Vol. 35, No. 2, 2019, pp. 135–143. https://www.redalyc.org/journal/2313/231360295010/231360295010.pdf
40 Cross, Simon and Barbara Bagilhole. "Girls' Jobs for the Boys? Men, Masculinity and Non-Traditional Occupations," *Gender, Work and Organization*, Vol. 9, No. 2, 2002, pp. 204–226. https://onlinelibrary.wiley.com/doi/abs/10.1111/1468-0432.00156
41 Equimundo, The Cost of the Man Box, Research Report, 2017. https://www.equimundo.org/resources/the-cost-of-the-man-box-a-study-on-the-economic-impacts-of-harmful-masculine-stereotypes-in-the-us-uk-and-mexico-executive-summary/
42 Bacevich, Andrew. *The Limits of Power: The End of American Exceptionalism*, Holt Paperbacks, 2005.
43 Labor Day speech at Liberty State Park, Jersey City, New Jersey, September 1, 1980. https://www.reaganlibrary.gov/archives/speech/labor-day-speech-liberty-state-park-jersey-city-new-jersey
44 Scherer, Steve. "Canada's Trudeau Vows to Run in Next Election at Liberal Party Convention," *Reuters*, May 4, 2023. https://www.reuters.com/world/americas/canadas-justin-trudeau-may-be-struggling-he-still-commands-his-party-2023-05-04/
45 Rodrick, Stephen. "Justin Trudeau: Canadian Prime Minister, Free World's Best Hope?" *Rolling Stone*, July 26, 2017. https://www.rollingstone.com/politics/politics-features/justin-trudeau-the-north-star-194313/
46 Rodrick, 2017.
47 Marche, Stephen. "Justin Trudeau is No Match for a Polarized World," *The New York Times*, April 28, 2024. https://www.nytimes.com/2024/04/28/opinion/justin-trudeau-right-wing-canada.html?searchResultPosition=4
48 Marche, 2024.
49 Jacobson, Louis. "Fact Check: President Donald Trump Called John McCain a Loser," *The Detroit Free Press*, September 8, 2020. https://www.freep.com/story/news/politics/elections/2020/09/08/president-donald-trump-john-mccain-loser-fact-check/5741070002/
50 Clemens, Danny. "John McCain Defended Barack Obama on 2008 Campaign Trail," August 26, 2018. https://abc7chicago.com/mccain-defends-obama-arab-2008-campaign-john/4058948/
51 "John McCain Withdraws Support for Donald Trump Over Groping Boosts," *The Guardian*, October 8, 2016. https://www.theguardian.com/us-news/2016/oct/08/john-mccain-donald-trump-sex-boast-tape
52 Benac, Nancy. "For McCain, a Life of Courage, Politics Came Down to One Vote," *AP News*, August 26, 2018. https://apnews.com/article/north-america-donald-trump-us-news-ap-top-news-bills-0bd309f182de44d9bc320f334be94875
53 Dugan, Andrew. "John McCain Well-Known, Well-Liked for Much of His Career," *Gallup*, August 26, 2018. https://news.gallup.com/opinion/gallup/237764/john-mccain-known-liked-career.aspx

54 Ben-Ghiat, R. *Strongmen: Mussolini to the Present*, W.W. Norton and Company, 2021.
55 "Ex-classmate Bares Details of Shooting Incident between Duterte, Friend," *GMA News Online*, April 22, 2018. https://www.gmanetwork.com/news/topstories/nation/563671/ex-classmate-bares-details-of-shooting-incident-between-duterte-friend/story/
56 Teehankee, Julio. "The Philippines in 2021," *Asian Survey*, Vol. 62, No. 1, 2022. https://online.ucpress.edu/as/article/62/1/126/120111/The-Philippines-in-2021Twilight-of-the-Duterte
57 Hollingsworth, Julia. "Philippine President Duterte Says He ''Used to be Gay'' before He ''Cured'' Himself," *CNN*, June 2, 2019. https://www.cnn.com/2019/06/02/asia/philippines-duterte-gay-intl/index.html
58 Timberman, David. "Philippine Politics Under Duterte: A Midterm Analysis," Carnegie Endowment for International Peace, January 10, 2019. https://carnegieendowment.org/research/2019/01/philippine-politics-under-duterte-a-midterm-assessment?lang=en
59 Ellis-Petersen, E. "Philippines: Rodrigo Duterte Orders Soldiers to Shot Female Rebels 'in the Vagina,'" *The Guardian*, February 12, 2018. https://www.theguardian.com/world/2018/feb/13/philippines-rodrigo-duterte-orders-soldiers-to-shoot-female-rebels-in-the-vagina
60 Timberman, 2019.
61 Teehankee, 2022.
62 "Brazil's Bolsonaro Extols Convicted Torturer as a 'National Hero,'" *Reuters*, August 8, 2019. https://www.reuters.com/article/us-brazil-politics-torture/brazils-bolsonaro-extols-convicted-torturer-as-a-national-hero-idUSKCN1UY2TJ
63 "Brazilian Potential Candidate Announces He Is Gay," *Al Jazeera*, July 2, 2021. https://www.aljazeera.com/news/2021/7/2/brazilian-potential-presidential-candidate-announces-he-is-gay
64 Winter, Brian. "'It's Complicated': Inside Bolsonaro's Relationship with Brazil's Military," *Americas Quarterly*, December 16, 2019. https://www.americasquarterly.org/article/its-complicated-inside-bolsonaros-relationship-with-brazils-military/
65 Winter, 2019.
66 Winter, 2019.
67 "COVID: Bolsonaro Tells Brazilians To 'Stop Whining' as Deaths Spike," *BBC News*, March 5, 2021. https://www.bbc.com/news/world-latin-america-56288548
68 Pašović, Maja, et al. "Countries Hit Hardest by COVID-19," *Think Global Health*, November 17, 2021. https://www.thinkglobalhealth.org/article/countries-hit-hardest-covid-19#:~:text=When%20we%20took%20an%20initial,Brazil%2C%20Russia%2C%20and%20Mexico
69 Kukutschka, Roberto. "CPI 2022: Corruption as a Fundamental Threat to Peace and Security," Transparency International, January 31, 2023. https://www.transparency.org/en/news/cpi-2022-corruption-fundamental-threat-peace-security
70 Lemoine, Joseph, et al. "False Promises: The Authoritarian Development Models of China and Russia," Atlantic Council, January 11, 2024. https://www.atlanticcouncil.org/in-depth-research-reports/report/false-promises-the-authoritarian-development-models-of-china-and-russia/
71 Zeufack, Albert. "Changing Social Norms and Values to End Widespread Violence against Women and Girls in DRC," The World Bank, December 22, 2022. https://blogs.worldbank.org/en/africacan/changing-social-norms-and-values-end-widespread-violence-against-women-and-girls-drc#:~:text=DRC%20ranks%20151st%20out%20of,of%20women%20occupying%20parliamentary%20seats
72 "Child Soldiers in the Democratic Republic of the Congo," The Borden Project, October 2023. https://borgenproject.org/child-soldiers-in-the-democratic-republic-of-the-congo/#:~:text=Children%20as%20young%20as%206,front%20lines%20for%20differing%20warlords

73 Kumar, Arild. "Baba Bora: Toxic Masculinity and Sexual Violence in the Democratic Republic of the Congo," *The Atlantic*, December 13, 2018. https://www.theatlantic.com/video/index/578113/baba-bora/
74 Nagel, Robert, Joshua Allen and Kristine Baekgaard. "Beyond Engaging Men: Masculinities, (Non) Violence and Peacebuilding," Georgetown Institute for Women, Peace and Security and Sisakawa Peace Foundation, 2023, pp. 20–21.
75 https://www.equimundo.org/formerly-known-as-promundo-us/ (accessed August 23, 2024)
76 https://nomore.org/ten-men-redefining-manhood/ (accessed June 20, 2024)
77 French, David. "Hulk Hogan Is Not the Only Way to Be a Man," *The New York Times*, July 28, 2024. https://www.nytimes.com/2024/07/28/opinion/hulk-hogan-vance-harris.html
78 https://www.youtube.com/watch?v=pxBQLFLei70
79 Caprioli, Mary. "Gender Equality and State Aggression: The Impact of Domestic Gender Equality on State First Use of Force," *International Interactions*, Vol. 29, No. 3, 2003, pp. 195–214.
80 Blake, John. "Why Some Women Stay in Religious Groups That Don't Let Them Become Leaders," *CNN*. https://www.cnn.com/2024/07/15/us/religious-groups-women-leaders-blake-cec/index.html

6

WOMEN AND LEADERSHIP

Admiral Grace Hopper was named "Man of the Year" in 1969 by the Data Processing Management Association. That was not the first time her sex was wrongly designated. When she joined the Navy to assist with the war effort in 1943 at age 36, accepted on her second enlistment attempt, her commission read: I do hereby appoint *him* a Lieutenant (junior grade) of the US Naval Reserve.[1] (Many professional women, even today, still receive corrrespondence addressed as "Dear Sir," evidencing gender-stereotyping.) With advanced academic degrees in mathematics from Vassar and Yale, highly unusual for a woman at the time, Hopper smashed gender barriers in the emerging field of computer science, a field assumed to be the purview of men.

But the barriers were there, largely originating from stereotypical assumptions stemming from culture; again, culture being a system of control. In 1960, Hopper and several other computing pioneers were part of a team that developed COBOL (Common Business-Oriented Language). But the male elite computing "priesthood" was skeptical, even predicting its rapid demise, having concluded that "the fruits of such an unstructured, female-dominated process could not be expected to survive, let alone flourish."[2] Yet within 40 years, COBOL was among the most widely used computer codes globally.

During her lifetime, when newspapers wrote wondrous stories speculating about the oncoming computer age and photographers took pictures of extraordinary technological breakthroughs, she and other women were left out, and their contributions were initially erased. For many years, that left women without a role model to follow and helped to build the myth that women "don't do" STEM fields. Gender stereotyping hurts men and women and helps only those who support the status quo, even when the status quo is counterproductive at the individual, national, and strategic levels.

DOI: 10.4324/9781003564065-7

And still, a 2016 study found that code written by women was more likely to be approved by other coders than code written by men – but only if their peers didn't know that the code came from women.[3] With the increased contemporary reliance on technology, including cyber, space, and artificial intelligence, effective leadership demands that organizational profiles be expanded not just in allowance, but in acceptance and accommodation: inclusion, not just integration. Cultural changes are needed.

Two Paths to Three Stars

There isn't one path to leadership, for men or women. Leaders develop at different paces, in different situations (and sometimes a situation will reveal a leader when they rise to the occasion), and in different ways. For women especially, though, it is important that they have goals but can also be open to new possibilities and opportunities, and be ready to seize them.

Michelle Skubic[4] was managing five nightclubs south of Los Angeles by the time she was 19, before she was old enough to drink at any of those nightclubs. That was just one step on her lifelong path to learning about life, business, and leadership. She joined the Navy at age 27, naïve about the military but already steeped in business experience. Conversely, Nina Armagno[5] attended the Air Force Academy right after high school. Her intent was to become a doctor as a road to achieving her ultimate goal of being an astronaut. Sally Ride was her hero and spaceflight her dream. The Air Force was a means to an end. Neither Michelle Skubic nor Nina Armagno intended to make the military a career. However, both of their military careers turned out quite differently than intended.

Vice Admiral Skubic retired from the Navy in 2024 as director of the Defense Logistics Agency, an organization that manages the end-to-end global defense supply chain for all military services. She was the first woman to serve in that position. Nina Armagno never became an astronaut but retired as a three-star Lieutenant General from the Space Force in 2023. She was the first woman to command both the 30th Space Wing and the 45th Space Wing of the Air Force, and upon her transfer, the first woman to serve as a general officer in the US Space Force, created in 2019. Perhaps ironically, the rough statistical odds of becoming an astronaut traditionally have been about the same as a woman reaching the rank of a three-star flag officer.

Admiral Skubic hailed from a loving but troubled family. Her mother and father divorced when she was very young. Until age 11, she lived with her mother in Southern California but then relocated to Massachusetts to live with her father and stepmother while her dad, a naval officer, served as commanding officer of USS *Constitution*. Graduating from high school at 16 and unsure what she wanted to do next, she "dabbled" in both college and employment, including taking a job at a bank in Boston while attending Harvard Extension School courses at night. Her job was to call Massachusetts city and town treasurers and convince them to invest in the bank's products. At 17 and gaining self-confidence, she was on a first-name phone basis with the treasurer of the city of Boston, among others, already learning life skills and leadership.

From there, she moved back to California and was hired as a nightclub cashier and bookkeeper. But her boss recognized her business and leadership acumen and began giving her more and more responsibility. Soon she was managing not just that club but a total of five that her boss owned. Officially, she "co-managed" the clubs with an over-21 bouncer, but he and everyone else in the clubs called her "boss." A friend's father convinced her to apply to California State University Fullerton, where she later graduated in 1988 with a business degree that she paid for herself. By that time, she was working in financial services, increasingly understanding her own value, learning to trust herself, and already experienced at managing and leading others. And then, a casual conversation with a navy reservist and a personally impactful day-trip to Newport, RI naval station with her father set her course. Although the required initial four-year commitment seemed daunting, she signed up. She joined the Navy. Subsequently, though, she gladly "re-upped" repeatedly over the next 35 years, never looking back. Admiral Skubic reflects that a military career likely would not have worked out for her had she joined when she was younger.

Nina Armagno's father was an Italian immigrant. Both he and her mother were teachers, instilling "dream big" and "work hard" ethics into her and her two younger brothers, often involving tough love. Talk at the dinner table focused the siblings on consistently proving and improving themselves so that they could get into the best schools – like Stanford or MIT – to further themselves. In Nina's case, that meant to best prepare to be a doctor, for a future as an astronaut. But when the time for college approached, family money was tight and the likes of Stanford and MIT appeared out of reach. But Nina wasn't willing to settle for anything less than an education that would allow her to fulfill her lifelong aspiration and so, with stellar grades to back her, she applied to and was accepted at the Air Force Academy.

Her approach at both the Academy and her military assignments was to make sure she became indispensable to the unit. She excelled in all that she took on. Balancing her first assignment at Beale Air Force Base, working on a phased array radar system, with taking classes and the required accompanying labs toward becoming a doctor was hard, but she did it. She thought about getting out so that she could focus on going to medical school but found herself enjoying her work, especially the leadership part. As a Lieutenant, she got to know herself as a leader and then, as a captain, still in her twenties, how to lead people. She began to understand, for example, that the mood of those in her unit often mirrored her own mood, and so she strove for personal professionalism, competence, and positivity every day. She saw success reflected in her unit's effectiveness and stopped thinking about medical school. She had found her calling: leading people. The Air Force afforded Nina Armagno a place to mature as a woman and a leader.

Michelle Skubic and Nina Armagno had very different motivations, backgrounds, and military career paths. Both have said they had positive opportunities and experiences in the military that would not have been afforded to them in many other careers. One described herself as a girly-girl; the other said she stopped wearing perfume after joining the military. Both considered personal authenticity as a "must" for a leader. Michelle Skubic is divorced and has two children (with one, she went into labor while on a military flight); Nina Armagno is married but does not have children. One describes her leadership style as a "servant leader," leading by authority achieved through mutual respect rather than power, an approach often associated with leadership guru John Maxwell, the other simply as "engaged and inclusive," but again, through mutual respect. They both felt that they had been able to positively affect situations – making connections, changing attitudes, seeing things from a different perspective – by virtue of their sex. They both consider themselves lifelong learners of leadership.

Neither Michelle Skubic nor Nina Armagno saw their career advancement as either helped or hindered based on their sex, but rather, appropriately, on merit. Like Skubic and Armagno, Michelle Howard, US Naval Academy class of 1982, also had an exemplary military career, hers as a surface warfare officer. Howard was another person of many "firsts," including: the first woman of color to command a US Navy ship, the first female to command operational forces, and in 2014 she became the first female four-star admiral in US naval history. While her career advancement was a significant event for the Navy, the military, and for women, Howard herself admitted in 2012, "There were individuals who didn't want me there or wanted to undermine what I was trying to do."[6] Admiral Howard retired in 2017 after nearly 36 years of service. But her experience demonstrates even women who achieve top leadership positions are not immune to prejudice along the way. A *Navy Times* article chronicled the prejudice, resistance, and resentment Howard had encountered "from her Induction Day in 1978," and that continued even as a flag officer.[7] A Navy investigation report cited one of her peers, Rear Adm. Chuck Gaouette, as suggesting to others that Howard "may not have had to cross as many hurdles in the same fashion to get where she was at," and her race and gender may have "sped up" her selection for vice admiral,[8] thus trying to depreciate her accomplishments. Gaouette was relieved of command of the John C. Stennis Carrier Strike Group mid-deployment in 2012 for conduct related to an incident with a crew member.[9] The kind of accusations openly made by Gaouette, and even more often privately by individuals, can undermine a leader's credibility.

Nor is the professional pettiness often directed at women confined to the United States. A male colleague sued Louise Dedichen when, in 2008 as a Rear Admiral, Norway's first female admiral, she was appointed as Commandant of the Norwegian Defense College. The colleague claimed she received the position due to her sex. Admiral Dedichen won her case but was then sued again, this time claiming she had received favoritism through family ties, but eventually exhausted her colleague's unfounded claims at the Norwegian Supreme Court.

The male dominated Norwegian Military Officers Union noted that they were disappointed by the Supreme Court's ruling.[10]

An American female Lt. General conceded that she too had once felt her leadership undermined, as a three-star general, when her boss made it clear to subordinates that she could be circumvented without reprisal. Yet another woman, a Major General I spoke with, told me of working for great male leaders and having outstanding male mentors throughout her operational career, only to find herself, as a general officer, working for a male general officer whose leadership mantra was "let people be happy." While she too wanted her subordinates to be happy, not at the price of substantive operational standards, which she felt were suffering. His emphasis on keeping people happy and hers on mission effectiveness caused them to clash, with her boss subsequently making it clear to others that it was okay to circumvent her. When she spoke with him, respectfully providing feedback, his response was to further distance himself from her. Even at the highest levels, women leaders can still face gender-based resistance that impedes their ability to lead and be effective in their positions.

Traditional Women Leaders: Warriors, Daughters, Wives, and Unifiers

There are certainly historical instances of women in military leadership positions. After her capture, Zenobia, the Warrior Queen of the Palmyrene Empire (Syria), who fought the Romans in 267, was marched through Rome in golden chains. The Celtic Queen Boudicca fought and banished the Romans after Nero ordered her daughters raped. Third-century warrior Trieu Thi Trinh is called the Vietnamese Joan of Arc, cutting a striking figure in bright yellow clothing when riding to battle against the Chinese on a war elephant. Joan of Arc commanded the French army at the age of 17 before being captured and burned at the stake by the English in 1430 at age 19 for charges including crossdressing. Rejected by the all-male Japanese army, Nakano Takeko formed a women's army with her peers and fought as samurais in the Japanese Boshin civil war in the 1860s. But notable examples notwithstanding, the role of women in war has been "largely associated with weeping, waiting and working: as wives, mothers and sweethearts."[11]

In politics, traditionally kinship has been a well-used route to power for both men and women; for women, it was sometimes the only route. Indira Gandhi was the daughter of India's first Prime Minister, Jawaharlal Nehru. Argentina's Cristina Fernandez de Kirchner succeeded her husband Carlos as president. She had held national office before assuming the presidency while he had not. Benazir Bhutto, another daughter of a former prime minister, served as Pakistani prime minister and then Chair of the Pakistan People's Party until her assassination in 2007. The Kennedy and Bush political dynasties in the United States have seen mostly males politically benefiting from family names. Having recognizable family names can help, or hurt, male or female candidates, as both Hillary Clinton and Jeb Bush learned in 2016.

Researchers have studied under what circumstances women in political dynasties rise to power. In some cases, for example, a woman may be assumed as not independently politically ambitious as a man and therefore is supported by status quo advocates who assume her malleable. The aging politicians who initially supported Indira Gandhi assumed her to be a *gungi gudiya*, Hindi for "dumb doll," which turned out to be far from the case. Gandhi's cumulative leadership tenure spanned almost 16 years, and Henry Kissinger once nicknamed her the "Iron Lady" for her tough personality and style of leadership. Gandhi's period of greatest achievement and highest public approval is associated with her 1971 leadership during India's decisive and swift victory over Pakistan in the Indo-Pakistani War, which resulted in the formation of an independent Bangladesh.

Or, since women are often viewed as family unifiers, they can be seen as symbols, as was Aung San Suu Kyi, or called upon to heal and unite a country after a period of conflict, as was the case with Liberia's Ellen Johnson Sirleaf. Liberia suffered decades of brutal internal conflict, with the use of child soldiers and gender-based violence prevalent, the most recent ending in 2003 with the ouster of strongman dictator Charles Taylor. Women played a big part in ousting Taylor through a mass action campaign, and three women, including Sirleaf and Leymah Gbowee from Liberia, were awarded the 2011 Nobel Peace Prize for their efforts. Not surprisingly, post-conflict Liberia remains riddled with institutional and societal issues that continue to tug at the social fabric, but the peace treaty has held. When women are involved in peace processes, the probability of the resultant treaties holding for two years or more increases by 20%, and 35% for holding 15 years or more. Women's inclusion increases the potential for the root causes of conflict to be addressed, not just the symptoms. Liberian women were intent on giving the agreement they had fought and sacrificed for every chance of success, and so after the conflict ended, they next focused on electing a woman president.

Ellen Johnson Sirleaf, another woman dubbed an "Iron Lady," served as the first elected president of an African country, Liberia, from 2006 to 2018. Born and raised in Monrovia, like many African women, she was married early and had four children by age 21. She followed her husband to the United States in 1961 and there earned a degree in accounting. Her academic success was met with jealousy-prompted abuse from her husband, and the abuse only heightened when they went back to patriarchal Liberia. She courageously left him and got a job at the Ministry of Finance. Having an education allowed her to leave the abusive marriage, which is often not an option for women, and too often not without retribution if they try. Hanifa Nakiryowa, a Ugandan woman I have had the pleasure to work with over the years, had acid thrown on her and her daughter by her husband, a college professor, when she attempted to leave their abusive marriage. He suffered no consequences in an(other) example of women being penalty-free targets of abuse and violence.

Sirleaf earned a degree in economics from the University of Colorado, Boulder, and later a Master's of Public Administration at the Harvard Kennedy School. But by 1980, she had returned to Liberia and was appointed the Minister of Finance in William Tolbert's administration. Sirleaf had become, according to biographer Helene Cooper, a cat with a number of lives.[12]

In 1980, there was a military coup in Liberia. New strongman Samuel Doe overthrew the government, his forces killing Tolbert in his mansion. Within a week, they had executed everyone in his cabinet, except Ellen Johnson Sirleaf. Cooper shared her views on why Sirleaf was spared.

> They spared her because she was a woman. Women were to be raped, to be attacked but not to be killed like that in a public way. And the second reason is because of all those speeches she had been making, complaining – in which she criticized the government. She was viewed by even people opposed to the government as having some street cred. So she was spared, and then Samuel Doe made himself president and invited her to join his government.

Sirleaf briefly joined Doe's government but remained critical of strongman governance and was soon forced to flee Liberia again.

During this period of exile, she held posts at multiple international financial institutions. But she was also active in the Liberian ex-pat community and still critical of Samuel Doe. In 1985, she went back to Liberia to contest a disputed election she had run in for a Senatorial seat and was promptly jailed for almost a year on a charge of sedition.[13] Like Mandela, her time in prison was personally transformational, as from prison she set her sights on running for the presidency. Doe was murdered in 1990, but internal strife kept the presidency vacant from 1990 to 1997. She finished second in the 1997 presidential election that was won by Charles Taylor, which led to years of internal conflict, not ending until 2003.

Sirleaf's leading contender in the 2005 elections was George Weah, an athlete who had once been named FIFA player of the year and African player of the century. He carried with him no political baggage, which worked in his favor, but Liberian women were concerned that he also had no experience with governance and they were unwilling to risk the hard-earned peace settlement on a political novice. Men had already run the country into the ground before.

Liberian women again mobilized to motivate women to register and vote. Their message in the campaign between the grandmother and the soccer star was simple: "Vote for Women!" One Liberian woman told of seeing:

> young men laughing as she campaigned for a female president. The boys had taken women's panties, had smeared the crotches with tomato paste and were waving them at the women – their unsubtle way of saying that a woman could not be president.[14]

Crass tactics only further motivated Liberian women.

Mr Weah's supporters utilized the politics of fear in his campaign, promising that if he lost the election the country would go back to war. The women had heard that argument before from Samuel Doe and rejected it. They campaigned hard and resorted to trickery when they felt it necessary, buying men's voter registration cards with beer, and even hiding voting cards from male family members. They brought babies to long voting lines, urging women to use the babies as props or to pretend to be pregnant to get to the front of the line. Mrs Sirleaf won in a tight runoff election.

Ellen Johnson Sirleaf's presidency focused on rebuilding Liberian society. As part of her presidential efforts to clean up endemic corruption in Liberia and attract foreign investment, she fired the entire Ministry of Finance staff and brought in women to serve as finance minister, chief of police, commerce minister, and justice minister, among others. Additionally, the first all-female UN Peacekeeping unit arrived in Liberia in 2007 from India, charged with providing 24-hour guard duty and public order management, and conducting night patrols in and around the capital city of Monrovia while assisting local security institutions with capability-building. Multiple rotations of the 125 Indian women and supporting personnel in the unit stayed until 2016, with Sirleaf Johnson saying, "We see you as family," upon their departure. Not only did Liberian women feel safer dealing with the women peacekeepers than men in the same roles, but they also saw the women Peacekeepers as role models.

But Sirleaf was also criticized for nepotism, giving her sons plum positions in government, and for not doing enough for women at the local level, where changes often have the most impact on women's daily lives. For example, she did not support a 2010 legislative proposal to mandate that women occupy at least 30 percent of political party leadership, with a trust fund to be established to finance their electoral campaigns, and so it was never ratified. Liberia's inclusion of women in the national legislature remains consistently lower than the average of other West African and Sub-Saharan countries, fluctuating between 11% and 16%.[15]

Ellen Johnson Sirleaf's presidential tenure was most remarkable in Liberia's enjoyment of more than a decade without internal armed conflict. For Liberian men, women, boys, and girls, that was a huge triumph. Domestically, in terms of policy achievements, her tenure has been described as "good enough."[16] Sirleaf stepped down as president in 2017, succeeded by her previous opponent, George Weah, and she was subsequently elected Chair of the Economic Community of West African States, the first woman to hold that position.

Factors that affect and potentially impair women's leadership are both external and self-imposed, with crossover between them. An exhaustive and comprehensive consideration of all the challenges facing women leaders is beyond the scope of this work. Some of the most prevalent, however, must be considered. External factors include glass cliffs, bias, gender stereotyping, cultural/traditional norms, social dominance orientation, the "broken ladder" of advancement at middle management, and lack of mentorship. Internal, or self-imposed, factors include imposter syndrome and women trying to be "one of the boys" or lead through traits more attributable to men, what has been called "gender changing."

Gendered Challenges

Women sometimes rise to power during times of crises. In a 2007 study at the UK's University of Exeter, researchers found that in male-led companies facing crises, study subjects preferred that a woman take over to calm the waters.[17] Also, in times of crises, the chance of leadership failure is high. The "glass cliff" theory that evolved from that study holds that women are often placed in positions of power when the situation is dire, with men uninterested because the likelihood of success is low and they don't want to be tagged as failures. Glass cliff failures, however, can reinforce broad-brush presumptions that women can't lead.

Britain's vote to leave the European Union in 2016, Brexit, passed by a very narrow margin –51.89% for leave, 48.1% for remain. Consequently, regardless of what a leader proposed as an exit plan, around half of the British people would be unhappy. Theresa May served as Britain's Prime Minister from 2016 to 2019 to navigate that minefield. She did not do well.

May was elected as leader of the Conservative Party in 2016 in an election against another woman, Andrea Leadsom, in a campaign that included Leadsom suggesting that motherhood made her a better candidate.[18] Making motherhood and children an election issue seems increasingly common. Comments by then US vice presidential candidate J.D. Vance that America was being run by "childless cat ladies," referencing Kamala Harris as "childless," and suggesting that individuals without children "don't really have a stake in it" went viral in 2024.[19]

In Britain, the two women became their parties' compromise candidates after the men who had pushed Brexit, Boris Johnson and Nigel Farage, stepped away. May announced her resignation as the leader of Britain's Conservative Party and as Prime Minister in 2019 after failing to deliver a Brexit plan during her three-year tenure. Her rise and demise are exemplary of both the undeniable glass cliff she stepped onto, and what often happens when women try to lead one-dimensionally using primarily masculine traits.

May exhibited few of the leadership traits normally attributed to women in conflict-management scenarios: communication, collaboration, inclusivity, prudence. In her resignation speech, May concluded, "I will shortly be leaving the position it was the honor of my life to hold – the second female prime minister." May clearly considered Britain's first woman prime minister, Margaret Thatcher, as her role model – another "Iron Lady" – but failed to recognize that hers was a different time and different circumstances. She seemingly ignored "context."

May, however, never had the initial political backing or wartime public popularity as Thatcher and made three major mistakes resulting in her Brexit-related demise. Though she entered office with a solid majority, she called for another general election almost immediately and lost support. The Conservatives mechanically fixated on pushing Brexit with slogans like "Strong and Steady" and "Brexit is Brexit" while the Labour Party switched their focus to fixing Britain's declining social services, thereby appealing to voters. After the 2017 election losses, May had to make a deal with Northern Ireland's pro-Brexit Democratic Union Party, or DUP, headed by another woman, Arlene Foster, and consequently became shackled to its often stringent and socially-conservative demands.[20] Then, rather than taking a gradual approach, May triggered Article 50 of the European Union Treaty (the process to withdraw from the EU) with no plan, little analysis, and a two-year deadline for reaching an agreement with the EU. Finally, with little consultation, she presented Parliament with a last-minute plan for EU withdrawal – a my-way-or-the-highway approach – and no Plan B.

May brought nothing remotely "feminine" to the Brexit negotiations or the healing of the internal rift within Britain consequent to the Brexit vote. A more feminine approach, including empathy and attention to voter issues, may have had a better chance of success. But, in fairness, the obstacles in her path for doing so were not inconsequential. May began from a position of internal divisiveness, and she faced many gender-related challenges.

During the 2017 election, May was nicknamed "Maybot,"[21] as in "wooden and emotionless." That persona was intensified after she failed to meet with survivors of the West London Grenfell Tower fire in June 2017, where 72 people died. Facing strong rebukes, May later said her response was "not good enough" and that she "regretted"[22] her reaction.

But women politicians walk a fine line in terms of being perceived as either too emotional or emotionless. Showing emotion can be used against them as well. Indeed, when May resigned, the media was quick to zero in on the (apparently too much) emotion in her speech. Newspapers described it as a "teary farewell"[23] and headlined that her voice[24] cracked. Similar flip-flopped claims of being both emotionless (with "robotic" imagery used against her as well) and too emotional were similarly made against Hillary Clinton during the 2016 presidential campaign. But a female British journalist put the emotion and precariousness of May's tenure into perspective. She noted both that "it will take decades to turn back the clock on that dismal [gender equality] record, no matter how hard she tries to push the 'second-ever female PM' line" and "that the conclusion of her resignation speech was like watching a woman shake off the patriarchal shackles she's been chained with for more than two years, and finally exhaling."[25]

Theresa May stood on a glass cliff and virtually jumped off in demonstrating little contextual intelligence of her situation. She also tried to govern using one-dimensional male traits, likely in an attempt to win over the men she was tasked to work with. In some instances, this "gender changing" has also been associated with what has been called internalized misogyny[26] – when women subconsciously impart sexist ideas onto themselves and other women – including discriminating against and berating other women. Often, this is done to gain the favor of men they perceive as powerful and able to help them advance. Rarely, however, does that kind of behavior resonate over the long term with those they are trying to impress, and it creates and perpetuates the Queen Bee typecast. Behavior associated with gender changing generally, and internalized misogyny more specifically, can backfire, making recovery difficult.

Women are expected to exhibit feminine traits, including kindness, compassion, and honesty, and stay within gender-stereotypical roles. For women political leaders who have already stepped outside of these expected stereotypical roles, expectations are especially high, and the public is far less forgiving of women's transgressions,[27] real or alleged, than for men. When women leaders are perceived to have failed, reverting to (often "ultra") conservative male leadership often follows, with women's rights and gender equality subsequently set back. Besides May, certainly that was also the case with Dilma Rousseff in Brazil, Cristina Kirchner in Argentina, and Michelle Bachelet in Chile.

In 2011, Dilma Rousseff became president of Brazil, Christina Kirchner began a second term as president in Argentina, and Michelle Bachelet had an approval rating of more than 80% after completing her first presidential term in Chile. By 2016, Kirchner had been indicted, Rousseff was impeached, and Bachelet's approval rating had plunged to below 30%. Crises and corruption are more or less staples of Latin American politics, leading analysts to ask what is behind the more-than-normal outrage against these politicians. Gender stereotyping played a big role.

The Latin "machismo" culture resulted in strong backlash against women politicians perceived to have let the populace down, and swiftly boomeranged voters back to traditional role expectations. Rousseff's, Kirchner's, and Bachelet's successors all reflected a cultural shift back to more traditionally acceptable, machismo politicians. Rousseff's former Vice President, Michel Temer, succeeded her. The cover of the Brazilian magazine *Piaui* portrayed the cultural shift, depicting "the 1950s-style suburban idyll" in which the gray-haired 75-year-old president is greeted by his spouse, Marcela, a soft-spoken former beauty pageant contestant 42 years younger.[28] Temer appointed a cabinet devoid of women. By May 2017, Temer too was under investigation for corruption and obstruction of justice and did not run for reelection. He was succeeded by openly (proudly) misogynistic Jair Bolsonaro.

Kirchner's successor in Argentina was Mauricio Macri, who served as president from 2015 to 2019. His third wife, fashion designer Juliana Awada, is 15 years his junior. Macri proudly told a television reporter that she was "insatiable" in bed.[29]

Chilean billionaire business executive Sebastian Pinera followed Bachelet as president, having already served as president from 2010 to 2014. During that tenure, he was censured by women's groups for "joking" on a state visit to Mexico, that when a woman says "no" it means "maybe," when a woman says "maybe" it means "yes," and when she says "yes" she's not a lady. Cultural proclivities and gender stereotypes can hinder women leaders beginning at young ages and follow them through their careers. One constant: women receive swift blame for perceived failure. Women walk a leadership tightrope.

Three highly related factors have been found key to all employee hiring, retention, and promotion: competence, confidence, and mentorship. However, they work entirely differently for men and women, as issues related to Social Dominance Orientation (SDO) come into play for women.[30] SDO is a personality trait measuring an individual's support for a standing social hierarchy (gender stereotyping) and the extent to which they feel justified in viewing their in-group as superior to out-groups. In male-dominated professions, organizations, and cultures, SDO represents the status quo. So, while not all women are more, or even equally, qualified for all or particular positions than all men, SDO-based assumptions made about women's competency, what competencies are career relevant, and whether women's competency is perceived to pose a threat to the status quo when it is demonstrated can work against women trying to climb nontraditional career ladders, typical of those that are national security-related careers. Perhaps most insidiously, when women are competent, or more competent than men currently in positions, that competency can work against them.

Studies have consistently evidenced a general tendency to evaluate men and women differently on performance reviews. Reviewers, regardless of gender, tend to give female employees more negative feedback than they give to male employees. Negative feedback, using very masculine language, given to women often includes personality criticism of some sort, such as being "abrasive," "judgmental," or "strident," not often found in men's reviews. Women are judged by different standards than their male counterparts, and in personalized ways that can mar confidence.[31] Dating back to a 2000 Harvard study commonly known as the Heidi/Howard study, it is known that women struggle with the dilemma of being perceived as either competent or likable, whereas men can be both.

Women with backgrounds in competitive sports have sometimes found those backgrounds advantageous. Admiral Kristin Acquavella, for example, cites having been in sports competitions as accustoming her to high levels of mental and physical exertion, thereby building stamina, and experience in building teams.[32] And as Macaela MacKenzie chronicles in her 2023 book *Money, Power, Respect: How Women in Sports Are Shaping the Future of Feminism,* women athletes have had noteworthy success in working together to improve conditions for all. Overall, too, previous sports competition experience simply develops a thick skin, useful and necessary in often personally critical male-dominated environments.

A study of a large-scale US military leader performance evaluation dataset similarly found that women were subjectively assigned significantly more negative attributes than men, such as being scattered, opportunistic, excitable, and temperamental, even though their performances were the same by objective measures.[33] These findings have held true in a variety of organizations. Research conducted based on data gathered through the website RateMyProfessor has found that students evaluate women professors differently than men. Men professors are more often considered brilliant and funny, while women are either nice, or rude and bossy. These evaluation practices – focusing on a woman's appearance or personality and on a man's skills and intelligence – reinforce people thinking more highly of men than women in professional settings and criticizing women for the same things for which men are praised.[34]

Many of the issues associated with competence, confidence, and mentorship are especially problematic for women "climbing the ladder." Women consistently tell me that as they advance in both age and position, they are more sure of themselves and willing to work together to push back against obstacles and "judgements." A woman aerospace executive I've known since she was an undergraduate – and always the smartest student in the class – shared a great example.[35]

She and her boss, a crusty, retired male Navy Captain old enough to be her father, were on a conference call with the Polycom SoundStation between them on one end, and multiple individuals on the other. The individuals on the other end were equivocating about providing some data that was needed, thereby unnecessarily and annoyingly prolonging the meeting. This exasperated woman finally reached forward, muted the Polycom, and "strongly suggested" to her boss that he just tell the individuals to send the required data and she would deal with it. To that, her boss replied with a bit of a chuckle, "Wow. Now I see why you're not married. You're bossy." But she pushed back, pointing out to him that had a man said the same thing as she just had, he would have lauded the man for being assertive. A while after the meeting ended, a colleague stopped by my friend's office to tell her that he had just spoken with their boss, and the boss was still reflecting on her assertion, and that he recognized she was right. Not all leaders do though, many of them at the middle-management level.

In 2019, women held the top three positions at the Central Intelligence Agency. That same year, women led four of the top five defense contractors in the United States. Certainly, that indicates that the glass ceiling is shattered regarding national security institutions and that everything is "fine;" all gender equity issues have been solved. Or, maybe not. A key finding of the 2023 annual "Women in the Workplace" study was that the corporate pipeline narrows for women, especially women of color, with advancement.[36] Much of that narrowing has been associated with women feeling stalled at the middle management level,[37] often by male middle managers, due to factors such as unconscious bias, SDO, and the absence of, or unawareness of, effective institutional policies promoting diversity. Consequently, "the bench" behind women leaders is often thin.

Although women in nontraditional career fields win awards and commendations for outstanding performance, whether competence is in fact a workplace benefit in performance evaluations has been questioned. London Business School researchers conducted a study of 200 US military commanders responsible for performance evaluations. They found a high correlation between SDO and performance evaluations "when the evaluator was male and high social-dominance oriented and when the female subordinate's objective on-the-job performance was high."[38] They concluded that in hierarchical organizations, past accomplishments can actually be detrimental to women in evaluations from men who want to maintain the traditional gender balance because women's accomplishments can be viewed as threatening. Simply stated, equal consideration of qualified women cannot be assumed. Further, once hired, advancement and retention in nontraditional fields are riddled with challenges. While competency remains an entrance and advancement prerequisite, it is not enough. Confidence comes into play as well.

There is, however, evidence that self-doubt among women is abating. The long-held notion that women only apply for jobs when they meet 100% of the asked-for qualifications while men will apply if they meet only 60% has recently been challenged, as a 2022 study conducted in Britain found otherwise.

> According to our study, men apply for a job when they meet 52.1% of the qualifications, where women apply if they meet 55.7%. The gender difference was explained by less qualified men's greater self-perceptions in meeting the overall requirements than similarly qualified women. This is supported by wider research that finds that men are more likely to overestimate their capabilities in stereotypically masculine domains.[39]

Hopefully, this new finding indicates a change toward women recognizing their own strengths and capabilities.

Women, including women in top leadership positions, often suffer from what is known as imposter syndrome, or self-doubt stemming from a lack of confidence. Journalists Katty Kay and Claire Shipman wrote about it in their 2014 book *The Confidence Code: The Science and Art of Self-Assurance – What Women Should Know*. Former Facebook COO Sheryl Sandberg's 2013 bestseller, *Lean In*, is largely self-reflective, talking about her many fears – and overcoming them – when she began her job at Facebook. She admitted to Kay and Shipman, "There are still days I wake up feeling like a fraud, not sure I should be where I am."[40] This imposter syndrome is backed by numerous studies. A 2024 survey by an executive search firm found that women seeking to advance their careers are nearly twice as likely as men to believe that they are not qualified for their manager's job.[41] This self-doubt can lead to women giving up on a task before even starting, fearing failure or demonstrating incompetence.

The link between competence and confidence is important and deserves consideration as well. The International Space University hosted a panel of four highly trained, highly competent women astronauts, from the United States, China, South Korea, and Canada during its 2014 Summer Session in Montreal. Asked by an audience member what their biggest challenge day-to-day in being an astronaut, Canadian astronaut Julie Payette answered without hesitation, "Getting male colleagues to take me seriously and having to prove my competence over and over again."[42] Her astronaut colleagues nodded vigorously in agreement. Confidence can be hard to sustain if your colleagues do not take you seriously. Research cites having to repeatedly prove themselves as one of five reasons women, particularly women of color, leave STEM fields.[43]

It must be noted as well that challenges faced by women generally are intensified as intersectionality comes into play. Sarah McBride became the first transgender person elected to the US Congress in 2024. Congresswoman Marjorie Taylor Greene reported responded by saying she would "fight" a transgender woman if she attempted to use the women's bathroom on the House side of the Capitol.[44] Lt. Colonel Anastasia Biefang, the first transgender commander in the German army, served two tours in Afghanistan and, as of 2024, serves as a branch head in Cyber and Information Domain Services. While she says, both the German military and lawmakers have increasingly worked to make gender transitioning legally easier and socially acceptable, the rise in homophobic violence and abuse toward transgender individuals in Germany and in general is concerning. She has compared the hateful rhetoric used against trans individuals to that used by the Nazis.[45]

Between having to overcome doubting themselves, doubt sometimes reinforced by male colleagues and generated by years of societal acculturation, and feeling the need to be hyper-competent, women are left in a precarious position. Yet according to *Forbes* contributor Bruce Kasanoff, "senior leaders perceive that they perpetually confront the same problem…they can't find women who are both confident and competent."[46] Nevertheless, perceived "overconfidence" and ambition can be a problem for women as well.

Gender-based stereotypical perceptions remain a key issue for women in nontraditional career fields. Researchers have conducted studies regarding gender-expected attributes for decades, such as one where participants were shown fictional biographies of two state senators. The biographies were identical except for the names associated with them; one was John Burr and the other, Ann Burr.

> When quotations were added that described the state senators as "ambitious" and possessing "a strong will to power," John Burr became more popular. But the changes provoked "moral outrage" toward Ann Burr, whom both men and women became less willing to support.[47]

Ann Burr had stepped beyond the culturally acceptable lanes of women's behavior.

Studies continue to document what many women already know: if women behave in too feminine a manner, they are seen as weak and not as leaders, but if they are too masculine, they can experience backlash for being seen as too aggressive. Women have already had to learn to switch on and off masculine behaviors of assertiveness and confidence. For example, while speaking up first can get a woman viewed as bossy, piggybacking on a male comment would likely be more acceptable to male colleagues. Or, rather than directly disagreeing with male colleagues, first stating the merit of his premise before gently suggesting another option would be less threatening to male colleagues. *Engaging Men: Reducing Resistance and Gaining Support* (2021) was written by Australian sociologists as a kind of practical "how-to" for women who work with men. While admittedly pragmatic, having to cajole the male ego can put women in a position of having to "mommy" their male colleagues. It can be very helpful for women to have other women to lead them through the minefield of gender relations in the workplace. More generally, mentors can be the difference between success and failure in the workplace.

Mentors are key to helping individuals learn both how to do their jobs and be leaders, and the rules of the organization. Mentors are in many ways teachers. A woman GFO I spoke to said that the first advice she was given at her first assignment by her male boss was "don't get pregnant" as it would add to the workload of others, which was a point well taken but didn't help her learn much. Fortunately, she later had two great women mentors. The first, she said, taught her how to give feedback. Her mentor sat her down and began by asking how she felt things were going, thereby providing her with the opportunity to share her thoughts. Then, with the feedback form in front of them, her mentor nonconfrontationally gave her thorough, helpful, positive, and negative feedback – what she was doing well, and where she could do better. Her second mentor talked to her about (in her case) "what big Air Force is like." Specifically, what would make her valued, earn her a strong reputation, and get her promoted. Interestingly, that included the advice of "don't make things look hard," even though they often were very hard.

Every organization has rules, and generally speaking, those who join organizations tacitly (or explicitly) do so agreeing to follow those rules. But there are always official rules, provided and conveyed through organizational human resources departments, and unwritten rules, the latter equally or potentially more important for advancement in the organization. Mentors tell you unwritten organizational rules, give advice and feedback that mentees might not want to hear but will help them move forward, and generally help them navigate organizational cultures.

Telling women mentees what they don't want to hear can mean the little things that get discussed by men at the watercoolers after meetings, like hair twirling, saying "um" and "like" and mumbling, and, sometimes, attire. But women in non-traditional careers are far less likely to have mentors than men.

While mentorship is sometimes imagined as a one-on-one, career-lifetime relationship, it is more likely individuals will have multiple mentors throughout their careers. A mentor is not necessarily a jack-of-all-trades person who spends hours with a mentee. An individual may meet and speak with – be mentored by – someone for ten minutes and gain considerable wisdom from that person, but never speak with them again. The value of mentors can be job-specific as well. Being open to having many mentors, including professional peers, is a more realistic option.

W. Brad Johnson and David Smith argue in support of more men mentoring women in *Athena Rising: How and Why Men Should Mentor Women* (2016).[48]

They assert that mentorship is key to attracting, retaining, and promoting the women needed to develop an inclusively diverse workforce for the future, and they assert that men mentoring women is hindered by six issues – all rooted in gender stereotyping – and called "reluctant male syndrome." These issues are persistent gender bias, men being socialized to "protect" women, men being uncomfortable with nonsexual intimate relationships, men fearing public or office perception and gossip if they are thought to spend too much time with a woman, fear (even inadvertently) of saying or doing the wrong thing, and worry about what their spouse will think. All of these concerns make it easier for men to simply keep their distance and maintain sterile relationships with women colleagues.

Women can be reluctant to mentor women as well. Sometimes, women are worn down from years of negotiating their own career gauntlet. A bright young woman I had worked with when she was in active-duty Air Force sent me a quote she had received from a still active-duty friend – a quote attributed to a recently pinned-on woman Colonel – that both bothered and resonated with her, and then with me. "I swam through a shark tank to achieve the success I have earned, I don't have the capacity to open myself up to other women for mentorship. I have given up too much to be here." Many women are exhausted. An active-duty female Army Ranger also reminded me that there can be a stigma attached to women who mentor other women, painting them as too feminist, something I certainly saw in my own career.

It is important to note than men can and do mentor men as well. As a Marine First Sargeant Diana Bacolod was assigned to the 1st Tank Battalion, where she held the senior enlisted billet. Well respected and supported by her male Captain, a new male Executive Officer (XO), a lieutenant, joined the battalion and immediately made of point snarking to her, "You're here, but we don't need you here." The "you" meaning "a woman." She replied saying only, "yes, Sir, as long as you realize we have to work closely together." Both the Captain and Bacolod knew well that the XO actually did need her to effectively do his job, and so the Captain suggested that he speak to the XO. Bacolod declined his offer, and suggested instead that they just let the XO learn for himself. Eventually, he did, and he was forced to come to her asking for her help, which she gave. By acting professionally rather than emotionally – having had every right to push back at his misplaced assumption and poor attitude – she provided the young XO a lesson in leadership.[49]

Mentorship and sponsorship are two different things but equally important in terms of furthering women through leadership pipelines. Sometimes a mentor is also a sponsor, but not always. A sponsor is someone in a position of influence who is willing to advocate for you, look out for opportunities for you, and to draw attention to you to those who can advance your career and/or advance you as they themselves advance. The Navy has long had the term "Sea Daddy," referring to the practice of leaders bringing their mentees up the ladder with them. But the very term "Sea Daddy" clearly indicates the traditional role has been masculine. A senior enlisted woman I spoke with said she calls out people by name to leaders when she hears of positions opening and knows a qualified woman to fill them, but acknowledged that this can come with risks for her.

Both mentorship and sponsorship come with risks to mentors and sponsors, and consequently, fewer young women than men are afforded either. Before entering into a mentoring relationship, mentors weigh the expected costs – whether mentoring will be more trouble than it is worth, the possibility of a dysfunctional relationship, if a protégé will reflect poorly on the mentor – and how much energy it will require. For women mentors, top on the list of expectations is a low-risk profile and a relationship where the rewards outweigh the costs, as even after women have climbed the career ladder, they still face more challenges and hostilities than their male colleagues.[50] Women at the top of their fields cannot afford mentoring someone who will reflect poorly on them or their organizations. Consequently, with fewer mentors to guide them on their path, women often feel isolated and frustrated by seeing others, including those less competent than themselves, advancing over them. Those frustrations, along with other factors such as subtle forms of bias and harassment, push women to self-select out of leadership-track positions.

The reality is that in testosterone-heavy career fields, men often nitpick women's behavior, looking for signs of weakness, signs of immaturity, being "too girly," or not being girly enough. When General Mike Flynn was Director at the Defense Intelligence Agency, women were sent a memo from his office telling them "to monitor their levels of makeup, avoid flats, and err on the side of skirts and dresses" and that "make-up helps women look more attractive."[51] Women were told to avoid the "plain Jane" look. Women walk a very thin line of behavior and deportment. Women mentors are acutely aware (having heard all jabs about wrong-doers in the halls and in meetings) of the multitude of potential faux pas young women can make and have no choice but to limit themselves to protégés who understand organizational culture and expectations.

Finally, networking is increasingly viewed as a way for women to professionally stay connected, avoid feeling isolated, and increase job security and advancement, with different types of networks fulfilling different roles. Some professional networks largely provide and exchange information of interest to those who belong. Others are more social, providing members with an opportunity to share stories, make friends, and generally feel less isolated. In terms of job security, a woman military officer I spoke with said she deliberately nurtured a close network with her subordinates and coworkers (by making herself valuable to them) so they would give her a "heads up" if someone was going to try to scapegoat her. Sadly, scapegoating women does happen; witness Janice Karpinski, discussed in Chapter 4, and the female Secret Service members of former President Donald Trump, who were immediately targeted with blame when he was shot at in July 2024.[52] A network can help prevent a woman from being blindsided. And as part of sharing information, networks can alert others to job openings and advancement potential. Networks can serve a number of roles relevant to women maneuvering professional and leadership challenges.

Women might be allowed into all career fields, but their rise and tenure are still determined by factors very different from those of their male counterparts. Rather than "climb the ladder" some women opt out in order to raise families or attend to other personal issues. Accommodation of women's overlapping career and biological clocks, and later care of aging parents, is a structural issue rarely addressed by organizations. Whereas women in the past often simply expected to have to choose between a career and family life, women today more often expect to have both.

Women often base their decision on whether to stay or leave a career path on what has been called the "fight-or-flight" moment, about ten years into their career. Dubbed the Athena Factor, researchers have found that multiple reasons contribute to highly qualified, talented women opting out at about the ten-year mark, many of which are gender-centered. Many women in nontraditional career fields find hostile environments, work in isolation or near-isolation, and face mysterious career paths tied to not having an internal support network, along with having to walk the precarious line between being perceived as negatively aggressive and positively confident, which can often derail women's careers.

Two women general officers I spoke with, both military reservists, independently suggested that transitioning from active-duty to the reserves had allowed them to continue serving their country, offer their talents, and avoid many of the family related issues associated with active-duty. In one case, she felt that her private sector cyber career added to what she was able to contribute in her military cyber role. In both cases, they felt the reserves were very family oriented and caring about their personnel, and an excellent way for women to serve and lead.

Lt. General Jody Daniels, Chief of Army Reserves, has gone out of her way to both demonstrate her own approachability and make the reserves family friendly, toward taking care of her people and the organization she leads. Her intent is not to push feminism but to diversify the reserves to make it the best organization possible. With two Master's degrees and a PhD, she has worked in the fields of mathematics, computer science, and artificial intelligence and recognizes the challenges facing the Army in the future require a well-trained, long-serving, diverse, STEM-heavy workforce comprised of citizen soldiers. As of 2024, nearly half of the Army Reserve force identifies as Black, Hispanic, Asian/Pacific Islander, or Native American, with women as 25% of all Army Reserve soldiers.[53]

An interesting commonality emerged among the women leaders I spoke with, well characterized by retired Air Force Major General Kim Crider.[54] "My superpower is common sense." She said she could sense what people wanted and needed and could just get it done, and that made her valuable. Many other women in many professions, military, business, and political, including Ambassadors, made similar comments, along with using the word "persistent." When career barriers were encountered, they found a way around them. Women are socialized to be more organized and efficient than men, which can work to their advantage.

Women Leaders Navigating the Gauntlet

When America dropped the mantle of global leadership in 2016, other countries were called upon or tried on their own to fill the void that the United States had left. German Chancellor Angela Merkel began being referred to as the new head of the free world because of her strong support of liberalism in the face of increasing right-wing populist, often authoritarian, governments. Polls repeatedly showed she was the world's most respected political leader. Though she was fiercely criticized within Germany and Europe for her 2015 decision to allow thousands of asylum seekers to cross the border into Germany, a key concern being a potential "pull effect" for subsequent migration that turned out to be unfounded,[55] her leadership capacity was never questioned. That was perhaps because, as Princeton professor Andrew Moravcsik suggests, "she cuts against the stereotype of modern politicians as egotists pandering to public opinion. She is unglamorous and reserved, instinctively moderate, slow to make decisions, and prone to communicate in cerebral, fact-based monologues."[56] After a decade and a half as the Chancellor of Germany, she stepped down in 2021.

Christine Lagarde described Merkel's leadership style at a 2019 event honoring Merkel as measured, methodical, and well-tempered. Referencing Merkel's love of opera, Lagarde went on to say: "She knows how to strike the right note, and she is especially skilled at playing what I would call the Four D's: *diplomacy*, *diligence*, *determination*, and *duty*."[57] Using that approach, Merkel persevered and rose in global respect against illiberal and misogynistic male leaders like Vladimir Putin, Donald Trump, and Jair Bolsonaro.

Merkel was born in what was then East Germany to modest parents, a teacher and a preacher, and was always an excellent student. Trained as a quantum chemist, she is analytic by both nature and education. Having spent the first 35 years of her life in East Germany, she also understood German history well, thereby understanding how power, politics, and ego can ravage a country. In terms of her leadership style, that conveyed a strong sense of self, humility, and fierceness when needed.

Her career included, like many women leaders, a career of many "firsts." She was the first female German Chancellor, the youngest German Chancellor since World War II, and the first born after 1945. She was also the first female leader of a German political party and the first in Germany to have a background in the natural sciences, a commonality she shared with Margaret Thatcher.

When it came to dealing with Covid-19, she based her decisions on scientific data and conveyed them to the German public with transparency and confidence, instilling their trust. A survey studying anxiety and depression levels[58] among the German public during Covid-19 found to drop substantially after Merkel gave an infrequent, non-sensationalist, and thereby extraordinary speech on March 18, 2020. It began, "*Es ist ernst.*" (This is serious.) The tone was direct, honest, and "searingly empathic."[59] A member of the research team conducting the survey stated that "our results highlight the tremendous importance of political leadership for mental health and psychological well-being. Strong and transparent leadership can reduce citizens' anxiety and depression in times of crisis."[60] Merkel also stressed the need for unity of effort, thanking workers on the front lines, "without accusations, boasts, hedges, obfuscations, dubious claims, or apocalyptic metaphors she did what a leader is supposed to do: explain the gravity of the situation and promise that the government's help would flow to everyone who needed it."[61]

Her views on gender were always understated; that gender parity in all areas is simply self-evident and thereby not needing special attention. Though many of her closest advisors were women, her ambiguity caused many people to question whether Merkel was/is a feminist, and for many years Merkel herself resisted being dubbed a feminist hero. In fact, in 2017 at a public event when asked outright if she was a feminist, she refused to answer, dodging the question. Merkel stated in 2019 that "parity (for women) in all areas seems logical to me. I don't need to constantly mention it specifically."[62]

But another woman member of the German parliament, from an opposition party, suggested Merkel's ambiguity was intentional, like a smokescreen. "'It was like armor,' she said. 'A type of protection against being considered a woman...She always refrained from almost all polarizing themes – and gender rights themes are always polarizing.'"[63] And while she largely supported feminine-friendly legislation and programs, she advanced few of her own. Even her clothing – black, boxy suits most often – shied away from feminine associations that Merkel feared could impair her effectiveness as a national and global leader. Other women have said the same thing, especially women in the military, that their professional clothing becomes like armor. Finally, at a 2021 speaking event, the year she stepped down as chancellor, Merkel declared on stage that given she believed men and women are equal: "I am a feminist."

New Zealand's Jacinda Ardern has become globally known as the model for a new generation of progressive women leaders, using both masculine and feminine traits according to the needs of specific situations. She multitasked as a national leader, partner, and new mother while Prime Minister. During her leadership tenure, she led one of the most successful, by most metrics, Covid-19 "elimination" strategies during the global pandemic and acted with both empathy and tough resolve to outlaw military-style semiautomatic weapons after a tragic 2019 mass shooting at two New Zealand mosques by a White supremacist.

Ardern stepped down in 2023, saying she had "no more in the tank" to lead the country or run for reelection. Not surprisingly, that she did so "holding back tears" was widely noted in media coverage. Analysis has cited the toll of dealing with Covid-19, increasing economic issues in New Zealand weakening her popularity, and personal attacks as among the reasons for her departure from office. Personal attacks are common for all leaders, with a healthy ego and thick skin required by all, but it is worth noting the extreme version with which she, and others, have dealt.

Disinformation/misinformation campaigns against women leaders are increasingly frequent, many of them coordinated rather than random. Manipulated imagery purporting to show Jacinda Ardern smoking crack went viral on Facebook in 2021, resulting in commentary such as "what else is she partaking of behind closed doors, is she really fit to run this country" and "I actually think it might be true. Her boyfriend is a dealer."[64] The Wilson Center, a nonpartisan US think tank, conducted a 2020 study on how gender, sex, and lies are weaponized against women online, specifically women politicians. The report concluded that online gendered abuse and disinformation is a national security threat, as many of the bad actors responsible are associated with Russia, Iran, and China, and that the threat has been largely ignored. They further concluded that gendered and sexualized disinformation is distinctly different from broad-based gendered abuse. It is often conducted through "malign creativity," or coded language, context-based visual and textual themes, and other tactics to avoid detection on social media platforms, making it extremely challenging to address.

The study focused on words and visuals used to imply or spread disinformation on selected social media platforms (platforms selected primarily based on researcher access to data) in conjunction with 13 women politicians: Jacinda Ardern (New Zealand), Priti Patel (UK), Chrystia Freeland (Canada), and from the US, Susan Collins, Kirsten Gillibrand, Kamala Harris, Jaime Herrera Beutler, Alexandria Ocasio-Cortez, Ilhan Omar, Elissa Slotkin, Elise Stefanik, Lauren Underwood, and Gretchen Whitmer. It found abuse and disinformation widespread, including gendered disinformation narratives of a racist, transphobic, or sexual nature. The overwhelming majority of keywords relating to those were directed at Kamala Harris on Twitter, at 78% of the total amount of recorded instances.

Sexual narratives about the women were the most common, accounting for 31% of the total data collected, again primarily targeted at Kamala Harris. To be clear, the transphobic narratives implied that the target was *actually a man*. Though the numbers are low, they were relatively widespread, thereby affecting a number of different research subjects. Apparently originating through QAnon, a photo of Kamala Harris was circulated next to her supposed former male identity, "Kamal Aroush," complete with a backstory. A video of Jacinda Ardern showing a pleat in her dress was interpreted and circulated as evidence of Ardern having male genitalia. Gretchen Whitmer's facial features were compared to transgender celebrity Caitlyn Jenner, with targeters asserting that her similar bone structure was "proof" of Whitmer's male identity. Alexandria Ocasio-Cortez has also been targeted online through the frequent use of words like "tranny" or "transsexual." Online gendered abuse and disinformation are often intersectional in nature, with abusers frequently engaging in both sex- and race-based narratives, compounding the threat for women of color. The purpose of implying that women leaders are transsexual is to suggest that leadership is reserved for males, thereby supporting misogyny and reinforcing homophobia – both being ways to discredit the women. Ardern's comment about "no more in the tank" upon stepping down to some extent likely reflected the psychological strain that is produced from this kind of gender-related abuse.

Misogynistic abuse falls largely, but not exclusively, on liberal-leaning women politicians. In August 2021, Kristi Noem, the Republican Governor of South Dakota, was already being talked about as a potential 2024 Republican presidential candidate, popular in her largely rural state for her populist policies and rhetoric. Nevertheless, she was targeted by conservative political commentator Matt Walsh on social media. Walsh made comments in a podcast about Noem's decision not to ban businesses from implementing coronavirus vaccine requirements, something other Republican governors had done. But then he went on to say:

> No use for Noem. Kristi Noem is a very attractive woman, so she's got that going for her. As far as I can tell that's the only reasons why she was ever looked at as some sort of 2024 potential frontrunner...The hype and everything she's gotten from conservative media is entirely based on the fact that she's an extremely attractive woman, which she is.

When Noem fired back at Walsh for what she called his "horrible misogyny," Walsh just kept going, insisting that his remarks were an "obvious truth" and calling those offended by his remarks "a bunch of ridiculous, whiney babies."[65] With more conservative women entering politics, they find themselves facing the same kind of critique liberal women politicians have long endured, and both have a vested interest in addressing it.

Italian Prime Minister Giorgia Meloni sued two men in 2024 for $108,200 in damages after they superimposed her face on adult film stars' bodies and posted them on a US-based porn site in 2020.[66] She is relatively new to the leadership podium and Italian women have divided feelings about a populist, far-right woman serving as Italy's first female Prime Minister. Meloni was elected in 2022 on a platform of "God, homeland and family," and is considered as leading Europe's tilt to the far-right. She touted her sex while running for office, in terms of breaking a glass ceiling, but didn't particularly court women's votes, given her support for potentially regressive women's rights. She ended a press conference once because, she said, her high heels were killing her. She gains support from Italian women for her efforts to prevent and abate domestic violence, including faster trials and tougher sentences for offenders. In other areas, however, specifically economic policies, women are facing cutbacks. Meloni opposes a minimum wage, which would primarily benefit women, and Meloni's government began restricting previously available women's access to pensions with fewer years of contributions than men.[67]

Meloni has been internationally praised, however, for her willingness and success in reaching out to Hungarian Prime Minister Viktor Orbán and getting him onboard regarding European Union aid to Ukraine. Meloni spent months using her longtime friendship with Viktor Orbán, with whom she shares a similar conservative political ideology, to convince him of the need and overall benefit to the EU and Hungary of the aid package.[68]

Especially as numbers grow, there will be as many leadership styles exhibited and issues surrounding women political leaders as there are for men. That will mean both opportunity and scrutiny for women leaders. Admiral Lisa Franchetti became the first woman to serve as Chief of Naval Operations (CNO) in 2023. It is likely every aspect of her tenure will be examined and analyzed as or more closely than those of her male predecessors, and through a gendered lens. Speaking at the 2024 Joint Women's Leadership Symposium in Washington DC, Franchetti provided the audience with what she labeled the "CNO's Top 7" leadership essentials. (1) Define "success": what does it mean to you individually, as it will vary among individuals. (2) Understand your organization: know organizational goals and what it takes to be considered valuable and promotable. (3) Set goals: she suggested both big goals and interim goals. (4) Develop a good network: networks serve multiple purposes, including as a support system. (5) Create balance: work-life balance is a challenge but a must for long-term survival. (6) Embrace excellence: make excellence your standard. (7) Create an empowering environment: don't wait for someone higher up to do it; take up the challenge personally at every level of leadership.

Franchetti spent a few minutes elaborating on work-life balance, explaining that she saw three overlapping areas of balance (presented as PowerPoint bubbles) that serve as her "checklist": me (personal time), friends and family, and profession/work life. She admitted that there were times when work was the biggest bubble by far, but having a checklist prompted her to remember not to ignore the other two. She also acknowledged "can women have it all?" as the perpetually asked question of women. Her answer, as a wife, mother, and woman holding a high-intensity career, was that women can have it all (however they define "all"), but perhaps not all at the same time and with the same level of intensity.

Conclusion

Theresa May's tenure as the British Prime Minister has been considered a failure, but would things have been different if a man had served during that tense time period? Perhaps she served a valuable purpose by stepping on all the political landmines to make it easier for her successor to then move an agenda forward. And what about Liz Truss in 2023? She holds the record for being the British Prime Minister with the shortest tenure in office, serving only 49 days. Several media outlets sardonically suggested that lettuce lasts longer in the refrigerator than Liz Truss did in office. Will she be judged as an individual, or as a woman? And why must so many successful women leaders be dubbed as "Iron Ladies"? Is that their only path to success?

It is still a risk for a woman leader to serve as a "woman leader," or to push gender-related initiatives. Chilean President Michelle Bachelet pushed for the integration of women into the Chilean navy in 2018 during her tenure and appointed an equal number of men and women to her cabinet. But she acknowledged the risks of being a woman leader. "I took a gamble to exercise leadership without losing my feminine nature."[69] Others, like Angela Merkel, strove to be seen as a leader, without a gendered prefix. Doing so appears to work well as long as the leadership style subsequently employed includes both masculine and feminine traits. That will be the key to the future for both men and women leaders.

Notes

1 "Rediscover Grace Murray Hopper," Arlington Public Library. https://library.arlingtonva.us/2019/08/19/rediscover-grace-murray-hopper/
2 Poole, Steven. "The Most Important Female Coder You've Never Heard Of," *New Yorker Magazine*, November 4, 2016. https://nymag.com/vindicated/2016/11/the-most-important-female-coder-youve-never-heard-of.html
3 Poole, 2016, referencing: Terrell, J., A. Kofink, J. Middleton, C. Rainear, E. Murphy-Hill, C. Parnin and J. Stallings. "Gender Differences and Bias in Open Source: Pull Request Acceptance of Women versus Men," *Computer Science,* Vol. 3, 2017. https://peerj.com/articles/cs-111/
4 Personal interview, April 11, 2024.
5 Personal interview, April 11, 2024.
6 "Vice Admiral Michelle Howard First African-American Woman to Reach the Rank of Three Star," WJLA-TV Washington, October 12, 2012. http://www.wjla.com/articles/2012/10/vice-admiral-michelle-howard-first-african-american-woman-to-reach-rank-of-three-star-officer-80588.html
7 "Howard's Path to Navy History," *Navy Times*, January 4, 2014.
8 Lerman, David. "Black Woman Named to a Top US Navy Job Says Wimps Fail," *Bloomberg News*, December 20, 2013. https://www.bloomberg.com/news/articles/2013-12-20/black-woman-named-to-a-top-u-s-navy-job-says-wimps-fail
9 Lagrone, Sam. "Gauoette Inspector General Report," *USNI News*, April 15, 2013. https://news.usni.org/2013/04/15/document-an-admirals-downfall
10 Ringnes, Isabella and Marie Louise Sunde, Hvem Spanderer/She's Got This, English translation © Ian Giles, pp.10-11.
11 "The She-Soldiers of World War One." http://ww1centenary.oucs.ox.ac.uk/unconventionalsoldiers/the-she-soldiers-of-world-war-one/
12 "'Madame President' Author on 'Street Cred' Economic Power of Ellen Johnson Sirleaf," *NPR*, April 1, 2017.
13 "Citibank Executive on Trial in Liberia," *UPI*, August 23, 1985. http://www.upi.com/Archives/1985/08/23/Citibank-executive-on-trial-in-Liberia/6574493617600/
14 Cooper, Helene. "How Liberian Women Delivered Africa's First Female President," *The New York Times*, March 5, 2017.
15 Pailey, Robtel Neajai and Korto Reeves Williams. "Is Liberia's Sirleaf Really Standing Up for Women?" *Al Jazeera*, August 31, 2017. https://www.aljazeera.com/opinions/2017/8/31/is-liberias-sirleaf-really-standing-up-for-women
16 "Praise for the Woman Who Put Liberia Back on its Feet," *The Economist*, October 5, 2017. https://www.economist.com/news/leaders/21730015-ellen-johnson-sirleaf-has-not-been-perfect-president-she-has-been-good-enough-praise

17 Ryan, Michael K. and S. Alexander Haslam. “The Glass Cliff: Exploring the Dynamics Surrounding the Appointment of Women to Precarious Leadership Positions,” *The Academy of Management Review*, Vol. 32, No. 2, April 2007, pp. 549–572.
18 Hyde, Marina. “Andrea Leadsom Apologises to Theresa May for Motherhood Remarks,” *The Guardian*, July 11, 2016. https://www.theguardian.com/politics/2016/jul/10/andrea-leadsom-apologises-for-motherhood-remarks
19 Treisman, Rachel. “The History behind JD Vance’s ‘Childless Cat Ladies’ Comments,” NPR, July 29, 2024. https://www.npr.org/2024/07/29/nx-s1-5055616/jd-vance-childless-cat-lady-history
20 Sayal, Rajeev. “From Climate Denial to Abortion: Six DUP Stances You Should Know About,” *The Guardian*, June 9, 2017. https://www.theguardian.com/politics/2017/jun/09/from-climate-denial-to-abortion-heres-six-dup-policies-you-should-know-about
21 Crace, John. “As She Says Goodbye, Maybot Finally Shows Her Humanity,” *The Guardian,* May 24, 2019. https://www.theguardian.com/politics/2019/may/24/theresa-may-end-resignation-speech-politics-sketch-maybot
22 Walker, Peter. “Theresa May Calls Her Response to Grenfell Fire ‘Not Good Enough,’” *The Guardian*, June 11, 2018. https://www.theguardian.com/politics/2018/jun/11/theresa-may-grenfell-tower-fire-response-not-good-enough
23 Shakhnazarova, Nika. “Theresa May Resignation Speech,” *The Sun*, June 8, 2019. https://www.thesun.co.uk/news/9146569/what-theresa-may-resignation-speech-quit-cry/
24 Reuters. “Theresa May’s Voice Cracked at the End of Resignation Speech,” *The Guardian*, May 24, 2019. https://www.theguardian.com/politics/video/2019/may/24/theresa-may-resignation-speech-downing-street-video
25 Hull, Harriet. “When She Allowed Her Emotion to Show During Her Resignation Speech, Theresa May Finally Did Something Good for Women,” *The Independent*, May 24, 2019. https://www.independent.co.uk/voices/theresa-may-resignation-speech-cry-tears-brexit-women-a8929361.html
26 Szymanski, D. M., A. Gupta, E. R. Carr and D. Stewart. “Internalized Misogyny as a Moderator of the Link between Sexist Events and Women’s Psychological Distress,” *Sex Roles: A Journal of Research*, Vol. 61, Nos. 1–2, 2009, pp. 101–109. https://doi.org/10.1007/s11199-009-9611-y
27 Dunaway, Joanna, et al. “Traits Versus Issues: How Female Candidates Shape Coverage of Senate and Gubernatorial Races,” *Political Research Quarterly*, Vol. 66, No. 3, 2013, pp. 715–726.
28 Romero and Kaiser, 2016.
29 Alejandro Rebossio. “Juliana Awada, Fashion Mogul and Future First Lady of Argentina,” *El Pais*, November 25, 2015. http://elpais.com/elpais/2015/11/25/inenglish/1448466351_432980.html
30 See: Cohn, Carol. “How Can She Claim Equal Rights When She Doesn’t Have to Do as Many Push-Ups as I Do?” *Men and Masculinity*, Vol. 3, No. 2, pp. 131–151.
31 Correll, Shelley, et al. “Inside the Black Box of Organizational Life: The Gendered Language of Performance Assessments,” *American Sociological Review,* Vol. 85, No. 6, December 2020, pp. 1022–1050.
32 Personal interview, April 15, 2024.
33 Smith, David G., Judith E. Rosenstein and Margaret C. Nikolov. “The Different Words We Use to Describe Male and Female Leaders,” *Harvard Business Review*, May 25, 2018.
34 McNell, Lillia, et al. “What’s in a Name: Gender Bias in Student Ratings of Teaching,” *Journal of Collective Bargaining in the Academy,* April 2015. https://thekeep.eiu.edu/cgi/viewcontent.cgi?article=1509&context=jcba
35 Personal interview, April 25, 2024.

36 Lean In. https://leanin.org/women-in-the-workplace?gad_source=1&gclid=CjwKCAjwoa2xBhACEiwA1sb1BO_ZP9UmtB4xU965NJgtyR8r5p3txLxy3hRCvMlo9fJB-oYMRvOoHxoCuA8QAvD_BwE

37 Einarsdottir, U. D., T. H. Christiansen and E. S. Kristjansdottir. "'It's a Man Who Runs the Show': How Women Middle-Managers Experience Their Professional Position, Opportunities, and Barriers," *Sage Open*, Vol. 8, No. 1, 2018. https://doi.org/10.1177/2158244017753989

38 Ena Inesi, M. and Daniel M. Cable. "When Accomplishments Come Back to Haunt You: The Negative Effects of Competence Signals on Women's Performance Evaluations," *Personnel Psychology*, Vol. 67, No. 3, 2014.

39 Nicks, Leonie, et al. *Gender Differences in Response to Requirements in Job Adverts,* UK Government Equalities Office, March 2022. https://www.bi.team/wp-content/uploads/2022/03/Gender-differences-in-response-to-requirements-in-job-adverts-March-2022.pdf

40 Kay, Katty, and Claire Shipman. "The Confidence Gap," *The Atlantic*, May 2014, 59.

41 Reynold, Russel. "Why Aren't There More Women CEO's What You Might Not Know About Your Women Leaders." 2024. https://www.russellreynolds.com/en/insights/reports-surveys/why-arent-there-more-women-ceos?utm_source=marketo&utm_medium=next-leadership&utm_campaign=artemis&mkt_tok=MzM3LUdFUi0yMTAAAAGRivE-RAJVxbKOFf4qjzkvImitMCykl4Bdr7RP5ciW0Ofyc0KFxmPg_6d57qGcFCKxCdnurmmuNrg190eckpbb1uSbCZgxh-XKT4X-PROK879E&

42 The author was in attendance at that presentation on July 10, 2014. See also: Oberhaus, Daniel. "Sexism in Space," *Motherboard*, April 2, 2015. http://motherboard.vice.com/read/sexism-in-space

43 Williams, Joan C., Katherine W. Phillips, and Erika V. Hall. *Double Jeopardy*, UC Hastings College of Law, 2015. http://www.uchastings.edu/news/articles/2015/01/double-jeopardy-report.pdf

44 Beavers, Olivia. "MTG threatens to fight transgender woman," Politico, 19 November 2024. https://www.politico.com/live-updates/2024/11/19/congress/mtg-threatens-to-fight-transgender-woman-00190344

45 Wohlleben, Nadja. "German LGBTQ+ Activist Warns Over 'Worrying' Hate Crime Rise," *Reuters*, July 23, 2023. https://www.reuters.com/world/europe/german-lgbtq-activist-warns-over-worrying-hate-crime-rise-2023-07-23/

46 Kasanoff, Bruce. "Women: If You're Competent, It's Time to be Confident," *Forbes*, March 23, 2015. http://www.forbes.com/sites/brucekasanoff/2015/03/23/women-if-youre-competent-its-time-to-be-confident/

47 Brescoll, Victoria and Tyler Okimoto. "The Price of Power: Power Seeking and Backlash Against Female Politicians," *Personality and Social Psychology Bulletin*, June 2, 2010.

48 Smith, David and W. Brad Johnson. *Athena Rising: How and Why Men Should Mentor Women*, Bibliomotion, 2016.

49 Personal interview 5 July 2024.

50 Lyness, K. and D. E. Thompson. "Climbing the Corporate Ladder: Do Female and Male Executives Follow the Same Route?" *Journal of Applied Psychology*, Vol. 85, No. 1, 2000, p. 101.

51 Zavadski, Katie. "Gen. Mike Flynn's Office Told Women to Wear Makeup, Heels, and Skirts," *The Daily Beast*, November 18, 2016. http://www.thedailybeast.com/articles/2016/11/18/gen-mike-flynn-s-office-told-women-to-wear-makeup-heels-and-skirts.html

52 Miller, Joe. "Secret Service Target of Misogynistic Backlash after Donald Trump Assassination Attempt," *Financial Times,* July 17, 2024. https://www.ft.com/content/3d032aa6-08ca-462a-9e1d-e7a345de71f6

53 Garfinkle, Xeriqua. "Lt. Gen. Jody Daniels: A Thought Leader Reframing the Army Reserve Culture," Army Reserve, March 7, 2024. https://www.usar.army.mil/News/News-Display/Article/3701248/lt-gen-jody-daniels-a-thought-leader-reframing-the-army-reserve-culture/
54 Personal interview, May 1, 2024.
55 Tjaden, Jasper and Tobias Heidland. "Did Merkel's 2015 Decision Attract More Migrants to Germany?" *European Journal of Political Research*, March 6, 2024. https://ejpr.onlinelibrary.wiley.com/doi/10.1111/1475-6765.12669
56 Moravcsik, Andrew. Reviewing *The Chancellor*, Kati Marton, Simon and Schuster, 2021, in *Foreign Affairs*, September/October 2021.
57 Lagarde, Christine. "Angela Merkel – Striking the Right Note on Leadership," *IMF News*, August 31, 2019. https://www.imf.org/en/News/Articles/2019/08/31/sp083119-Angela-Merkel-Striking-the-Right-Note-on-Leadership
58 Teufel, Martin, et al. "Not all World Leaders Use Twitter in Response to the COVID-19 Pandemic," *Journal of Public Health*, Vol. 42, No. 3, September 2020, pp. 644–646. https://academic.oup.com/jpubhealth/article/42/3/644/5835923?login=false
59 Davidson, Justin. "The Leader of the Free World Gives a Speech, and She Nails It," *Intelligencer*, March 18, 2020. https://nymag.com/intelligencer/2020/03/angela-merkel-nails-coronavirus-speech-unlike-trump.html
60 Oklenburg, Sebastian. "The Merkel Effect: How Leadership Reduces COVID-19 Anxiety," *Psychology Today*, June 3, 2020. https://www.psychologytoday.com/us/blog/the-asymmetric-brain/202006/the-merkel-effect-how-leadership-reduces-covid-19-anxiety
61 Davidson, 2020.
62 Petzinger, Jill. "Did Angela Merkel Matter For Women?" *Foreign Policy*, December 13, 2021. https://foreignpolicy.com/2021/12/13/did-angela-merkel-matter-for-women/
63 Petzinger, Jill. "Angela Merkel's Feminist Legacy," *Foreign Policy*, December 13, 2021. https://foreignpolicy.com/2021/12/13/did-angela-merkel-matter-for-women/#:~:text=But%20in%20September%20of%20this,%3A%20I%20am%20a%20feminist.%E2%80%9D
64 "Fact Check-Clip of Jacinda Ardern Smoking Cannabis is a Deepfake," *Reuters*, November 16, 2021. https://www.reuters.com/article/factcheck-newzealand-ardern/fact-check-clip-of-jacinda-ardern-smoking-cannabis-is-a-deepfake-idUSL1N2S71BZ
65 Greenwood, M. "Noem Rips Conservative Writer Matt Walsh Over 'Horrible Misogyny,'" *The Hill*, August 28, 2021. https://thehill.com/homenews/campaign/569535-noem-rips-conservative-writer-matt-walsh-over-horrible-misogyny/
66 Nadeau, Barbie Latza. "Italian Prime Minister Giorgia Meloni Seeking Damages of $108,200 in Deepfake Porn Trial," *CNN*, March 22, 2024. https://www.cnn.com/2024/03/22/europe/giorgia-meloni-italy-deepfake-porn-intl/index.html
67 Roberts, Hannah. "Is Italy's Meloni Failing to Deliver for Women?" *Politico*, August 6, 2023. https://www.politico.eu/article/italy-giorgia-meloni-women-rights-feminism-motherhood-abortion-rights/#:~:text=Women%20are%20underrepresented%20in%20both,linking%20unemployment%20benefits%20to%20children
68 Moens, Barbara. "How Georgia Meoni and French Hospitality Got Orban to OK Ukraine Aid," *Politico*, February 1, 2014. https://www.politico.eu/article/how-eu-leaders-pushed-hungary-orban-ukraine-aid-support-meloni-italy/
69 "Michelle Bachelet Quotes," *101Sharequotes.com*. 2016. http://101sharequotes.com/quote/michelle_bachelet-i-took-a-gamble-to-exercise-lead-64826

7

GENDER DIVERSE LEADERSHIP IN PRACTICE

A Nuclear Ambiguous Iran

Did it really matter that the European Union's (EU) foreign policy chief, Baroness Catherine Ashton, endeavored to get to know her Iranian counterparts as she negotiated the 2013 "Joint Plan of Action" to temporarily freeze Iran's nuclear program while a more permanent deal was worked out? Did it matter that, while the Iranians would not shake hands with her or any other women diplomats, they would share videos and stories of their families? Did it matter that three key negotiators of the historic second, more permanent deal reached in 2015 were women? Given the successful outcome of the negotiations where past efforts had failed, apparently, it did.

One of the pillars of the Women, Peace, and Security framework referenced in Chapter 1 is participation. It calls for increased participation of women in all aspects of security affairs. Regarding negotiations, as pointed out in conjunction with Ellen Johnson Sirleaf in Liberia, involving women in peace negotiations increases the potential for the resultant agreement to last longer than otherwise. In this case, women were front and center.

Rarely do China, France, Germany, Russia, the United Kingdom (UK), and United States agree on much, if anything. But in the case of Iran potentially developing a nuclear weapons arsenal, all agreed that it was not in the best interests of their countries individually, the region, or international stability generally, and so negotiations were undertaken. In 2011, when the negotiations began, relations were strained at best. Ashton wanted to create an environment conducive to compromise. She held a dinner the night before the negotiations commenced to break the interpersonal ice before the hard work began.

DOI: 10.4324/9781003564065-8

Though her title certainly rings of snobbishness, Baroness Catherine Ashton, Cathy as she is widely known, the lead negotiator for the West in 2011, comes from a tough, working-class (coal-mining) northern England background. Her title was bestowed during Tony Blair's administration in 1999 when she was named to the House of Lords. Given Britain's derision of the EU before its 2016 departure vote, it's not surprising that Ashton, as the EU high representative for foreign affairs, was ridiculed in the right-wing British media as a "national embarrassment," and her EU office as "useless" and "slow to respond to crises."[1] Among her peers, however, Ashton has been known for both being a consensus builder and not being easily pushed around. According to a colleague speaking in 2012, "Her manner and style are not that of a globe-trotting foreign minister. She has a subtle way of working. Her brand is relational diplomacy,"[2] as opposed to the more masculine, power-based coercive diplomacy. Ashton herself has said, "You can achieve an awful lot if you're prepared not to take the credit."[3]

In 2022, I co-authored an *Orbis* article[4] with attorney Melissa Deehring to demonstrate how and why a mixed masculine-feminist approach to dealing with a nuclear-ambitious Iran offered greater success than the strictly power-based masculine approaches already tried and failed. It does so through a case study of US deterrence strategy toward Iran during the most recent past presidential administrations, two Democratic and two Republican. Analysis focused on whether each administration's stance toward Iran had been traditionally masculine, feminine, or a mix. We found the mixed strategy most effective.

Since the taking of the American hostages in Iran in 1979 and the establishment of the Islamic Republic, US–Iranian relations have deteriorated into acrimony, misperceptions, mutual distrust, and bitter exchanges. Iran's place in US grand strategy has depreciated from ally to terrorism producer and source of proliferation of weapons of mass destruction.[5] Retired CIA officer Paul R. Pillar summarized the problem in 2013, "Each side's worst presumptions about the other side encourage words and actions that make the presumptions look true."[6] Iran, with China and Russia, is part of the geopolitical Great Power Competition that prevails in national security considerations.

While US Presidential administrations have adopted a variety of foreign policy strategies toward Iran, certain key objectives have remained constant: the United States seeks to deter Iran from becoming a nuclear-armed regional hegemon and wants to stop Tehran's support for what the United States deems terrorism. At the same time, while Iran has adopted at least two distinct foreign policy approaches since 1979,[7] détente and then containment, it has also retained one common undercurrent: Iran seeks independence from foreign influence and does not want to be told what it can or cannot do by dominant world powers, particularly the United States and its allies, either by deterrence or compellence, two variations of coercion as a political-diplomatic strategy.

To understand coercion as a US strategic response to prevent military escalation with Iran, it is first important to understand the differences between deterrence and compellence. Deterrence seeks to prevent something from happening, to dissuade an opponent from a particular course of action because the costs/risks outweigh the benefits.[8] Classical theories hold that deterrence "is the practice of discouraging or restraining someone – in world politics, usually a nation-state – from taking unwanted actions, such as an armed attack."[9] Compellence, on the other hand, responds to an action already taken by an opponent.[10] Compellence seeks to force an opponent to give up or stop doing something, to compel an opponent into a specific course of action. Because compellence involves accepting a loss while deterrence means abstaining from a possible gain, it has been argued that compellence is more difficult than deterrence because compellence induces risk-acceptant behavior.[11] Phrased differently, preventing a country from developing nuclear weapons is easier than convincing a country that already has them to give them up, particularly if the country in question is a rogue or pariah state that considers those weapons its primary guarantee of regime survival. Additionally, it must be remembered that both deterrence and compellence inherently include both a carrot and a stick; numerous studies have found "strictly coercive or bullying strategies are not optimal under most conditions."[12] For both deterrence and compellence to be effective, opponents must believe that they have something to gain, or less to lose, from actions.

As US hegemonic power wanes and US adversaries become significantly more capable, the development of effective deterrence strategies against threats has become increasingly difficult. Additionally, because deterrence must shape the thinking of a potential aggressor and therefore consider what it values and why,[13] the ever-widening gap between US–Iranian perceptions and relations makes the chances of the United States adopting an effective deterrence policy with Iran more elusive. This is particularly the case if the United States continues to adopt what national security scholars Valerie Hudson and Rose McDermott deem traditional masculine deterrence strategies that come with, in their words, a significant price tag measured in strategic loss and human insecurity.[14] Consequently, a successful long-term coercive strategy with Iran benefits from the inclusion of a feminist approach.

Referencing the masculine fight/flight and feminine tend/befriend propensities raised in Chapter 1, Hudson and McDermott argue that traditional US deterrence has a masculine bent as it is "conceived in 'fight or flight' terms," with the fight portion involving "looking very fierce, weapons in hand, prepared to meet any challenge in order to deter potential adversaries from attacking"[15] – the international equivalent, they say, of a haka dance – and post-deterrence resembling the "flight" alternative. Alternatively, they maintain that a "tend and befriend" approach focuses on post-deterrence to "mitigate threat through de-escalation ('befriend'), and seek to bolster human security in situations of deterrence failure ('tend')."[16] Consequently, a "blended deterrence stance of 'fight and befriend,' coupled with post-deterrence planning of 'tend and flight,' offers clear advantages over simple, conventionally masculinist 'fight or flight'" strategies.

Hudson and McDermott argue that with "fight and befriend," because as much effort is invested in "befriending" through diplomacy, economic development, and aid as "fighting" toward a longer-term goal, there is less chance of hostilities breaking out. It is a prudent option. They assert that when "fight and befriend" is coupled with strong "tend and flight" post-deterrence contingency planning, it provides greater human security and undermines the success of the opposing party's aggression. These arguments resemble other scholarly findings that successful deterrence requires "broad-based strategies to dissuade," more than mere threats, a combination of threats with concessions, and a mix of deterrence with conciliation.[17]

Using these premises, we examined the Bush 43, Obama, Trump, and Biden administrations' respective policies and rhetoric toward Iran. It was only under the Obama Administration, using both masculine and feminine approaches, that the stated objective, deterring Iran from the development of a nuclear weapon, was achieved. Not coincidentally, women negotiators were key among the multinational team negotiating the resulting Joint Comprehensive Plan of Action (JCPOA) signed between the P5+1 (the five permanent members of the Security Council: China, France, Russia, the UK, and the Unites States, plus Germany), the EU, and Iran on July 14, 2015.

Ayatollah Ali Khamenei, Iran's second Supreme Leader, ultimately controls all aspects of Iran's nuclear program. Prior to 2013, he had consistently argued that Iran's nuclear program was peaceful, but he was also consistent with his anti-American rhetoric and rejection of any notion of negotiations with the United States on Iran's nuclear ambitions. Then in a 2013 speech, his tone changed. Though he expressed skepticism about negotiations with the United States, he also said, "I don't oppose them."[18] Khamenei caveated, though, that talks would be possible only if Washington altered its approach of entitlement and pressure. Iranian President Hassan Rouhani, elected in 2013, ran for office on a platform of moderation, seeing a potential nuclear deal as a means to economic progress, ending Western sanctions, and consequently putting an end to Iran's international isolation, but needing to achieve it without being seen as selling out. Both Khamenei and Rouhani were facing severe potential backlash from hardliners if they felt that Iran was overly capitulating to the West. Rouhani had already been politically burned by the failed nuclear negotiations he had been associated with in 2003. Iranian politics put significant pressure on Foreign Minister Javad Zarif and chief negotiator Abbas Araghchi.

Javad Zarif came to the United States when he was 17 years old. He attended a private high school in California and went on to earn both a Bachelor's and a Master's degree in international relations from San Francisco State University. He then obtained a doctoral degree in international law and policy from the University of Denver in 1988. Before becoming Foreign Minister, he served as Iran's Ambassador to the United Nations from 2002 to 2007, where he gained a reputation for being articulate and reasoned. Zarif was officially "in charge" of the negotiations, and it was Zarif and Federica Mogherini, the EU's chief diplomat and former Italian foreign minister who took over for Ashton in 2014, who made the official 2015 announcement that an agreement had been reached. Chief negotiator Abbas Araghchi, a career Iranian diplomat, was also educated in the West, having a Bachelor's, Master's, and Doctoral degrees in politics and government from the University of Kent in Britain. Both were astute politicians and experienced negotiators rather than hardline ideologues. But both sides had red lines, and neither was willing to give what would be seen at home as "too much."

Given the hyper-tense geopolitical relations between the United States and Iran, the multinational aspect of the negotiations was also key. Iran was not just negotiating with the United States. While not all of the P5+1 delegations were headed by, or even included, women, three were, and they played key roles. Mogherini initially faced criticism, including from the West, that she was too young (she was in her early 40s at the time) and inexperienced. She proved, however, to be a tough negotiator, politically savvy and, according to a colleague, "never ideological."[19] Her deputy, Helga Schmidt, had significant negotiation experience, including with Iran, and has been credited with the technical knowledge to negotiate the agreement language and the five annexes. As a negotiator, she has been described as both tough and empathetic. According to a colleague: "She is German in the sense that she is cautious, she thinks a lot about the issue, and knows where the red lines are."[20] US State Department representative Wendy Sherman came to the negotiations in 2011 as a seasoned nuclear diplomat, having served as the chief strategist on the negotiations involving the North Korean nuclear program. Sherman coordinated with the US Security Council and played a major role in US–Iranian bilateral agreements. Sherman believed being a woman gave her some latitude in the negotiations.

> When I sat across from the Iranians I was the United States of America and perhaps as a woman I can say some things that don't come across as tough, but when I do get tough and when I do lose it, it makes a big impression because it's unexpected.[21]

Ashton had carefully worked in the first round of talks to create the idea that the negotiations represented a special opportunity for Iran that was easier and smarter to seize than reject. But creating that environment was a tightrope. Speaking at the time, a European diplomat described Ashton's intent.

> She wants to show [the Iranians] in word and deed that these negotiations are a genuine opportunity to move forward. But [she is also trying] not to be hoodwinked and fooled by negotiators who have [in the past] strung out and wrapped negotiators in games of politics.[22]

Mogherini recognized the value of maintaining the advantageous working environment in the second set of negotiations that Ashton had created in the first.

Nevertheless, tensions remained high. Initially, for example, the Iranians would speak only in Farsi, though most spoke English well. The women realized as well that the (all male) Iranians would likely not be entirely comfortable working with women. Consequently, they made a deliberate decision to dress conservatively to assuage some of the Iranian cultural angst.

The women worked as a team. Mogherini chaired the meetings within the P5+1 coalition, called for plenaries with the Iranians, set the agenda, and drove the process. Schmidt and her team built "technical bridging proposals" that allowed both sides to eventually get to the finish line. Sherman worked politics, saying:

> I sometimes joke that we certainly had negotiations within our own government; we had consultations and negotiations with the Congress, with outside interests in our own country; we negotiated with our negotiating partners; and then we negotiated with Iran. And we also negotiated with interested parties around the world.[23]

She described this complicated political negotiation as a "Rubik's Cube." Meanwhile, during the negotiations, Abba Araghchi became a grandfather, and Sherman became a grandmother. They shared videos of their grandchildren with each other. The women's presence and approach added value. It worked.

Both the Ashton/Mogherini approach and the multinational aspect of the negotiations were important to the ultimate success of the negotiations. A senior Western official at the negotiations described the environment.

> We tried hard to understand where the negotiators came from, the pressure they had, because it would not result in the same consequences from them as it would for us. Sometimes they were asking too much, but we were tough and we didn't give in easily.[24]

Further, according to Mogherini, "when the men veered off course and went on historical tangents or started to get tangled into debates about who gave more, the women walked them back to the present."[25] The women were prudent, goal-oriented, and used a mix of tend/befriend and fight/flight approaches.

But in 2018, the Trump Administration announced that the United States was withdrawing from the JPCOA. Critics and administration officials claimed that the agreement did not address Iran's missile development program (that was not the intent), cheating on the part of Iran (the agencies charged with monitoring compliance found none), and that there were sunset clauses in the agreement which made exiting necessary to get ahead of the threat (the sunset clauses were distant, not urgent). The complaints did not hold up to scrutiny and even some senior Israeli officials have suggested that US withdrawal from the JPCOA was a mistake.[26] Analysis of the withdrawal has included consideration of hubris again playing a role, this time the hubris of President Donald Trump personally.[27] As a presidential candidate, Trump had promised to force the Iranians back to the bargaining table to make a much better (nuclear) deal. That did not happen.

Since the collapse of the JPCOA, Iran has sped up production of its 60% enriched uranium program and is getting closer to the 90% needed for a nuclear weapon.[28] The International Atomic Energy Agency, which monitors Iran's nuclear program, has concerns about a worrisome lack of transparency from Iran regarding its efforts and intentions.[29] Analysts have suggested that heightened Middle East tensions surrounding the ongoing war in Gaza make an Iranian bomb more likely.[30] Had hubris not intervened, the JPCOA may have tamped down and certainly slowed down Iranian efforts.

Circumstances, the context for the negotiations, have changed since 2015 and consequent to the US pulling out of the JPCOA that led Biden to avoid - a masculine approach - dealing with Iran on deterrence. Hence, Sherman said in 2023 that "the Joint Comprehensive Plan of Action…is still on the table. But it's not on the agenda."[31] Hardliners came back into power in Iran. Subsequently, Iran supplying Russia with UAVs to use against Ukraine, the US supporting the Iranian protesters subsequent to the 2022 government murder of Mahsa Amini, and Americans still being wrongfully detained in Iran have all poisoned the waters. Though reformist candidate Masoud Pezeshkian was elected as President in Iran in 2024, with the re-election of Donald Trump as the US President also in 2024, improved US-Iranian relations seem unlikely But there was a moment in time in 2015 when diplomacy and diverse leadership worked.

The Intelligence Community

Nowhere is the need to avoid groupthink more obvious than in the intelligence community (IC). But the record and prospects for diverse leadership within the intelligence community are a mixed bag. The good news is that women are well experienced with intelligence operations, having been active in the intelligence world since Biblical times. During the American Revolutionary War, women played key intelligence roles through gender stereotypical activities, including socializing, cooking, laundry – hanging laundry outside to send secret messages to other operatives – and counterintelligence that resulted in Benedict Arnold's treason being revealed. Gender stereotyping resulted in a threat – women acting as part of intelligence networks – being overlooked. By World War I, women were serving as translators, telephone operators, drivers, and even cryptologists, as communications technology was not originally assumed as primarily a man's purview. And by World War II, a woman, Eloise Randolph Page – known as the "iron butterfly" – served as a station chief. Before the ban on women in combat was lifted, women wanting to serve their country often joined the military and served in intelligence, or in intelligence agencies, as it was the closest they could get to the fight.

Additionally, experience in Afghanistan demonstrated that the premises of the Women, Peace, and Security framework can be a valuable analytic and that gender considerations matter. With all the sophisticated, high-tech intelligence apparatus available to the United States and allies, the best indicator of an imminent Taliban attack was often when the women and children went inside because, through their homes and families, they were privy to information. It was recognized too that when the price men were required to pay for a bride went up, having a wife and children being an integral part of manhood in the country, the ability of the Taliban to recruit local men went up as well. Men were willing to join the Taliban to earn money to buy a bride and establish their manhood.

Similar issues have been found relevant to bride-prices and establishing manhood in other countries as well. The average age when men were marrying before the revolution erupted in Egypt in 2011 was 33. Men in Egypt, where marriage and children stereotypically define their masculinity, were frustrated and angry. Similarly, men unable to find wives in China are called "bare branches" and considered a security risk because they are untethered to society and therefore more willing and likely to engage in reckless and violent activity. We know this and yet gender-related information is still not mainstreamed as key analytic material. And though women have a history in intelligence roles, the position of women in intelligence organizations has been and sometimes remains precarious.

Janine Brookner began as a CIA operative in the 1970s. She served in the Philippines, Thailand, as a deputy CIA station chief in Caracas, Venezuela, and as a CIA branch chief in Manhattan, across from the United Nations. Between 1989 and 1991, she was the agency's station chief in Jamaica. Her supervisors called her performance there "superb." But then things changed. After disciplining a few subordinates for misconduct, including her male deputy whom she reported for repeatedly beating his wife, the malcontents went after her through the agency's IG, who backed up their report on Brookner. In the IG report, an early example of the IG system being weaponized, she was portrayed as a heavy drinker who sexually harassed men.

When friends questioned the IG's actions, they were threatened, and so colleagues began distancing themselves from her. Her promised assignment to Prague disappeared. Though she took legal action against the CIA and the CIA case against her quickly collapsed, her career was over. She received a cash settlement but no admission of wrongdoing by the agency.[32] Other women learned from Brookner's experience not to complain; some were rumored to be sent for psychological evaluation if they had.[33]

Consequently, the bad news is that often there are few women making it through the leadership promotion pipeline of intelligence organizations, a problem not unique to the intelligence community, but rather exemplary of a problem in many organizations and institutions. That problem must be addressed to optimize the potential of diverse leadership.

Brookner's field experience was also unique, as a 1991 CIA-commissioned study known as the glass ceiling study found that part of the reason women were not moving ahead at the same rate as men was that they were often being denied operational positions that placed them in positions for promotion. The study found that, at the time, women made up 40% of the CIA's workforce, but only 17% of operations officers were women. In the operations division, "there was a strong belief that women could not recruit agents, due to the low standing women have in the Arab culture, as well as the lack of acceptance of women in authority by the Latino culture."[34] Consequently, many women left the agency in frustration. But in some instances, the low status of women in many regions, and generally, has been found to be advantageous to women in recruiting and in other ways. Foreign men will often be more revealing with women because women are disarming, nurturing, and nonthreatening and so men are less likely to suspect them as intelligence officers. Women can add unique value.

Similarly in the State Department, Ambassador (ret.) Gene Christy[35] stated in an interview that during his time as the US Ambassador in Brunei, women diplomats often had an advantage. Women were allowed access to parts of the Sultan's palace not accessible to men, parts where talk often flowed freely. In particular, it was, he recalled, the female Ambassador from the Philippines who was often the most informed within the diplomatic community during his tenure in Brunei.

Ambassador Christy's view was reiterated by a female US Ambassador to the Middle East/North Africa (MENA) region, with an interesting note about the importance of what country a woman was representing and an acknowledgment of age as a source of prejudice.

> Being a female in the MENA region gave me entry into half of the society that my male foreign service counterparts could not enter, and I learned valuable insights that my male counterparts could not. Women have a LOT of influence in the Arab world, including influence on the men in their families who may be leaders of the country.
>
> As an American diplomat, representing both "the flag" and something host country interlocutors often wanted (access to American government officials for a multitude of purposes), I was not excluded from the male side of society. I think age PLUS gender was perhaps a hinderance when I was starting out in the MENA region, as twenty-something females were not seen as bringing much to the table. Having a more senior title and more experience mitigated what could have been gender bias.

> I worked equally with my male and female Ambassador counterparts – because in countries where I served, being an American ambassador meant everyone wanted to work with you and curried favor. This was NOT the same for my female ambassador counterparts from less prominent countries. So…it was the flag that made the difference.[36]

The foreign service and intelligence communities share many issues regarding the hiring, retention, and promotion of women, both structural and cultural.

Additional structural issues were identified in the CIA study as well.

> Women were not achieving at the same pace or to the same degree as men, and were receiving proportionately fewer awards while still being given the choice assignments. The report also noted that, in order to be accepted, female officers tolerated widespread sexual and racial harassment.[37]

That report led to a class action lawsuit by 250 female operations officers against the CIA for sexual discrimination and systematic denial of promotional opportunities for women. The CIA settled and provided some financial relief to the complainants, but little was achieved in terms of long-term change.

All types of diversity – sex, age, ethnicity, education, religion, geographic, etc. – bring intelligence benefits. Yet intelligence organizations have traditionally been comprised exclusively of individuals described as "pale, male, and Yale." But that demographic alone is inadequate to address the plethora of global issues, attitudes, and threats being faced. Though some skeptics still beat the drum of "excellence is being sacrificed to alter of diversity," that argument flies in the face of the diverse challenges being faced from diverse sources, thereby needing a broad spectrum of perspectives to identify and address them. Diversification has, however, proved difficult. As reported in 2022:

> Latinos make up about 18% of the American population but just 7% of the roughly 100,000-person intelligence community and 3.5% of senior officers. Black officers comprise 12% of the community – the same as the US population – but 6.5% at the most senior level. And while minorities comprise 27% of the total intelligence workforce, just 15% of senior executives are people of color.[38]

Here the diversity focus is on gender. Amy Martin, writing in the *Journal of Strategic Security,* says:

> Undervaluing women's talents and expertise directly and negatively impacts the mission…While men tend to identify things from point A to B and move on, women tend to have a psychological desire to create context for a situation, which can be better in the long run. Women usually have more patience than men, and can "smooth over edges and work through boundaries" more easily than men.[39]

The benefits of combining the differences in thinking and approaches between men and women intelligence officers have been shown effective in operations including finding Osama Bin Laden and Abu Musab al-Zarqawi.

In fact, women analysts had been tracking and analyzing Osama Bin Laden (OBL) and AQ since before 9/11. Unfortunately, however, it is now known that because it was mostly women who were charged with monitoring AQ, their analysis was sometimes, or often, downplayed. Even the competency of their male boss was questioned because "the only people who work for him are girls."[40] At one point, all the analysts at Alec Station, the unit charged with finding OBL, were women, and women always made up the majority. Known as "the sisterhood," some of the members have subsequently spoken out regarding how they saw being female was key to their success.

According to sisterhood member Nada Bakos, "We're aggressive in the protection of our children…We see risks differently, longer term."[41] Further, Carol Rollie Flynn, former executive director of the agency's Counter Terrorism Center, said she thinks "the real strengths of these women were their intense dedication and incredible attention to detail."[42] Women intelligence analysts also participated in the interrogation of terror suspects, and were at times particularly successful because they challenged the men's manhood. The men were both surprised to be interrogated by women, individuals they felt inferior to, and were shamed by it. Women in intelligence offer added value when utilized.

It will take both structural and cultural changes to achieve the kind of diversity clearly needed to maximize intelligence operations. While acknowledging that the goal is cognitive diversity, not diversity simply for the sake of diversity, realistically, demographics are important to achieving cognitive diversity. Diversity is about experience, background, and everything that individuals bring to the table, with demographics being a key part of determining that. And diversity is not just important in intelligence analysis and operations, but also in the development of technology used in association with those.

Whether artificial intelligence (AI), space, cyber, or another potentially disruptive technology, not having available the additive value of half the population in its development and utilization inherently diminishes its capabilities and potential value, including in the intelligence world. Canadian Joy Buolamwini was a black woman researcher at the Massachusetts Institute of Technology Media Lab when she discovered that the facial recognition software she was using for a project there didn't recognize her face. Some black faces were recognized by the software as gorillas or other primates. The problem was that the AI had been taught to recognize only part of the spectrum of facial structures and skin tones. Only about 12% of machine-learning researchers are women, and only a small portion of those black. AI is only as good as those teaching it. "Who codes matters," Buolamwini has pointed out.[43] Now imagine if the intelligence community was relying on AI technology in a national security crisis to identify someone who had been left off the facial recognition spectrum. In the case of AI as well, since it is made by humans, it internalizes the same biases found in its developers and society, which means gender bias.

Lack of diversity among coders is evident in other key databases as well, potentially devaluing use by intelligence agencies. American anthropologist Nina Jablonski has studied skin coloring around the world. Her work shows that the majority of the world's people have skin that would be classified as on the darker end of the majority of skin classification scales. However, the US government IJB-A dataset, specifically created to be used in conjunction with facial recognition technology and intending to have the widest geographic collection of facial images in a wide variety of poses, illumination, expression, resolution, and occlusion has more than 80% lighter-skin individuals.[44] Diversity is a matter of national security.

Yet, according to a 2023 report from the Office of the Director of Intelligence, women remain underrepresented in the leadership ranks throughout the 18 organizations and agencies that comprise the IC in the United States, though some organizations are doing better than others. Women and men begin at the same GS-10 level at about 50/50 each. However, as individuals rise in rank, a gap begins to be evident. At the GS-15 level, it is 65% men and 35% women, and it narrows further from there.[45] Within different organizations and agencies, there are both success stories and indicators of gender-based issues.

At the Central Intelligence Agency (CIA), for example, in 1976 there was only one woman among the agency's 98 key officials; in 2015 women made up one-third of the senior staff, and three of the top four officers and five of the top eight officers were women, including the CIA's deputy director, executive director, chief information officer, director of support, director of intelligence, human resources director, deputy chief financial officer, and the Chief of Staff.[46] How deep the pool is behind them, however, is unclear. Between 2013 and 2019, for example, female representation at the GS-13 level actually decreased, and the attrition rate for women remains higher than that for men.[47]

At the National Security Agency (NSA), a 2019 report by the agency's IG found that "female employees received only 14% of 'individual retention incentives,' discretionary bonuses, even though women make up 41% of the agency's civilian workforce.'"[48] Testifying before Congress in 2021, NSA Director General Paul Nakasone provided sobering statistics: NSA's senior cadre of Defense Intelligence Senior Executive (DISES) and Defense Intelligence Senior Leaders (DISLs) had seen an increase of only 0.3% women over three years and that, notably,

> representation of minorities and women in Senior ranks is roughly 10% lower than their overall representation among the graded workforce. Representation of women in the DISL ranks is even lower, at only 18.3% of the population, a 1.2% increase in representation in 3 years.[49]

Clearly barriers to leadership advancement for women (and minorities) remain.

What will it take to hire, retain, and promote women to positions of leadership in the intelligence community and other male-dominated security organizations? That question has been addressed, formally and informally.

Individual incentive on the part of interested women is a key theme, one raised by multiple women leaders I've spoken with, and referenced by the women college professors in Chapter 2 who were harder on young women associates than their male counterparts. Women have to be ambitious, persistent, and be willing to push boundaries and find ways around obstacles if they are to succeed. This is certainly true for cisgender women and even more so for transgender women.

Recommendations have been made in various studies and from groups organized in the intelligence community to look at ways to improve the promotion rates and hiring of women (and other minority groups). Early suggestions for improvement ranged from ensuring that promotion and selection panels included minority representation, to conducting formal training for upwardly mobile GS-15 women, and to strengthening mentoring for junior officers. More recently, in 2015, specific recommendations for improvement in the CIA were provided by a group organized by David Petraeus when he was Director. Included in those recommendations was the establishment of clear promotion criteria. Without clear, specific criteria, promotion processes can become "atta boy" rewards.

Leadership and management principles for State Department employees are laid out in three FAM 1214, the Foreign Affairs Manual, which guides Department operations. Amb. (ret.) Gene Christy talks about the importance of criteria in evaluations.

> As a DOS inspection team leader for my last two years of active duty and part-time for the next five years, I was charged to evaluate the leadership and management skills of ambassadors, deputy chiefs of mission, and other senior mission leaders. Along with several of my OIG [Office of the Inspector General] colleagues, we fought to have the Department develop and publish a set of leadership and management criteria. Until that was done, all of our written evaluations of leadership were subject to challenge, as we had no criteria beyond our own experiences and observations of leaders. Having criteria was great; the propensity to challenge our conclusions did not subside, especially when we were critical.[50]

More generally, the issues confronting women in intelligence are much the same as those facing women in other male-dominated career fields: lack of both mentorship and sponsorship, subtle forms of bias and harassment, insufficient workplace flexibility, an increasing number of "extreme jobs," and "the pull of outside responsibilities."

Microaggressions, subtle forms of bias and harassment, are exhausting and happen to women at every level. A female Major General I spoke with told of, at her two-star rank, repeatedly making a suggestion at a meeting only to have it ignored until a male colleague said the exact same thing and the boss praised it effusively. She said her phone blew up, with colleagues in the room texting her after noting the slight. Other microaggressions include nonrecognition of titles and being interrupted. A female military officer in Jordan from the medical community said her "doctor" title was regularly dropped by her male colleagues. Women Supreme Court justices in the United States are interrupted more than men justices. Speaking over women, being ignored, mansplaining, etc. are all examples of microaggressions commonly experienced by women. Besides being annoying and exhausting, microaggressions also wear on confidence.

Insufficient workplace flexibility is perhaps the barrier to women's leadership advancement and self-selecting out of advancement pipelines most amenable to organizational behavior changes. Too often, organizational procedures operate on a "that's the way we always done it" basis, rather than thinking through how something can be done in ways to better accommodate employees within organizational parameters. When employees are required, for example, to drive government vehicles to work but doing so restricts them from dropping off their kids at school, maybe it's time to look at that policy. Perhaps a simple, reasonable change can be made. Too often though, it is women who are affected by these policies, but they are reluctant to ask for change and subsequently risk being perceived as asking for special treatment.

Extreme jobs are those which entail more than 60 hours a week, and often some combination of unpredictable workflows, fast-paced work within tight deadlines, an inordinate scope of responsibility that means someone is working more than one job, work-related events outside of work hours, 24/7 availability, large amounts of travel, responsibility for successes and failures, mentoring and recruiting expectations, many direct reports, and a physical presence of more than ten hours per day.[51] Research has found that most individuals who take these jobs don't feel exploited; they love the "rush" of the job. But research also suggests that women are at a disadvantage. "Although they don't shirk the pressure or responsibility of extreme work, they are not matching the hours logged by their male colleagues. This constitutes a barrier for ambitious women."[52] Part of that work-life balance is the pull of outside responsibilities and the accompanying guilt that women tend to experience more than men for not being available for family matters as much as other women in less time-intensive professions.

Anne-Marie Slaughter is a Princeton professor and was the first woman to serve as Deputy Director for Policy Planning at the State Department under Hillary Clinton. She caused somewhat of a firestorm among women when she resigned from her State Department position in 2012 and wrote a cover story for *The Atlantic* magazine titled "Why Women Still Can't Have It All." In it she said, "juggling high-level government work with the needs of two teenage boys was not possible."[53] While some women welcomed the acknowledgment of the difficulties women face juggling family and career, others considered Slaughter's rationale for leaving what she had called her "dream job" as providing ammunition to individuals who wanted excuses not to hire women, especially mothers, for high-intensity, extreme jobs.

After Slaughter's 2012 proclamation, her former boss Hillary Clinton was asked her view. Clinton replied in an interview to *Marie-Claire* magazine, "some women are not comfortable working at the pace and intensity you have to work at in these jobs...Other women don't break a sweat."[54] Anne-Marie Slaughter couldn't make "having it all" work for her, but Hillary Clinton and Lisa Franchetti have, again pointing out the differences and individuality among even high-powered leaders. Slaughter later revised her proclamation to say that she had realized no one could have it all, and that sacrifices have to be made by men too. My son's first job after college at a New York hedge fund had an annual Saturday event when spouses and children were welcomed at the office. It was sardonically referred to by the primarily male employees as "Meet Daddy Day." The only women in the office were single.

Women leaving professional positions remains a challenge and women sometimes still blame themselves. The American Bar Association (ABA) issued reports in 2019 and 2020 focusing on the long-term experiences of women in the nation's 500 largest firms, concluding that women's relative lack of advancement in the profession was largely a structural issue. Similar to Slaughter's experience in 2012, when attorney Susan Smith Blakely suggested in a June 29, 2021 *ABA Journal* article that perhaps the lack of women attorneys' advancement was due to "distractions" and that women couldn't or didn't invest the time needed for career advancement,[55] another firestorm again resulted. Ten ABA women past presidents responded with an open letter stating that "women lawyers deserve a fair and equitable workplace where the policies and ethos allow them to thrive and does not drive them away."[56] Too often, "distractions" like those Susan Smith Blakely referred to are a euphemism for children, seen as women's responsibility, not a family – male included – responsibility.

Further, it is laudable that there were ten women ABA presidents, that there was consensus in their view about barriers to women in the profession, and that they were willing to state so in an open letter. But the letter also raises the question of why no male ABA presidents signed or spoke out in support of the women's letter. The inclusion of men's support would have made the statement even stronger. This is an example of where male allies could have played an important role.

Male allies for gender equality work in partnership with women to change harmful gender relations and stereotypes into relationships better for everyone, men and women, and the organizations and institutions where they work. Smith and Johnson's 2020 research-based book, *Good Guys: How Men Can Be Better Allies in the Workplace*, evidences that when men are deliberately engaged in gender-inclusion programs, 96% of the women in those organizations perceive real progress in gender equality compared to 30% of women in organizations without strong male engagement.[57] The roles that men can play as allies, from amplifying women's voices and providing them space to have a voice, to addressing microaggressions and reducing women's feelings of isolation, are all important. Actively being an ally in small ways is more important to women than a performative-only leader who provides one-and-done rhetorical support for women on stage, but then forgotten.

Organizations like Our Secure Future have conducted studies on how and why men internalize the importance of gender equality (and the Women, Peace, and Security framework) to national security, including through interviews with male leaders. "The experiences and perspectives of a number of men in leadership positions who understand gender equality as a strategic capability and transformational policy tool point toward a window of opportunity."[58] That is, once gender equality and gender value are recognized and understood, they are accepted. Male allies are key in making that recognition and understanding happen as women's advocacy is often seen as coming from a place of having a vested interest in change, rather than it being for the greater good.

For leaders and organizations committed to exploiting the value of diversity, both extreme jobs and the pull of outside responsibilities present an opportunity for these leaders and organizations to find ways to tap the talents of all individuals, especially women, who will commit to hard work and responsibility but cannot put in over-long days without sacrificing a healthy work-life balance. Having more men as allies, mentors, and sponsors will also open the pipeline for women to advance in the leadership pipeline. For women, competence, confidence, mentorship, and persistence remain key to developing a reputation strong for advancement. A former CIA officer said bluntly, "Never assume you can't do something until you try and never communicate your doubts."[59] Never communicating doubts is similar to the "don't make things look hard" comment told to the female GFO and conveyed in Chapter 5. It is unfortunate but true that women must continually strive to make it all – work and work-life balance – look easy, when it's not.

Space Force

In the spirit of full disclosure, I was not a supporter of the creation of Space Force as the sixth branch of the US military. Space security was my area of expertise for a long arc in my academic career. I authored or co-authored seven books and scores of articles on different aspects of space security, including international cooperation and competition in space and the Chinese space program. I also held the Charles F. Bolden, Jr. Chair in Science, Space and Technology at the Naval War College and testified before Congress on multiple occasions on space-related topics. I had certainly witnessed the rise in military importance of space technology, due to space technology enabling information-related capabilities key to deterring conflicts and prevailing in conflicts. But the US military is already the biggest bureaucracy in the world and my feeling was that enlarging it would not solve the budget prioritization issues space advocates faced within the Air Force. I certainly recognized that fighter pilots were the fair-haired children in the Air Force, as evidenced by their disproportionate representation in leadership,[60] while space advocates flying desks were the stepchildren. But it took the Department of Homeland Security ten years to establish itself after 9/11, so a new military bureaucracy – with the bands, uniforms, golf courses, and intra-service rivalry that inevitably accompanies establishment – seemed unnecessary to me. Nevertheless, Space Force was launched in December 2019.

From a positive perspective, the establishment of Space Force presented an opportunity. One of the pillars of the Women, Peace and Security framework is to take a gendered perspective on "relief and recovery." Relief and recovery occur after a crisis, usually an event involving destruction and a consequent need for rebuilding. In practice, it has meant understanding that in responding to humanitarian needs after an earthquake or hurricane, like the provision of latrines, a gendered approach is necessary. An often-used example is that latrine facilities for men and women must be placed apart from each other, with the women's located near their housing, and with lighting and locks on the doors provided. Otherwise, the women will be afraid to use them, fearing gender-based violence, and the effort will be for naught.[61] The premise of taking a gendered perspective is that there is an opportunity to not simply rebuild old structures that perpetuate patriarchal systems and subsequent problems, but to take a different approach, to create something better. The same premise can be applied to the creation of a new organization, like Space Force, and in fact was.

Nobody expected Space Force to happen as quickly as it did. Rather, it was thought Congress would dictate a planning phase before the "stand up," but that didn't happen. Consequently, the early days were a bit chaotic, but in ways many people described as fun and exciting.

Initially, about 30 people were brought in to build the framework for Space Force, about half from the Air Force and half were "bodies" from other services who knew little or nothing about space. But they were eager and professional, and many were sent early on to special, introductory courses on space at Vandenberg Air Force Base. Upon the return of one group in February 2020, however, many of them were ill with what they humorously dubbed the "space flu," but later found out to be Covid-19. To add to other challenges, Space Force was created during the pandemic.

Initial discussions among the stand-up group specifically recognized that they had an opportunity to do things differently. When looking through files of individuals seeking to move to Space Force from other services, the stand-up team intentionally looked for diversity. Accepted individuals were identified first by those who could do the job, second, best performers, and if there was a tie, diversity, including military backgrounds, was the third deciding criterion.

The internal stand-up group also considered that Space Force be comprised of 50% women. However, there simply weren't enough women with the requisite skills and in appropriate positions to do that. But the need and desire for diversity and inclusion in Space Force were recognized. Being a small force, for Fiscal Year 2025, Space Force has asked to grow from 9,400 to 9,800 in uniform, Space Force needed to be flatter and leaner than the other services, and in fact, that has been accomplished through the elimination of some traditional layers of military bureaucracy.

Air Force Major General Nina Armagno was promoted to Lieutenant General and brought to Space Force in 2020 to assist with the stand-up as Chief of Staff. In her case, "assisting" meant holding so many roles, usually designated by numbers with individuals holding one number, that she was dubbed "the 42" for all the roles she played. There were big things and seemingly small things (that actually were big things) included in the "doing things differently" approach taken by Armagno and Space Force. One of the big "little things" was the Space Force uniform. For the first time, the woman's uniform was designed first, and the men's uniform retrofitted, rather than the traditional other-way-around. Consequently, issues of fit, comfort, and style (like where the ribbons and medals are placed on the chest) could be considered. Subsequently, others have continued the approach of doing things differently and thinking differently, within the constraints of being nested with the Department of the Air Force and component of the Department of Defense, both in terms of approaches to national security and caring for personnel.

Space Force is a noncombatant command responsible for organizing, training, and equipping the majority of forces for US Space Command, a unified combatant command for all US military operations. Space Force personnel, for example, are known as "Guardians," a defensive rather than offensive-sounding term. Space war, and particularly kinetic space war, serves no one well, especially the United States. That is well recognized by everyone who works on space security issues. As one Space Force officer said, "you can't win a space war, you can only lose." Any action that creates space debris, as blowing up anything in space would do, endangers satellites critical to national security, with the United States having more satellites and being more dependent on them than any other country. Make no mistake, US Space Command has copious capabilities at its disposal and General Jay Raymond, the first Space Force Chief of Space Operations, said, "We are forging a warfighting Service that is always above."[62] But the branding of Space Force as defensive tempers the "space war" rhetoric prevalent in many US circles that can make diplomacy, even discussions, with other countries difficult.

Space Force announced its mission statement in 2023 – Secure our Nation's Interests In, From and To Space – the product of a process led by Guardians. For many years my academic career was focused on space security, and there was only one question being asked within space security related communities, and only one answer. Question: how to win a space war; answer: technology. It is a legitimate and important question, but not the only one. And while technology is the answer to some problems, it is not the answer to all problems. Deterrence strategies to avoid conflict, and more focus on issues of an inherently multinational nature, like space debris and space traffic, serve US and global purposes as well, and receive the attention needed through the Space Force. "Securing" space protects assets that enable the American way of life, and an increasing number of other countries as well through systems like the US-owned and operated Global Positioning System (GPS). Like the internet, GPS is considered a global utility given its use in areas like airline safety and efficiency and facilitating the entire global financial system.

In 2021, the *Guardian Ideal*[63] was published, intended to provide the vision and values of Space Force. Recruitment, retention, and development of each individual

Guardian, and a culture of diversity and inclusion is emphasized. Recognizing that there would be skeptics to a talent management approach that emphasized diversity, the rationale and citing of empirical evidence of benefits were included.

> This focus on attracting, identifying, developing, and retaining a diverse workforce intentionally placed into high-performing teams will enable the Space Force to achieve the Chief of Space Operation's priorities, as defined in the CSO's Planning Guidance, in support of the National Defense Strategy. We will purposefully integrate evidence-based approaches to ensure our Guardians more closely reflect the population they serve because it is a national security imperative. [64]

Holistic attention is given to the 5Rs: recruitment, retention, readiness, resources, and risk to force/risk to mission.

Guardian Ideals also recognize the aspirational nature of this new approach, necessary in recognition that problems persist. The 2021 Space Force Racial Disparity Review noted, for example, issues with the underrepresentation of minorities, sexism, sexual harassment, and stigma attached to pregnancy and women who took maternity leave.[65] Problems plaguing other services plague Space Force as well. Perhaps a difference with Space Force is that individuals are encouraged to speak up about issues, not remain silent as has been the unwritten code in other services for too long.

Speaking at an April 2024 event at the Women's Military Memorial in DC, Lieutenant General Deanna Burt reiterated that while there are certainly many issues still needing to be addressed, on the positive side in areas like work/family life balance, Space Force continues to find and implement better ways of addressing personnel concerns. She said that, for example, joint spouse assignments, working spouses, and family issues like having a child who is a senior in high school are all taken into consideration in Space Force assignments, and both maternity and paternity leave are made available.[66] Space being a highly technical, STEM-heavy field, recruiting and retaining good people is key to keeping Space Force mission-ready.

The individualized consideration that the Space Force has embraced as part of its talent management (and development) plan can take the needs and desires of each member into account and minimize the number of people who choose to leave in lieu of undesirable assignments. For example, Bree Fram[67] is a Colonel in the US Space Force, an astronautical engineer, and has held command at the squadron level, led Air Force security cooperation in Iraq, and led space acquisition programs. She was also President of SPARTA, an organization that advocates and educates about transgender military service, and Co-Lead of the Air Force LGBTQ+ Initiatives Team, one of seven Barrier Analysis Working Groups in the Department of the Air Force, and advocates for pilots who "come out" as transgender, as they are subject to medical policies that can be interpreted as the transgender individual having a mental health condition that grounds them. These barriers inhibit retention, and so readiness.

Fram came out as transgender on the day the transgender ban in the military was dropped in 2016. The barriers faced by transgender members of the military in some ways reflect the barriers faced by minorities, but in others are very unique. She has said she would have to refuse assignments to Texas or Florida because of both medical and legal issues she and her family members could face there due to hostile transgender state laws and policies. She would choose to retire rather than go, but so far hasn't had to do that.

Advocating for change for the LGBTQ military community is difficult, however, because requests for change are most effective when backed by data, and there is no way to track data about LGBTQ military members because of privacy policies. While those policies were intended to protect individuals from being tracked down after the "don't ask, don't tell" era, they now make it impossible to collect data regarding retention rates, promotion rates, etc. One of the goals of the Barrier Analysis Group is to allow individuals to self-identify as members of the LGBTQ community, basically saying "I want to be tracked," so that relevant data can begin to be gathered to supplement already plentiful anecdotal evidence.

Space Force is only five years old as of 2024, with growing pains still evident. But signs of it being a learning organization, with people and culture as key elements of its focus, are also evident. Space Force may present a diverse workforce model for other services to emulate, if their leaders so choose.

Conclusion

The inclusion of women diplomats, military officers, intelligence officers, and in other security-related positions has been shown to change the calculus of interactions and policies between countries. At one point in 2022, there were some dozen female Ambassadors to Nigeria who met weekly on Zoom, recognizing the importance of working together, including five from significant partner countries. They coordinated their actions on issues such as elections. Imagine, one said, the image of the female Ambassadors from the US, UK, France, Germany, and the EU "going as a gaggle to talk to presidential candidates."[68] In a patriarchal country like Nigeria, that image of female leadership is impactful to both men and women. How might their presence and stature affect both the men and women they work with? The women also shone a bright light on women's empowerment through a high-profile gala awards ceremony recognizing stellar achievements by women in areas ranging from government to business, to the arts – and one award for a "he for she" for noteworthy work advancing and including women.

Men and women working together in leadership roles can provide a strategic advantage over adversaries that maintain reliance on one-dimensional, masculine leadership. The purpose of diverse leadership, as advocated in this book, is not social justice, it is for policies, decision-making, and workforce motivation that will give countries that utilize it an edge. Doing so, however, requires leaders who put organization and country over self, partisan politics, and ideology, which has been a problem of late.

Notes

1 Shipman, Tim. "At Last, EU Wakes Up to 'Useless' Ashton," *The Daily Mail*, April 24, 2013. https://www.dailymail.co.uk/news/article-2314043/At-EU-wakes-useless-Ashton-MEPS-condemn-indecision-foreign-policy-chief.html
2 Rozen, Laura and Barbara Slavin. "Can Western Women Tame Iran's Nuclear Negotiators?" *New Atlanticist*, April 26, 2012. https://www.atlanticcouncil.org/blogs/new-atlanticist/can-western-women-tame-irans-nuclear-negotiators/
3 Mayer, Catherine. "Catherine Ashton: Female Diplomat Who Helped Broker Iran Nuclear Deal," *TIME*, November 25, 2013. https://world.time.com/2013/11/25/meet-the-woman-who-helped-negotiate-the-iran-nuclear-deal/
4 Deehring, Melissa and Joan Johnson-Freese. "A More Feminine Approach? Rethinking How America Deters a Nuclear-Capable Iran," *Orbis,* Vol. 66, No. 4, 2022, pp. 509–525.
5 Edelman Eric S. and Ray Takeyh. *Revolution and Aftermath: Forging a New Strategy Toward Iran*, Hoover Institution Press, 2018, pp. 110–111.
6 Pillar, Paul R. "The Role of Villain: Iran and U.S. Foreign Policy," *Political Science Quarterly*, Vol. 128, No. 2, Summer 2013, p. 217.
7 For a discussion of Iran's foreign policy shift from détente to containment, *see* Hassan Ahmadian and Payam Mohseni. "From Detente to Containment: The Emergence of Iran's New Saudi Strategy," *International Affairs*, Vol. 97, No. 3, 2021, pp. 779–799.
8 *See* George, Alexander L. and Richard Smoke. *Deterrence in American Foreign Policy: Theory and Practice*, Columbia University Press, 11 1974.
9 Mazarr, Michael J. "Understanding Deterrence," *Perspective*, RAND Corporation, 2018. https://www.rand.org/pubs/perspectives/PE295.html
10 *See* Levy, Jack. "Deterrence and Coercive Diplomacy: The Contributions of Alexander George," *Political Psychology*, Vol. 29, No. 4, 2008. pp. 537–552.
11 Levy, 2008, p. 542.
12 Levy, 2008, p. 541.
13 Mazarr, 2018.
14 Hudson, Valerie and Rose McDermott. *Feminist Foreign Policy and Deterrence*, Center for Feminist Foreign Policy, July 7, 2021. https://web.archive.org/web/20211219000933/https:/centreforfeministforeignpolicy.org/journal/feministforeignpolicyanddeterrence
15 Hudson and McDermott, 2021.
16 Hudson and McDermott, 2021.
17 Mazarr, 2018, p. 11; *see also*, Morgan, Patrick M. *Deterrence Now*, Cambridge University Press, 2003, pp. 162–163.
18 Hu, Zoe. "Meet the Men behind Iran's Nuclear Deal," *Al Jazeera*, July 14, 2015. https://www.aljazeera.com/news/2015/7/14/meet-the-men-behind-irans-nuclear-deal
19 de la Baume, Maïa. "The Women beyond the Iran Nuclear Deal," *Politico*, July 17, 2015. https://www.politico.eu/article/the-women-behind-the-nuclear-deal/
20 de la Baume, 2015.
21 Kianpour, Suzanne. "Iran Negotiations: The Women Who Made the Iran Nuclear Deal Happen," *BBC,* August 6, 2015. https://www.bbc.com/news/world-us-canada-33728879
22 Rozen and Slavin, 2012.
23 Pazzanesse, Christine. "Inside the Iran Nuclear Deal," *Harvard Gazette,* October 6, 2015. https://news.harvard.edu/gazette/story/2015/10/inside-the-iran-nuclear-deal/
24 de la Baume, 2015.

25 Kianpour, 2015.
26 "Top Israeli Security Experts Agree – Withdrawal From the JPCOA Nuclear Agreement Has Been a Total Failure," *J Street.* https://jstreet.org/top-israeli-security-experts-agree-withdrawing-from-jcpoa-has-been-a-total-failure/ (accessed March 12, 2024)
27 Larison, Daniel. "Trump's Foreign Policy Hubris is Already a Disaster," *The American Conservative*, February 5, 2020. https://www.theamericanconservative.com/trumps-foreign-policy-hubris-is-already-a-disaster/; "The Guardian View of Iran's Nuclear Deal: Trump Creates a Narrative for War," *The Guardian*, May 9, 2018. https://www.theguardian.com/commentisfree/2018/may/09/the-guardian-view-on-irans-nuclear-deal-trump-creates-a-narrative-for-war
28 Azodi, Sina. "Will Iran Get the Bomb in 2024?" Stimson Center, January 31, 2024. https://www.theguardian.com/commentisfree/2018/may/09/the-guardian-view-on-irans-nuclear-deal-trump-creates-a-narrative-for-war
29 Gambrell, Jon. "The Head of the UN's Nuclear Watchdog Warns Iran is 'Not Entirely Transparent' about its Atomic Program," *AP*, February 13, 2024. https://apnews.com/article/iran-nuclear-program-iaea-gross-israel-hamas-gaza-war-ee164aefb63a533548a54179c952b5e1
30 Vaez, Ali. "Why the War in Gaza Makes a Nuclear Iran More Likely," *Foreign Affairs*, January 25, 2024. https://www.foreignaffairs.com/israel/why-war-gaza-makes-nuclear-iran-more-likely
31 "Wendy Sherman on Iran," The Iran Primer, US Institute of Peace, January 25, 2023. https://iranprimer.usip.org/blog/2021/jan/26/wendy-sherman-iran
32 Sandomir, Richard. "Janine Brookner, Punished CIA Officer Who Got Revenge, Dies at 80," *The New York Times*, May 26, 2021. https://www.nytimes.com/2021/05/26/us/janine-brookner-dead.html
33 Newman, Lily Hay. "The Opportunities – and Obstacles – for Women at NSA and Cyber Command," *Wired*, April 6, 2021. https://www.wired.com/story/women-cyber-security-nsa-cyber-command/
34 Martin, 2015, p. 102.
35 Personal interview, June 27, 2024.
36 Email correspondence, June 28, 2024.
37 Newman, 2021.
38 Merchant, Nomaan. "Spy Agencies Urged to Fix Open Secret: A Lack of Diversity," *AP News*, May 19, 2022. https://apnews.com/article/racial-injustice-national-security-us-intelligence-agencies-7149db22d9da96efba8396ba89cc977e
39 Martin, Amy. "America's Evolution of Women and Their Roles in the Intelligence Community," *Journal of Strategic Security*, Vol. 8, No. 5, Fall 2015. https://digitalcommons.usf.edu/cgi/viewcontent.cgi?article=1479&context=jss
40 Mundy, Liz. "The Women Who Saw 9/11 Coming," *The Atlantic*, November 18, 2023. https://www.theatlantic.com/ideas/archive/2023/11/cia-women-counterterrorism-9-11-al-qaeda-warnings/676041/
41 "Hunting Osama Bin Laden was Women's Work," *NBC News*, November 14, 2013. https://www.nbcnews.com/news/world/hunting-osama-bin-laden-was-womens-work-flna2d11594091
42 "Hunting Osama Bin Laden was Women's Work," *NBC News*, November 14, 2013. https://www.nbcnews.com/news/world/hunting-osama-bin-laden-was-womens-work-flna2d11594091
43 Pressman, Aaron. "Biased Artificial Intelligence Aps Could Cause Problems," *Fortune,* September 14, 2018. https://fortune.com/2018/09/14/fight-algorithmic-bias-joy-buolamwini
44 Buolawini, Joy. "Unmasking the Bias in Facial Recognition Algorithms," MIT Sloan, December 13, 2023. https://mitsloan.mit.edu/ideas-made-to-matter/unmasking-bias-facial-recognition-algorithms

45 Annual Statistical Transparency Report, 2024. Office of the Director of National Intelligence. https://www.dni.gov/index.php/newsroom/reports-publications/reports-publications-2024/3811-annual-statistical-transparency-report-regarding-national-security-authorities-calendar-year-2023
46 Martin, 2015, p. 106.
47 CIA, Diversity in Leadership Report, 2019. https://www.cia.gov/static/6c3dcb22cd19b11dbd8352082286f225/DLS_Year_4_Report.pdf
48 Newman, 2021.
49 Nakasone, Paul. "Statement for the Record before the House Permanent Select Committee on Intelligence," October 27, 2021. https://docs.house.gov/meetings/IG/IG00/20211027/114177/HHRG-117-IG00-Bio-NakasoneP-20211027.pdf
50 Email correspondence September 12, 2024.
51 Hewlett, Sylvia Anne and Cheryl Luce. "Extreme Jobs: The Dangerous Allure of the 70-hour Workweek," *Harvard Business Review,* December 2006, pp. 249–259.
52 Hewlett and Luce, 2006, p. 249.
53 Slaughter, Anne-Marie. "Why Women Still Can't Have it All," *The Atlantic*, July–August, 2012. https://www.theatlantic.com/magazine/archive/2012/07/why-women-still-cant-have-it-all/309020/
54 Waldman, Ayelet. "Is this Really Goodbye?" *Marie-Claire*, October 18, 2012. https://www.marieclaire.com/politics/news/a7354/hillary-clinton-farewell/
55 Blakely, Susan. "Are Women Lawyers Paying Enough Attention to Upward Mobility?" *ABA Journal*, June 29, 2021. https://www.abajournal.com/columns/article/are-women-lawyers-paying-enough-attention-to-upward-mobility
56 Refo, Patricia Lee. "Women's Success in Legal Careers," *ABA Journal*, July 6, 2021. https://www.abajournal.com/news/article/womens-success-in-legal-careers-lack-of-advancement-is-not-a-woman-problem-its-a-profession-problem#:~:text=Women%20lawyers%20deserve%20a%20fair,profession%20and%20for%20our%20clients
57 Smith, David and W. Brad Johnson. *Good Guys*, Harvard Business Review Press, 2020.
58 Shoemaker, Jolynn and Sahana Dharmapuri. "Not the Usual Suspects," Our Secure Future, October 2017. https://oursecurefuture.org/sites/default/files/2022-06/Not-The-Usual-Suspects-Report.pdf
59 Newman, 2021.
60 Sebren, Jr., C. Hall. "Air Force Leadership Diversity," *One Team, One, Fight*, Air University Press, 2024, pp. 107–111.
61 "Gender_ABC_Haiti_Emergency." https://www3.paho.org/hq/dmdocuments/2010/Gender_ABC_Haiti_emergency.pdf (accessed June 9, 2024)
62 https://www.airandspaceforces.com/app/uploads/2021/09/21SEPT-USSF-GUARDIAN-IDEAL.pdf
63 https://www.airandspaceforces.com/app/uploads/2021/09/21SEPT-USSF-GUARDIAN-IDEAL.pdf
64 https://www.airandspaceforces.com/app/uploads/2021/09/21SEPT-USSF-GUARDIAN-IDEAL.pdf (accessed June 12, 2023)
65 https://www.spaceforce.mil/News/Article/2769196/department-of-the-air-force-releases-reports-on-racial-disparity-review-update/ (Accessed June 12, 2023)
66 Military Women's Memorial. Women, Peace & Security – Air & Space Event, April 1, 2024. https://www.youtube.com/watch?v=SySXKTZ21P0
67 Personal interview, June 26, 2024.
68 Email correspondence, June 30, 2024.

8

THE FUTURE OF LEADERSHIP

To reiterate from the book Introduction: leadership is in crisis. That is a truism in the United States and globally, or so say respondents in survey after survey.[1] Not surprisingly, politics is singled out as especially problematic. A 2023 Pew report on American views said: "Majorities say the political process is dominated by special interests, flooded with campaign cash and mired in partisan warfare. Elected officials are widely viewed as self-serving and ineffective."[2]

Institutions usually highly rated, like the military, are not faring well either, for reasons including leadership. The topic of "toxic leadership" is one regularly addressed in military publications and opinion pieces. A 2020 OpEd titled "Why toxic seniors survive – and sometimes thrive – in the military" addresses a question many people have asked. The answers given include the desire to retain experience, lack of accountability by those who sponsored "bad apples," and, perhaps most importantly, the military's "desire to avoid scrutiny and additional loss of confidence."[3] Relatedly, a 2023 Gallup poll showed confidence in the US military at the lowest it's been in over two decades.[4] It is not partisanship that most divides Americans having a positive or negative view of the military, but age, with those 18–29 being the most negative,[5] which, of course, affects recruiting.

Throughout this book, examples of historical and contemporary leaders have been offered for consideration of why diverse leadership and considerations of gender matter, lessons learned, and dilemmas posed by their leadership styles as related to national security. Looking forward, however, compels us to begin with consideration of "where we are" and then "where we want to go." Futurists do not predict the future; they create a future by setting a goal and then constructing a path to get there. Similarly, nations, organizations and people individually will have to decide what they want the future to look like, and select and support leaders who will take them there.

DOI: 10.4324/9781003564065-9

The personal desire for power, position, and gain, along with an organizational desire to present a perfect picture rather than address reality, appears near epidemic within today's leadership environment. I have provided examples of both bad and good leadership to prompt discussion and learning from in this book. Pointing out leadership foibles and failures is not an exercise in disparaging individuals or institutions. It is a plea to do better, in the United States for the sake of preserving American democracy and national security, globally to support positive peace. Like disinformation and domestic terrorism, leadership issues threaten national security. "Doing better" will require consideration of gender as well as other, more traditional aspects of leadership. Whether even those traditional aspects still hold, however, is uncertain.

Authenticity vs. Rebranding

Leaders I have known and have interviewed have, to a person, men and women, cited authenticity as a touchstone for good leadership, necessary to establish and maintain trust with those they led. Americans say that they know what they want in a leader and that being "authentic" is among the top desired traits.[6] While cultures sometimes value different character traits in their leaders - directness in the Netherlands and Germany, for example, cordiality in Sweden, Canada and much of Latin America[7] - authenticity, sticking to your principles, is also expected and respected.

American diplomat Wendy Sherman spoke of Angela Merkel as an authentic leader, having worked with her for many years.

> She is extraordinary. She knows who she is. She does not try to be anything other. She is an authentic leader, which is critical. She has a strong set of values, and she understands German's history exceedingly well, in part because she comes from East Germany. So she has a certain humility that comes from her particular biography. She fights for her country and her people. She is analytical, she's fierce, she's a very skilled politician. She didn't start out that way, but she certainly has become that. And she knows how to operate on the world stage – no easy task.[8]

Merkel learned to be a leader, evolving over time, but she was steadfast and consistent in her personal values.

Mahatma Gandhi, with his consistent simplicity, honesty, and dedication to his vision – ending British rule in India – is also considered exemplary of an authentic leader. Gandhi inspired others, including US Civil Rights Movement leader Martin Luther King Jr. in the 1960s.

A lawyer by trade, Gandhi gave up his law practice and materialism to lead the Non-Cooperation Movement. Between 1915 and 1947, he led his fellow citizens in boycotting British institutions, services, and goods, as well as in marches and peaceful protests, in support of the movement. In 1930, he led his followers on a

240-mile march to the Arabian Sea to produce salt from saltwater, in defiance of the British salt tax.

Gandhi *inspired* others – different from goading or inciting – by keeping his focus on the interests of his country and his people, and by empowering those around him, rather than acquiring power for himself. Being truthful, regardless of circumstance and potential risk (he was imprisoned many times), was a core tenet of Gandhi's leadership. His courage to do so stemmed from his unwavering convictions and values. Followers sense the authenticity of their leaders, and authentic leadership is the only leadership that people are consistently willing to support over long periods.

Individuals evolve with time, age, and experience. People change. Gandhi changed. People change political affiliations. But in some cases there seems to be a point at which evolution, or change, becomes a total rebranding of who a person is and their principles. Does that matter regarding whether or not they are or can be desirable, effective leaders? I When is "change" "selling out" for power? Does authenticity still matter in leadership? Important to consider too, as a female Marine raised in a discussion, is whether evolution and rebranding are more personally acceptable if someone changes to be more akin to your own views.

Thoughtful, sophisticated, deep, eloquent, clear-thinking, brilliant, extraordinary, principled, unpretentious – special – are all words said about Josh Hawley as a young student and professional. Born and raised a conservative in Missouri, he was always the rising star, whether during high school as a National Merit Finalist, as a Stanford undergraduate, at Yale Law School, as a prominent member of the Federalist Society, or while clerking for Supreme Court Chief Justice John Roberts. Sworn into the Senate at 39 in 2019 after serving as Missouri's Attorney General, he was considered "an intellect in a movement that increasingly seemed to shun intellect…the intellectual heir of Trumpism."[9] There was also always an undercurrent of Hawley cultivating an image of himself as "special," one not uncommon or necessarily nefarious among ambitious professionals, especially where politics is concerned.[10] But some of his peers have suggested that beginning at Yale, advancing a conservative ideology became less Hawley's goal than winning accolades and prestigious posts, and he was very successful in that regard.

Fast forward to January 6, 2021 and the iconic image of Josh Hawley on the steps of the US Capitol, fist raised toward protesters who would shortly thereafter assault the institution and those dedicated to protecting it. Whether the photo shows a US Senator encouraging insurrection or a leader showing solidarity with law-abiding protestors depends on which side of the wide divide of American politics you stand on. Hawley had the image put on a coffee mug, which is rather ironic, given that there are also iconic images of Hawley sprinting away from that same mob after it breached the Capitol barricades. To many people, this was a different Josh Hawley from the one they had known in the past.

Former Missouri Republican Senator John Danforth, Hawley's political mentor, fervently disavowed Hawley after January 6, saying that supporting Hawley:

> was the worst mistake I ever made in my life...I really was part of creating something that has just turned out in a really terrible way. So, yeah, I feel, I guess, a little like what Dr. Frankenstein must have felt. I was part of creating something that was really wrong.[11]

Danforth went so far as to say that Hawley shared in the blame for the riot based on his comments in the days leading up to the attack.[12]

Even before January 6, Hawley had overtly changed. His friends and peers, and his Stanford advisor who had once called him "arguably the most gifted student I taught in 50 years,"[13] no longer saw him as principled, but only angry, with ambition and having "eyes on the prize" as his North Star rather than ideology.

He confounded his own party leadership by assuming an increasingly Christian nationalist approach to politics, though only sometimes, depending on the political capital to be gained. For example, in 2019 he questioned the confirmation of some conservative judicial nominees as insufficiently pure on social issues like abortion and same-sex marriage. But in 2024, after elections in several states showed popular support for women's reproductive rights, he said he supported limited access to abortion.[14] He not only backed but also amplified Trump Administration claims of the election being stolen before January 6. Hawley clearly recognized that his environment was one where there was no cost to anger overtaking principles; indeed, there were perhaps gains to be found there. Hawley wasn't alone in that regard.

At the time she took office in 2014, Elise Stefanik, at age 30, was the youngest woman ever elected to Congress. Born and raised near Albany, Stefanik and her brother Matt were raised Catholic. Her family owned a lumber company where her father served as president and her mother as the company's Chief Financial Officer. She attended the Albany Academy for Girls and graduated with honors from Harvard in 2006. While at Harvard, she co-authored an article with longtime Democratic politician Jeanne Shaheen on getting the youth vote more involved in politics[15] as early evidence of her moderate, bipartisan inclinations. From there she went to Washington, DC and worked in several high-profile policy jobs, including in the Office of the Chief of Staff for President George W. Bush Administration and helping to prepare the Republican national platform in 2012. After the Republican loss in 2012, she went into the family business before running for Congress. During her first campaign in 2014, some voters questioned whether she was a fresh voice for upstate New York or a carpetbagger, given her ties to the area were only through a seasonal home her parents owned there.[16] She married marketing and communications executive Matthew Manda in 2017 and gave birth to their son in August 2021.

Health care initially was a particularly sticky policy issue for Stefanik. Four weeks into her term in 2015, she voted to repeal the Affordable Care Act (ACA) though no Republican replacement bill was on the horizon at the time, hence drawing constituent criticism. Her 2017 vote in support of the American Health Care Act (AHCA) to replace the ACA drew criticism from some constituents as well, including depictions of her as the Grim Reaper and receiving death threats. She responded with a myth-vs.-fact explanation of her vote, disparaging the use of misinformation in politics, particularly the claim that the AHCA would not disallow preexisting conditions. In other areas, her extensive policy background prepared her well for membership on the House Armed Services Committee, the only 2015 freshman member of Congress to be placed on that committee.

Her Congressional profile began as that of a moderate Republican: pro-choice and against leaving the Paris climate agreement, but supportive of the Keystone pipeline. She voted with the Trump Administration 78% of the time, less than many of her Republican colleagues.

Stefanik encouraged voters to see her as one of Congress' "most bipartisan" members, and in 2017, when nearly all GOP lawmakers rallied behind Trump's proposed tax breaks for the wealthy and big corporations, Stefanik voted against them, one of only 12 Republicans to do so.

The Republican Party has traditionally billed itself as "gender blind," implying that ignoring gender is positive, rather than its actual meaning of defaulting to a masculine preference. But Stefanik has spoken up in support of inclusive diversity in the Republican Party on the E-PAC (Engage, Empower, Elevate) website that she helped create. In 2018, she said:

> I am going to keep pointing out to my GOP colleagues that we are at a crisis level for GOP women. This election should be a wake-up call to Republicans that we need to be better...We need to be elevating women's voices.[17]

She has argued in support of "gender value." Elise Stefanik was the poster child for moderate Republicans. Her mentor, Paul Ryan, described her as "the future of hopeful, aspirational politics in America."[18]

Regarding the 2016 presidential election, Stefanik pledged her support to the Republican Party but declined to say Donald Trump's name, fearing that voters would see her as a Trump ally. Her district's newspaper reported that an alliance with Trump might well put her seat up for grabs to a Democrat,[19] explaining her fear of alienating voters.

Her profile changed dramatically in 2020 when she was named to be part of his legal defense team just hours before the Senate impeachment hearings were set to begin, becoming one of the most ardent and vocal supporters of President Trump. Because Stefanik had previously supported a special counsel probe into Russian interference in the 2016 elections, which Trump had virulently objected to, her 2020 support for him surprised many people. She gained considerable media attention for going head-to-head with Democratic Intelligence Committee Chair Adam Schiff in defense of the president. Republicans were giddy with praise and Democrats were infuriated by what they characterized as Stefanik's "attack dog" tactics and her ignoring committee rules with interruptions and grandstanding. Politically, Stefanik's support of Trump made sense.

While Stefanik's district leans Republican and she was up for reelection in 2020 (and won), the potential for political advancement in Democratic-Party-dominant New York is limited. So, high-profile support for Trump could have paid off in a role in his Administration had he won in 2020. While that didn't happen, then, Stefanik did successfully raise her profile among the Trump-dominated Republican Party. She became the third-ranking House Republican in 2021 as the party's conference chair. Stefanik was reelected again in 2022 with 59% of the votes.

In May 2024, Stefanik got into a heated exchange during an appearance on *Fox News* when the host reminded her of her past negative comments about Donald Trump, including calling him a "whack job" in a message obtained by the *New York Times*.[20] Stefanik's anger was all about timing. Her elevation within her party paid off as, in Spring 2024, Stefanik was considered to be "auditioning" as Trump's vice presidential running mate. "I was the only Republican elected woman from the Northeast who voted for him in 2016, who was strongly supporting him, and I'm proud to be one of his strongest allies today,"[21] Stefanik countered to the *Fox News* host. As part of her audition, Stefanik also said she was unwilling to commit to certifying the 2024 election. Elise Stefanik had undergone a Kafka-like metamorphosis. Though she wasn't selected to be Trump's 2024 running mate, shortly after the November 2024 election, president-elect Donald Trump nominated Stefanik as the US Ambassador to the United Nations.

Rebranding can come in many forms. With the approach of the 2024 election, Kristi Noem was again in the news, this time for gender-related "backfires" in relation to also auditioning for the vice presidential spot on the Republican ticket with Donald Trump. In the aftermath of the *Access Hollywood* debacle, Noem said while she didn't approve of Trump's comments, she accepted his apology and intended to vote for him. (Though she also said: "I think this election has proven to us that we have two very flawed candidates."[22]) She was then quick to take up the Make America Great Again (MAGA) banner when Trump entered office, so Noem's makeover wasn't really ideological, it was physical. The question is whether a physical makeover is different than a "principles" makeover.

Noem, who over the years had billed herself as a grassroots cowgirl, sported short haircuts, wore khaki shirtdresses, donned cowboy hats, and rode horses in South Dakota, rebranded herself in 2024 with the more "girly-girl," sexy look favored by the Trump camp. According to analysts, the newer version of Noem, with long wavy hair, lip gloss, a bright smile, and form-fitting dresses, was intended to signal her as a "Miss America-like white femininity"[23] woman who would complement Trump but not challenge him. But the makeover proved problematic.

Part of the makeover included dental work, revealed in an infomercial-type video, that got her in legal trouble.[24] Then, in her 2024 book *No Going Back: The Truth on What's Wrong with Politics and How We Move America Forward*, she told a story of how she shot and killed her 14-month-old dog Crickett for having an aggressive personality. Though intended to show her as having Sarah-Palin-like "grit," she was quickly removed as a contender for Donald Trump's running mate, with media reporting that Trump couldn't run with a "puppy-killer."[25]Nevertheless, president-elect Trump noted and rewarded Noem's loyalty, nominating her to head head the Department of Homeland Security after his reelection. Noem, while a Member of Congress between 2007-2019, was a sponsor and champion of the 2017 Women, Peace and Security Act.

Authentic leadership is under fire for men and women. The rash of rebrandings that goes beyond Hawley and Stefanik might be argued as a political problem rather than a leadership problem. But it's not. It is a leadership problem that has created a political problem that could easily affect the politics of war and peace.

In 2020, Army General Mark Milley, then Chairman of the Joint Chiefs of Staff, made two calls to his Chinese counterpart. The first was prior to the election to ease Chinese fears, fears detected by US intelligence, that President Trump might attack China in an October surprise "wag the dog" effort to unite voters behind him to fight a foreign enemy. The call was authorized by the Secretary of Defense. A similar, second call was made on January 8, 2021, two days after the Capitol insurrection, again to assure the Chinese that the US government was stable and not going to attack China. In later testimony before Congress, Milley said the calls were intended to "prevent war between two great powers…My task at the time was to de-escalate."[26] Milley added that several top Trump officials were aware of and had authorized the calls. In September 2023, Donald Trump posted on his social-media network, Truth Social, that the calls were "an act so egregious that, in times gone by, the punishment would have been DEATH,"[27] a statement that has been interpreted as suggesting that Milley should be executed. Trump's ire, accusing Milley of "treason," followed an article in *The Atlantic* "detailing the ways in which Milley attempted to protect the Constitution from Trump."[28]

The Constitution has been called Milley's "North Star,"[29] and having a consistent North Star is an integral part of leadership. Admiral Mike Mullen, Chairman of the Joint Chiefs of Staff under Presidents George W. Bush and Barack Obama, explained why that is especially important for an individual in that position.

> You have to have a framework of values and principles that you adhere to – lines in the sand that you will not cross. Because standing in the presence of the most powerful person in the world, and having to adhere to those values in a consequential decision; you have to have those values and that framework or you will fail at it.[30]

An allegiance to the Constitution and a strong belief that the military must be apolitical drove Milley throughout his career, but especially between 2018 and 2020. Mark Milley, though a complex leader prone to both bluntness and banter, a combat veteran and Ivy League scholar, and appointed to the position of Chairman of the Joint Chiefs by Trump himself in 2018, nevertheless never rebranded himself though the president he was serving expected him to do so.

Milley grew up in the Greater Boston area of Irish-Catholic descent. Though patriotism and service-to-country were strong elements in his upbringing, he did not intend to make the military his career. His father, a World War II Marine who fought at Iwo Jima, did not want a military career for him either. Though Milley interviewed at West Point, he chose to go to Princeton on an ROTC scholarship instead. There he played on the hockey team and graduated in 1980 with a Bachelor of Arts degree in politics. His 185-page senior thesis was titled "The Irish Republican Army: A Critical Analysis of Revolutionary Guerilla Organization in Theory and Practice." He later earned a Master's degree in International Relations from Columbia University as well and remained a voracious reader and an avid student of history, military, and general history throughout his life.

Milley intended to serve in the Army as required by the ROTC scholarship money he had received, then get out and get a law degree or attend business school. But that didn't happen. His service-to-country inclinations were heightened during his initial military tour, and he ended up serving for 44 years before his 2023 retirement. He did combat tours in Afghanistan and Iraq, as well as deployments in Egypt, Panama, Haiti, and South Korea. Described as "built like a tank" and having "four-star eyebrows," Milley physically fit the bill as a "force of nature" with the Irish "gift of gab" as well.[31]

That gift of gab, appealing to Trump with comments about bloated military costs and having "an instinct for finding common ground with different types of people"[32] led Trump to announce Milley as the next chairman nearly a full year before the serving chairman's term was set to expire. That resulted in Milley serving during a time of unprecedented national political discord and divisiveness, under a president whose relationship with both the military and the country set the tone for both the discord and divisiveness. That environmental context resulted in needing an apolitical military leader being acutely aware of his political surroundings without being drawn in. Milley was usually good at that, but not always.

Milley was attending a White House meeting in June 2020 when, he thought, he was asked to accompany the president and Defense Secretary Mark Esper to visit National Guard troops and police near the White House. Instead, dressed in military fatigues, he found himself joining Trump in walking to a church near Lafayette Square, "a piece of theater that Trump intended as a response to the Black Lives Matter protestors who had been forcibly dispersed from the area,"[33] dispersed by the use of tear gas and rubber bullets. Milley soon realized that his participation created the impression that the military was involved in politics and considered resigning. Instead, however, he issued a public apology, saying, "I should not have been there."[34] The apology infuriated Trump.

Besides navigating the military and national security through rough waters surrounding the 2020 election and the Biden Administration taking office, Milley navigated other rough waters as well. After Donald Trump withdrew the United States from the JPCOA with Iran in 2018 and ordered the killing of one of Iran's most senior military officials, Qassem Soleimani (Suleimani), in January 2020 outside of Baghdad International Airport, war drums against Iran were again building. The legality of that killing has been repeatedly reviewed in the United States and international legal forums,[35] but after-the-fact Iran cared only that it had happened. While not wanting war (perhaps feeling not ready for it yet), Iran felt it nevertheless necessary to prepare for such, given that Trump followed the attack with tweets including threats to target sites "important to Iran and the Iranian culture"[36] indicating that de-escalation was not a White House priority. Milley is widely thought to have tamped down those White House inclinations.[37] He did not advise Trump to attack Iran, as the former president later claimed in conjunction with legal charges of mishandling classified documents.

Ironically, after the Biden Administration took office, Milley was accused by MAGA supporters in Congress of politicizing the military by becoming too "woke" during his tenure, as evidenced by, according to the supporters, including readings referencing critical race theory at some Professional Military Education (PME) institutions. Critical race theory, an academic theory dating back to the 1980s that addresses racial privilege, was relatively unknown beyond academia before a conservative activist and journalist named Christopher Rufo decided, by his own admission,[38] that it had sensationalist political potential. So, at a 2021 defense budget hearing, when Milley was challenged about critical race theory, he was ready. "I've read Mao Zedong. I've read Karl Marx. I've read Lenin," he said. "That doesn't make me a Communist." He further asked, "What is wrong with having some situational understanding about the country we are here to defend?" and stated "it's important for those of us in uniform to be open-minded and be widely read."[39] Milley made it clear that contextual intelligence is key to both effective leadership and deterrence.

In Milley's farewell address in 2023, he returned to his roots, talking about the importance of swearing allegiance to the Constitution.

> We don't take an oath to a king or a queen or to a tyrant or a dictator. And we don't take an oath to a wannabe dictator. We don't take an oath to an individual. We take an oath to the Constitution.[40]

Leaders without a touchstone, without a North Star, without principles, will fail. Milley was not one of those. Neither was Liz Cheney, the person Elise Stefanik replaced as Republic Party conference chair.

Liz Cheney voted with Trump over 90% of the time in Congress, a hard-core Republican from a deeply red state and a family of hard-core Republicans. Though she said she found his remarks about women appalling, Cheney supported Trump in his 2016 bid for the presidency because she felt Hillary Clinton's actions regarding the handling of emails while Secretary of State were far worse, as Cheney felt that Clinton had jeopardized national security. But she lost her seat in the House for swearing fealty to the Constitution after the January 6 insurrection, again in defense of national security, rather than swearing fealty to a cult of personality.

As a politician, Liz Cheney was known for being ambitious and for her willingness to "speak up to the boys." The eldest of two daughters of former Defense Secretary and Vice President Dick Cheney, Liz Cheney was elected to serve as Montana's lone Congressional representative in 2016. With just over a million constituents, overwhelmingly white, rural, and deeply conservative, the district is the largest by land area in the contiguous United States. Born in Wisconsin, Cheney grew up with her family splitting their time between Wyoming and Washington, DC as her father represented Wyoming in Congress. She attended college in Colorado, worked for several years in the State Department, and then received a law degree from the University of Chicago. Cheney has had extensive professional experience in foreign affairs and, like her father, has always supported a muscular US defense posture. Cheney married Washington lawyer Phillip Perry in 1993 and they have five children.

In 2013, Cheney announced that she would run for the Senate from Wyoming. Like Stefanik once had, Cheney faced carpetbagging criticism, this time from her Republican opponent in the primary since her family had only moved from Washington to Wyoming in 2012. She responded by noting her long family roots in the state. Cheney was among those *Newsmax* named as the 25 most influential women in the Republican Party in 2013.[41] But Cheney's campaign suffered from her decidedly hawkish foreign policy and defense views among a public weary of war, and from a public spat with her lesbian sister Mary over Liz's opposition to same-sex marriage, a view about which she has subsequently said she was "wrong." Seeing no road to victory, Cheney withdrew from the race in 2014 citing family health issues. But after overcoming those earlier issues, she was elected in 2016, reelected in 2018 by nearly 34 points, and then again in 2020 by 42 points. After only two terms, she was tapped by her colleagues in 2019 to fill the #3 spot in the Republican Party in the House, as party conference Chair, demonstrating her rising influence and success.

Male colleagues have described Liz Cheney as reminding them of Margaret Thatcher in terms of being a strong person in a big position in an organization dominated by men. Thatcher rose through party ranks, and so did Cheney. As the Republican conference committee chair, Cheney was responsible for communicating the party's message to party members. What that message was during Trump's presidency was often hard to decipher and could change quickly. Nevertheless, Cheney did well.

Cheney was one of the few Republicans to successfully walk the line between support for Trump, evidenced by her voting record with him, and criticizing Trump policies and supporters without alienating them. She aggressively defended Trump and his policies when and where she agreed with him, such as on matters concerning China, and didn't hesitate to lacerate Nancy Pelosi as House Speaker – not surprising given the two women are political opposites. Cheney's national security bona fides were second to none, perhaps giving her more latitude than some others, even with Trump.

Cheney openly questioned whether Trump was aware of reports that the Russians offered Afghan militants bounties to kill US troops when demanding that the administration take a more aggressive posture toward the Kremlin. She referred to Trump's plans to remove US troops from Germany as "dangerously misguided," strongly demurred to the idea of hosting peace talks with the Taliban at Camp David, and said it would be a "very serious mistake" to not retaliate against Iran for downing a US surveillance drone. "She's got values, she's got guts, and she says what's on her mind," said her Republican colleague John Shimkus in 2020.[42] For a time, many Republicans believed that she might be the poster child for the post-Trump Republican Party.

Liz Cheney and Jaime Herrera Beutler were the two Republican women among the ten Republican House members to vote in favor of impeaching Donald Trump for the second time, on the charge of incitement of insurrection. Both received blowback. Herrera Beutler lost her seat in Congress to a Democrat in 2022. Cheney's blowback came even sooner, initially focused on intra-party calls for her to step down from her leadership position. Cheney said she was acting as a matter of conscience. "The President of the United States summoned this mob, assembled the mob, and lit the flame of this attack," Cheney said in 2022 in her opening statement on the select committee to investigate January 6. "Everything that followed was his doing."[43]

Cheney is known for her thick skin, so sharp elbows from colleagues didn't faze her, and she survived another leadership challenge in February 2021 by a vote of 145–61. Just prior to that vote, Julie Conway, the Executive Director of the Republican women's political action committee VIEW PAC, held a virtual fundraiser for Cheney. "Liz's primary is absolutely the most symbolic race in the country right now," she said. Conway added,

> She's the proverbial canary in the coal mine. I mean, is the party ready to get back to principled leaders with substance and a moral compass? Or have we become a party that sees Congress as a source of entertainment and intellectual cotton candy?[44]

The women stood up for Liz Cheney.

But the attacks on Cheney continued, based solely on her refusal to bow to pressures to support Donald Trump. She was finally stripped of her party leadership position by a voice vote on May 12, 2021. So as not to be construed as a GOP attack on a woman in a leadership position, she was replaced by Elise Stefanik, who had actively campaigned for the job. Cheney told reporters in 2021 after her ouster that she would "do everything I can to make sure the former president never gets anywhere near the Oval Office."[45]

In June 2021, the Select Committee investigating the January 6 insurrection was created by a House resolution, by a vote of 222–190. Republicans Liz Cheney and Adam Kinzinger joined all Democratic members voting in favor of establishing that committee. Sixteen Republicans did not vote. Both Kinzinger and Cheney went on to serve on the committee, Cheney as Vice Chair. Cheney made no bones about her belief that Donald Trump was personally responsible for the events of January 6 and that he was "unfit" for office.[46] Perhaps ironically, she worked well with Nancy Pelosi regarding the committee, each woman commending the other for professionalism and principles. Principles cost Cheney her seat in Congress.

Harriet Hageman emerged as Donald Trump's choice to oppose Cheney in the 2022 Wyoming Republican primary. In 2016, Hageman had been a key player in trying to stop Donald Trump from getting the Republican presidential nomination, calling him racist and xenophobic. In 2021, however, she said she considered Trump the best president in her lifetime, in what a *New York Times* article referred to as "the Republican Party's marquee showdown over fealty to the former president."[47] Another case of rebranding. Hageman won the Republican primary with 66.3% of the vote to Cheney's 28.9%, and subsequently her seat in Congress.

In her December 2023 book *Oath and Honor*,[48] besides Trump, Cheney directs much of her negative leadership analysis toward former House Speaker Kevin McCarthy, referring to him as "sad" and "pathetic" there as elsewhere.[49] Many times, she says, McCarthy could have made a decision, sometimes just a procedural decision, to stop the Big Lie narrative and allow the government to get on with the business of governing and paying attention to national security threats, but didn't, thus enabling both Trump and the divisive political environment that weakens the United States in the eyes of its adversaries. After his 2024 reelection, Donald Trump specifically targeted Liz Cheney for punishment.

The Cost of Leadership

"Exhaustion" has been cited in conjunction with the retirement of Jacinda Ardern and potentially Justin Trudeau. Mark Milley's job was 24/7, including phone calls in the middle of the night. Leadership jobs generally allow for little "down time." Liz Cheney had to hire personal security in 2021 after receiving death threats. Nancy Pelosi's husband Paul was attacked with a hammer during a home invasion in 2022 perpetrated by a far-right conspiracy theorist. Fears for your physical safety or that of loved ones create accompanying mental strain. Leadership, even for those with seemingly unlimited energy, takes a physical, personal and mental toll on individuals.

When I was teaching leadership at the Naval War College, we had the students watch the 1949 movie *12 O'Clock High,* based on a novel[50] of the same name. Set in 1942, it depicts the leadership struggle behind the successful development of a precision aerial bombing unit during World War II in Europe. The hero, Brigadier General Frank Savage, assumes command of a bomber unit in England known as "the hard luck group" for all its losses. Initially, his no-nonsense leadership style is resented by both his pilots and his second-in-command, a West Point graduate and son of a general. The unit eventually pulls together and completes successful missions, but the leadership toll on Savage is tremendous, including, in his case, suffering a brief catatonic state, physically and mentally. That toll begs the question of how much stress a leader can take before reaching his or her breaking point?

The military has long recognized the impact of stress on individuals. In World War I, it was called "shell shock" and later "traumatic neurosis," specifically related to an external situation that is "overwhelming to the individual and puts him under such stress that psychological decompensation occurs."[51] The wartime goal was to successfully treat individuals and get them back to their operational units as quickly as possible. The aftereffects have more recently come to be known as Post Traumatic Stress Disorder. Away from combat, however, burnout among leadership is a separate problem.

"Burnout" is an occupational phenomenon, according to the World Health Organization, not a medical condition. According to the American Psychological Association, it "results from performing at a high level of stress and tension, especially from extreme and prolonged physical and mental exertion or an overburdening workload, take their toll."[52] It is physical and emotional exhaustion and often associates with the decreased motivation and lowered performance at work.

Jacinda Ardern speaking out about her exhaustion has been considered a plus by the mental health community, as it is hoped that her relatability, both as a person and a leader, would make talking about and admitting burnout more palatable to a wider range of individuals,[53] similar to the burnout admissions by high-performance athletes Simone Biles and Naomi Osaka. However, Danna Greenberg, a professor of organizational behavior, has pointed out the downside to Ardern's admission. "While I believe that Prime Minister Ardern's honesty might further normalize conversations around mental health, I worry that this will in fact do the opposite and simply fuel bias against working mothers and their ascent to leadership roles."[54] Further, says management consultant Adela Hussain, "The danger with Jacinda as a female leader sharing her vulnerability is that there's room for misogynists to question whether women are capable of high-profile leadership"[55] and, in fact, data from 2022 indicates that global trust in women's leadership has fallen.[56] The bigger problem, perhaps, is the reluctance – indeed stigma – felt by male leaders about similarly admitting burnout, instead trying to merely "push through" at a lower level of performance.

When leaders try to simply push through stress, they may "surface act," meaning to put on a game face that merely hides their real state of emotions. *Harvard Business Review* reports, however, that:

> suppressing and faking emotions has high costs for both the leader and the organization. The effort expended reduces self-control resources, making leaders likelier to lash out at work, for example, by belittling or making rude comments to a coworker. The stress of consistent surface acting can also impact leaders' health, making them more prone to bodily aches, burnout, insomnia and drinking heavily when they get home.[57]

Surface acting can also impair decision-making. "Burned out leaders become slow and indecisive when faced with important decisions, and they feel much less confident in their choices. This can lead to poor decisions and missed opportunities, as well as lower employee morale and engagement."[58]

Clearly, gender stereotyping impedes leadership for both men and women. With "real man" gender stereotyping, male leaders are reluctant to address burnout for fear of being stigmatized as weak.

> The primary cause of the stigma against men's mental health is the social definition of what it means to "be a man." While younger generations tend to have a better grasp on gender and the harmful effects of strict gender roles, it's still clear that people have been socialized to expect different behavior from people of different genders. When you have men in male-dominated fields (like the military), this societal expectation is even more pervasive.
>
> Men are expected to be stoic and strong. It's "unmanly" to cry or show distress in any form that isn't anger or aggression. Men in the military are expected to keep their emotions under wraps, and while this may have benefits while on the job, it leads to a mindset that says emotions are inconvenient and perhaps even embarrassing.[59]

This stigmatization can come with the potential for real costs.

One of the best students I ever had at the Naval War College, an Army officer, left soon after graduation for Iraq. He was a hot runner. Everyone knew he was on his way to being a general officer. A few years later I got a call from him, from Baghdad. By then, he was in the middle of his second tour. He was calling to ask me for a recommendation to a PhD program, which I gladly offered to write. He was, he told me, burnt out and knew it, had family issues that needed him to be present, and felt he and the Army could benefit from him getting more education. He was accepted into a top program. Years later, I was visiting him and his family, and he told me a story.

While still in Iraq, a helicopter landed at his base one day, and unexpectedly his commanding officer got out. My student assumed the general was there to motivationally talk to the troops, as the unit had recently seen a great deal of gritty combat and had taken losses. But that was not the case. The general immediately took my student aside and told him that he had heard he was going to take an educational billet rather than another combat tour. My student told him that was correct and explained why. The general told him point-blank that if he went ahead with that plan, he, his commanding officer, would ruin his career. He would make sure my student never made general officer. And then he got back on the helicopter and left. My student nevertheless took the educational billet.

Several questions flow from this anecdote. Are there circumstances where the commanding officer's style of leadership is appropriate and effective? Was this one of them? The risk my student took in stepping away from another operational assignment was substantial. How many other individuals would have the fortitude to do that even though they felt burned out? Had he stayed on for another combat tour, would or could he have been an effective leader? Would staying on have been a disservice to those who followed him?

The dilemma faced by men and women leaders presents a Catch-22 impossible situation. Women leaders, though they may be less reluctant to try to address burnout and seek help, can consequently then face a loss of trust by those within their organizations. But men who are more reluctant to address burnout, to maintain follower trust and confidence, may well be operating within less-than-optimal personal parameters. In both cases, an increase in burnout results in a decrease in good leadership.

Leaders face significant personal stress and work-life balance challenges. Leaders miss family events, good and bad. Nelson Mandela lost his eldest son, "Thembi," in a car accident while he was serving a life sentence in prison. Aung San Suu Kyi was separated from her husband and sons for almost twenty years. Many women politicians, from the local to national levels, have had to hire private security for themselves and their families due to the normalization of violence. World Wrestling Entertainment personality Hulk Hogan got cheers in the runnup to the 2024 election when he asked a crowd if he should body slam Kamala Harris. Studies in Sweden have shown that women elected to public office - mayors and parlimentarians - doubled their chances of splitting from their partners compared to those not elected, while there is no evidence of a similar effect on personal relationships for men.[60] Leadership comes at a personal price.

Learning Leadership

I began this book by saying I wasn't sure leadership could be taught, but certainly it could be learned if an individual is interested in doing so. There are two requisites to learning. First, there must be motivation and an openness to new ideas and having their ideas challenged. Leadership in 2024 is too often ideologically driven, and ideology is often not swayed by facts, and facts have often become fungible.

Democracy has been empirically shown to be the best type of government in terms of providing a road toward positive, sustainable peace. Government by the people, however, doesn't require much of individuals being elected. In an interview after his election, Republican Senator Tommy Tuberville, elected to the Senate from Alabama in 2021 after a decades-long career as a college football coach and sports commentator, misidentified the three branches of the US government (as the House, the Senate, and the executive), said the European theater of World War II was fought "to free Europe of socialism," and said he was looking forward to raising money from his Senate office, a violation of federal law.[61] A newly elected Democratic Congresswoman was surprised when I suggested in a discussion that the United States could veto an upcoming Security Council vote on a contentious issue. "We have one of those?" she asked. "When did we get that?" Certainly no one expects lawmakers to enter their office fully knowledgeable on all subjects, but it is hoped that they will want to learn and surround themselves with people who will assist them in that regard. I've also had (nonlawyer) military students emphatically describe to me parts of the Constitution that simply don't exist (I taught Constitutional Law for ten years early in my career). Nobody expects military officers to be Constitutional experts, but if they profess to be, their views should be based on fact. Alas, however, education, indeed even learning generally, has become deemed elitist in too many instances, given over to ideology. That does not bode well for leadership.

Second, there must be venues for learning. Saying that I wasn't sure leadership could be taught doesn't mean that I don't think leadership classes shouldn't or needn't be taught or that venues for discussion shouldn't be provided. Quite the contrary. It means I don't think leadership can be learned only by listening to others or self-taught through reading, though both can be an important part of learning. Leadership issues must be discussed. Pushing individuals to express their views and explain their rationales in discussions with others is an important learning experience. I push students to *write* as well, as nothing forces clarification of thoughts as much as having to put them succinctly into written words.

What I question, however, is whether really hard issues are being discussed in some venues. It has been my experience that even in PME classes, lectures, and workshop planning sessions, there is a surprising amount of consideration given to not wanting to offend anyone by questioning, for example, whether the Proud Boys are domestic terrorists, why toxic leadership is tolerated, or why sexual assault continues to be present in the military given the service's ethic. Those topics are too often reserved for op-ed consideration. Sometimes the "tread lightly" individuals are the same ones who might have accused General Milley of being too woke. It often seems easier instead to focus leadership learning sessions on "tests" – color personality tests, Myers-Briggs, perhaps but less likely the Harvard Implicit Bias Test, and others. These tests can be personally enlightening to those open to self-improvement but are not enough, especially in trying to identify and work with those not particularly open to self-improvement. Perpetuating the picture that "everything is fine" does not get problems addressed.

Kudos to the US Air Force for publishing a 2024 book titled *One Team, One Fight: Diversity and Inclusion in the Department of the Air Force*[62] that actually includes sections titled "Hard Discussions" on race, gender identification and sexual orientation, gender disparity, and Air Force culture. Hopefully, the contents of the book will be mandatory reading in Air Force leadership courses. Glaringly missing, however, was a section on masculinities, important given the pervasiveness of "real man" masculinity in the military, as discussed in Chapter 5, and the need to help men identify paths toward positive, healthy masculinity. The gap between the aspirational "good man" and aggressive and angry "real man," including in leadership, must be addressed.

Regarding issues of gender and the value of diverse leadership more specifically, in some cases, acceptance of changed norms is truly generational. I had a Navy Captain in one of my classes who, regardless of the topic of the class discussion, wanted to rail about training women as pilots when "everybody knew" they would only get pregnant when it was time to deploy so that they didn't have to go. I made a point of looking into statistics about his claim. Through some gender-differentiated statistics about losing work due to profession-related health issues (hurt on the job) or personal (which would include pregnancy for women), the figures showed more men than women missed deployments due to personal health issues. Consequently, I was able to stop his diatribe in class, but I was not at all certain I had been able to dispel the myth so strongly ingrained in his mind. His next assignment after graduation was to teach leadership at the Naval Academy, where his views would be passed on to another generation of military officers.

A woman flag officer I interviewed told me stories of women spouses complaining to her and her husband regarding "what was to happen to the spouse club?" with her, a woman, in command. With two-income families increasingly the norm in the military, as in the general population, those issues and spouse clubs, where husbands' ranks can transfer to wives' power bases, will go the way of the dinosaur. But with the retirement of the Old Guard it is required that the next generation of leaders be prepared to step in. In that regard, because of the Congressional requirements for professional military education, the military is better positioned in many ways than the civilian sector to assure that leadership is learned. All PME institutions have leadership classes and programs. The question is what is being taught and who is teaching it.

Civilian institutions, academic, business, and professional, all claim leadership initiatives as well and should be lauded for doing so. But one-and-done programs of any sort hold little sway over changing organizational culture. Leadership is, in many ways, a leadership issue. That is, it must be taken seriously by leadership, with accountability for follow-up and follow-through.

Contextual intelligence is best served through diverse leadership, to bring as much knowledge, consideration of as many variables, and differing perspectives to problem-solving as possible. Gender diversification has been evidenced as important in this regard. The first step is to recognize the role of gender in matters of national security. Though most of the security community is still in the nascent stages of doing so, the good news is once it is seen, it cannot be unseen.

Conclusion

Just as with the creation of Space Force and having the opportunity there to "build better" from scratch, leadership is in crisis, also providing an opportunity to "build better." The number of good leaders still outnumbers the bad, but which way the future will go will be determined by every individual, whether in politics, in the military, a leader themselves or not. What will they tolerate? What will they turn a blind eye to? Leaders must learn to balance empathy, prudence, and assertiveness, and support assertiveness rather than aggression. Women and men must work together toward more effective decision-making, which is critical to war and peace. These are all topics of discussion that I hope will be spurred by this book.

Finally, war and peace are issues of discussion and study in civilian and governmental international relations and security studies programs and professional communities. International relations theory is the lens through which participating individuals and decision-makers view the world and consequently develop and implement strategies and policies to address threats. Great Power Competition has spurred a return to realism as the guiding US theoretical lens, one focused on states, power, and Machiavellian rules, rather than liberal internationalism that prompted decades of attempts at democratization and nation-building in countries sometimes neither seeking nor prepared for either. Realism, however, requires seeing the world as it is. Consequently, political scientists Valerie Hudson and Rose McDermott have pointed out that realism requires gender-related issues and responses to issues, such as deterrence, to be considered.[63] That includes, indeed requires, consideration among leadership. But gender-related issues and responses to issues often aren't considered, even by professed realists.

As Capt. (ret.) David Reynolds, a former Naval War College student of mine and one of the best theorists I've ever worked with, has suggested, to a certain degree, "realism" seems to exist in the eye of the beholder. "I've read articles where the author appears to be simply putting forward his (always a he) collection of assumptions and cherry-picked observations and wrapping it up in a package of 'realism.'" Referencing Hudson and McDermott, he states further that while their "argument seems absolutely sound, I could see many men pushing against it simply because it doesn't fit their worldview, conveniently setting aside the evidence in an act of cognitive dissonance."[64]

But, knowing what we know about gender inequality directly affecting national security instability, if the situation regarding women, gender, and conflict isn't being regularly tracked and considered in decision-making, is the United States really pursuing a realist approach? Or perhaps better stated, is the United States most effectively pursuing a realist approach? Ideally, more diverse leadership will feel comfortable asking and answering those questions. A volatile, uncertain, complex and ambiguous environment can best be addressed with as close to full situational information as possible. Ignoring 50% of the population doesn't provide that, yet war and peace depend on it. More diverse leadership can push the United States in a more "real" realist direction.

Notes

1 Davis, Elliot. "Americans 'Disappointed' in Society's Leaders, Survey Finds," *U.S. News and World Report*, December 12, 2023. https://www.usnews.com/news/leaders/articles/2023-12-12/americans-disappointed-in-societys-leaders-survey-finds; "Outlook on the Global Agenda 2015," World Economic Forum, October 17, 2014. https://www.weforum.org/publications/outlook-global-agenda-2015/

2 "Highly Negative Views of American Politics in 2023," Pew Research Center, September 19, 2023. https://www.pewresearch.org/politics/2023/09/19/americans-dismal-views-of-the-nations-politics/
3 Lamb, Jason. "Why Toxic Senior Leaders Survive – and Sometimes Thrive – in the Military," *Air Force Times*. https://www.airforcetimes.com/opinion/commentary/2020/09/04/why-toxic-senior-leaders-survive-and-sometimes-thrive-in-the-military/
4 Younis, Mohamed. "Confidence in the US Military Lowest in Over Two Decades," *Gallup*, July 31, 2023. https://news.gallup.com/poll/509189/confidence-military-lowest-two-decades.aspx
5 "Americans View of the US Military," Pew Research Center, February 1, 2024. https://news.gallup.com/poll/509189/confidence-military-lowest-two-decades.aspx
6 Wolf, Christopher. "The Formula for the Perfect Leader," *US News and World Report*, December 12, 2023. https://www.usnews.com/news/leaders/articles/2023-12-12/survey-americans-want-trustworthy-leaders-above-all-else
7 Hutt, Rosamund. "The 6 Types of Leadership Styles," World Economic Forum, May 2019. https://www.weforum.org/stories/2019/05/leadership-style-types-around-the-world/
8 Pazzanese, Christina. "Those Who Have Known Angela Merkel Describe Her Rise to Prominence," *Harvard Gazette*, May 28, 2019. https://news.harvard.edu/gazette/story/2019/05/those-who-have-known-angela-merkel-describe-her-rise-to-prominence/
9 Plott, Elaina and Danny Hakim. "Josh Hawley is 'Not Going Anywhere.' How Did He Get Here?" *The New York Times,* March 7, 2021. https://www.nytimes.com/2021/03/07/us/politics/josh-hawley.html
10 Arrieta-Kenna, Ruairi and Emily Cadei. "The Education of Josh Hawley," *Politico*, January 19, 2021. https://www.politico.com/news/magazine/2021/01/19/josh-hawley-senator-stanford-history-capitol-insurrection-ambition-460481
11 Keller, Rudy. "Danforth Says Regrets Over Hawley Make Him 'Feel like Dr. Frankenstein,'" *Missouri Independent*, February 3, 2021. https://missouriindependent.com/2021/02/03/danforth-says-regrets-over-hawley-make-him-feel-like-dr-frankensein/#:~:text=In%20the%20aftermath%20of%20the,in%20a%20really%20terrible%20way
12 Keller, 2021.
13 Arrieta-Kenna, 2021.
14 Liss, Samantha. "Democrats Seeks to Make GOP Pay in November for Threats to Reproductive Rights," *CBS News*, May 9, 2024. https://www.cbsnews.com/news/election-2024-abortion-rights-ivf-missouri-lucas-kunce-josh-hawley/
15 Kaden, David, Jeanne Shaheen and Elise Stefanik. "Shaping Our Political Future," *The Harvard Crimson*, October 6, 2005. https://www.thecrimson.com/article/2005/10/6/shaping-our-political-future-the-aftermath/
16 Mann, Brian. "NY21: Is Elise Stefanik a Fresh New Voice or a Carpetbagger?" NCPR News, May 20, 2014. https://www.northcountrypublicradio.org/news/story/24896/20140520/ny21-is-elise-stefanik-a-fresh-new-voice-or-a-carpetbagger
17 Bade, Rachel and Sarah Ferris. "I Wasn't Asking for Permission: GOP Women Put Leaders on Notice," *Politico*, December 11, 2018. https://www.politico.com/story/2018/12/11/gop-women-leadership-1055195
18 Ryan, Paul. "The Next 100: Elise Stefanik," *Time*, 2019. https://time.com/collection/time-100-next-2019/5718823/elise-stefanik/?utm_source=twitter&utm_medium=social&utm_campaign=time-100-next&utm_term=_&linkId=77760091
19 Freedman, Dan. "Elise Stefanik Won't Say Donald Trump's Name, but Pledges GOP Loyalty," *Times Union,* May 5, 2016. https://www.timesunion.com/tuplus-local/article/Elise-Stefanik-won-t-say-Donald-Trump-s-name-but-7396796.php

20 Confessore, Nicholas. "The Invention of Elise Stefanik," *The New York Times*, December 31, 2022. https://www.nytimes.com/2022/12/31/us/politics/elise-stefanik.html
21 "Elise Stefanik, Fox News Host Shannon Bream Clash Over Question about Trump," *Politico*, May 19, 2024. https://www.politico.com/news/2024/05/19/stefanik-fox-host-clash-over-question-about-trump-00158793
22 Ferguson, Dana. "Noen Says She'll Vote for Trump Despite Lewd Comments," *Argus Leaders*, October 10, 2016. https://www.argusleader.com/story/blogs/danaferguson/2016/10/10/live-noon-kristi-noem-paula-hawks-debate-rotary/91848068/
23 Freidman, Vanessa. "Kristie Noem Gets a MAGA Makeover," *The New York Times*, March 20, 2024. https://www.nytimes.com/2024/03/20/style/kristi-noem-teeth-trump-vice-president.html?searchResultPosition=5
24 Freidman, 2024.
25 Adegoke, Favour. "Donald Trump 'Disappointed' in 'Puppy Killer' Kristi Noem as She Loses Vice Presidential Shot," *Yahoo News*, April 29, 2024. https://www.yahoo.com/news/donald-trump-disappointed-puppy-killer-224524273.html
26 Desiderio, Andrew. "Milley: Beijing's Fear of U.S. Attack Prompted Calls to Chinese General," *POLITICO*, September 28, 2021. https://www.politico.com/news/2021/09/28/milley-china-congress-hearing-514488
27 Klass, Brian. "Trump Floats the Idea of Executing Joint Chiefs Chairman Milley," *The Atlantic*, September 25, 2023. https://www.theatlantic.com/ideas/archive/2023/09/trump-milley-execution-incitement-violence/675435/
28 Klass, 2023; Goldberg, Jeffrey. "The Patriot," *The Atlantic*, November 2023. https://www.theatlantic.com/magazine/archive/2023/11/general-mark-milley-trump-coup/675375/
29 "Milley Says Farewell After 4 Years as Chairman," Association of the US Army, September 29, 2023. https://www.ausa.org/news/milley-says-farewell-after-4-years-chairman
30 Cooper, Helene. "How Mark Milley, a General Who Mixes Bluntness and Banter, Became Trump's Chief Military Advisor," *The New York Times*, September 29, 2021. https://www.nytimes.com/2019/09/29/us/politics/mark-milley-chairman-joint-chiefs.html
31 Sevastopulo, Demetri. "General Mark Milley: 'Americans Have Kind of Had it with Wars,'" *Financial Times*, March 1, 2024. https://www.ft.com/content/3a8ab059-4710-4e56-ad04-87eb623d79ac
32 Cooper, 2021.
33 Seveastopulo, 2024.
34 Cooper, Helene. "General Milley Apologized for Trump Photo Op Role," *The New York Times*, June 11, 2020. https://www.nytimes.com/2020/06/11/us/politics/trump-milley-military-protests-lafayette-square.html
35 Hodges, Scott. "The Killing of Qassam Soleimani," JAG reporter, October 29, 2020. https://www.jagreporter.af.mil/Post/Article-View-Post/Article/2539536/the-killing-of-qassem-soleimani/
36 "The Trump Administration's Escalating Tension with Iran," American Oversight, January 20, 2021. https://www.americanoversight.org/investigation/the-trump-administrations-escalating-tension-with-iran
37 Glaser, Susan. "You're Gonna Have A Fucking War: Mark Milley's Fight to Keep Trump From Striking Iran," *The New Yorker*, July 15, 2021. https://www.newyorker.com/news/letter-from-bidens-washington/youre-gonna-have-a-fucking-war-mark-milleys-fight-to-stop-trump-from-striking-iran
38 Wallace-Wells, Benjamin. "How a Conservative Activist Invented the Conflict Over Critical Race Theory," *The New Yorker*, June 18, 2021. https://www.newyorker.com/news/annals-of-inquiry/how-a-conservative-activist-invented-the-conflict-over-critical-race-theory

39 Full transcript found at: https://www.rev.com/blog/transcripts/general-milley-secretary-austin-full-testimony-transcript-on-2022-budget-request (accessed May 23, 2024)
40 "WATCH: Gen. Milley Delivers Defense of Democracy in Farewell Address," *PBS Newshour*, September 29, 2023. https://www.pbs.org/newshour/politics/watch-live-biden-speaks-at-farewell-event-for-retiring-joint-chiefs-chair-gen-milley
41 Meyers, Jim. "The 25 Most Influential Women of the GOP," *Newsmax,* July 31, 2013. https://www.newsmax.com/politics/newsmax-top-25-women/2013/07/31/id/518085/
42 Zanona, Melanie. "Cheney Takes on Trump," *POLITICO*, June 30, 2020. https://www.politico.com/news/2020/06/30/cheney-takes-on-trump-346089
43 Bradner, Eric and Jeff Zeleny. "How Liz Cheney Lost Wyoming's Lone Seat in the House," *CNN,* August 17, 2022. https://www.cnn.com/2022/08/17/politics/why-liz-cheney-lost/index.html
44 Draper, Robert. "Liz Cheney vs MAGA," *The New York Times*, 2021. https://www.nytimes.com/2021/04/22/magazine/liz-cheney-vs-maga.html
45 Hudak, Zachery. "Liz Cheney Removed from House GOP Leadership," *CBS News*, 2021. https://www.cbsnews.com/live-updates/liz-cheney-removed-gop-leadership/
46 Shapiro, Julia. "Liz Cheney: Jan. 6 Panel Work Shows Trump 'Unfit' for Office," Axios, July 21, 2022. https://www.axios.com/2022/07/21/liz-cheney-jan6-committee
47 Epstein, Reid J. "How an Anti-Trump Plotter Became His Champion," *New York Times,* September 27, 2021. https://www.nytimes.com/2021/09/27/us/politics/harriet-hageman-liz-cheney-trump.html
48 Cheney, Liz. *Oath and Honor*, Little, Brown and Company, 2023.
49 Robertson, Nick. "Cheney Calls McCarthy 'Sad' and 'Pathetic' for Saying He'd Serve in Trump Administration," *The Hill*, December 12, 2023. https://thehill.com/homenews/house/4355251-cheney-mccarthy-pathetic-serving-trump-administration/
50 Lay, Bernie and Sy Bartlett. *12 O'Clock High!* Harper and Brothers, 1948.
51 Daniels, Robert. "The Psychological Tolls of Leadership," University of Chicago Papers, March 18, 1971. https://www.chicagobooth.edu/review/psychological-tolls-leadership
52 APA Dictionary of Psychology. https://dictionary.apa.org/burnout
53 Baynes, Megan. "Burnout, Why Jacinda Ardern's 'Rare' Admission about her Mental Health Matters," *Sky World News*, January 20, 2023. https://news.sky.com/story/burnout-why-jacinda-arderns-rare-admission-about-her-mental-health-matters-12790047
54 Cox, Josie. "Is Burnout Finally 'High Profile' Enough for Leaders to Act?" *BBC*, January 24, 2023. https://www.bbc.com/worklife/article/20230123-is-burnout-finally-high-profile-enough-for-leaders-to-act
55 Cox, 2023.
56 Reykjavik Index for Leadership. https://kantar.turtl.co/story/reykjavik-index-2021/page/1?utm_source=Global%20web&utm_medium=website&utm_campaign=Reykjavik%20Index%202021&utm_id=Reykjavik%20Index&utm_term=Reykjavik%20Index%20for%20Leadership%202021
57 Smith, Dina Denham and Alicia A. Grandey. "The Emotional Labor of Being a Leader," *Harvard Business Review*, November 2, 2022. https://hbr.org/2022/11/the-emotional-labor-of-being-a-leader
58 "Why Leaders Have To Be Well To Do Well," *Human Psychology*. https://humanpsychology.com.au/heart-leadership-and-the-4-buckets-2/#:~:text=Burned%20out%20leaders%20become%20slow,lower%20employee%20morale%20and%20engagement
59 "Removing the Mental Health Stigma for Men," Operation Red Wings Foundation. https://orwfoundation.org/removing-the-mental-health-stimga-for-men/?gad_source=1&gclid=EAIaIQobChMI35fDmoGuhgMVujUIBR3P_AviEAAYAiAAEgLsC_D_BwE

60 Savage, Maddy. "Why promoted women are more likely to divorce," BBC, 22 January 2020. https://www.bbc.com/worklife/article/20200121-why-promoted-women-are-more-likely-to-divorce
61 Stacy, Todd. "In the Weeds with Tommy Tuberville, Alabama Next Senator," *Alabama Daily News.* https://aldailynews.com/in-the-weeds-w-tommy-tuberville-alabamas-next-senator/
62 https://www.osi.af.mil/Portals/29/B_183_Matherly_One_Team_One_Fight_1.pdf
63 Hudson, Valerie and Rose McDermott. "Feminist Foreign Policy and Deterrence," Center for Feminist Foreign Policy, July 7, 2021. https://web.archive.org/web/20211219000933/https://centreforfeministforeignpolicy.org/journal/feministforeignpolicyanddeterrence
64 Personal email correspondence, Capt. David Reynolds, United States Navy Reserve, August 6, 2024.

INDEX